THE INTERIOR DESIGN BIBLE

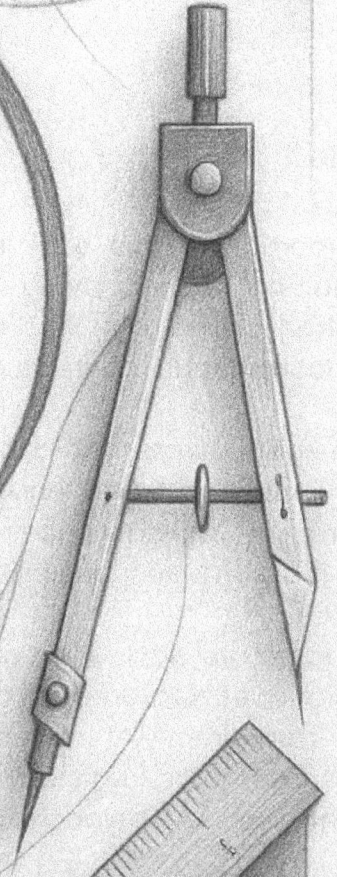

The Interior Design Bible

*by **StudioLux***

©2025 StudioLux. All Rights Reserved.

First Edition

Cover and Layout Design by StudioLux

BECOME ICONIC — MAKE YOUR STYLE VIRAL WITH US!

You've selected **"The Interior Design Bible"**, a statement addition to your beautiful home.

Now it's your moment in the spotlight! Create a captivating video or sophisticated photograph featuring **"The Interior Design Bible"** and share your creation on Instagram, TikTok, or Facebook using the hashtag **#StudioLux**. Your elegant post might just spark the next big social media trend!

WHY PARTICIPATE?

- Showcase your exquisite taste and inspire a wide audience.
- Gain the opportunity to be featured by StudioLux for greater visibility and recognition.

And there's more to come...

CLAIM YOUR EXCLUSIVE GIFTS!

To celebrate your creativity, we've designed an exclusive bonus filled with practical and inspiring ideas you can immediately use to enhance your home's style. Don't miss this special opportunity—it's your next step toward achieving interior excellence.

FOLLOW THESE SIMPLE STEPS TO CLAIM YOUR REWARD:

- Capture your unique photo or create a compelling video featuring the book.
- Share your creation on Instagram, TikTok, or Facebook using the hashtag #StudioLux.
- Scan the QR code below to instantly unlock your exclusive bonus content.

Your moment of viral fame awaits!

With style and appreciation,

StudioLux

SCAN ME

TABLE OF CONTENTS

TABLE OF CONTENTS

Introduction

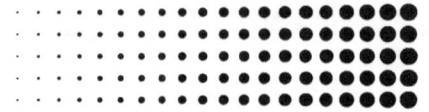

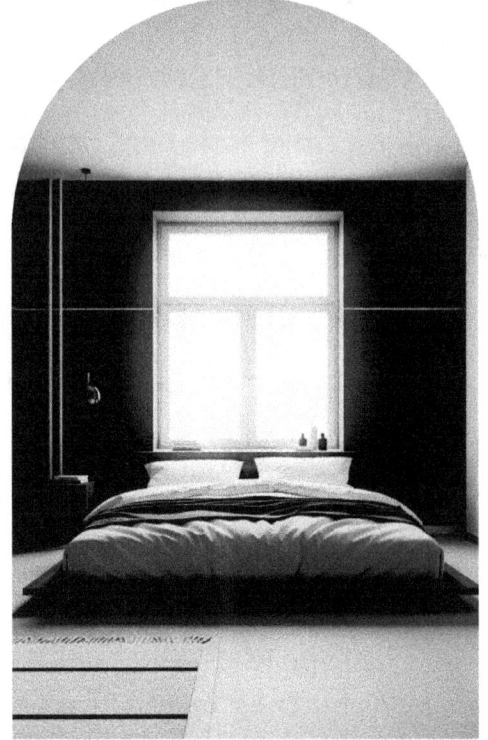

WELCOME TO YOUR
Design Journey

Welcome, friend! If you're holding this book in your hands right now, chances are you're ready for something special—something transformative. You've taken the first meaningful step toward turning your living space into more than just a place to eat, sleep, and relax. You're embarking on a deeply personal journey to create an environment that truly reflects your identity, comforts your soul, and fills you with joy every single day. Whether your home is a cozy studio apartment in the bustling heart of the city, a sprawling suburban house filled with family laughter, or something entirely different, rest assured: you're in the right place.

Interior design is not merely about decorating or making rooms look pretty; it's about storytelling. Your home should narrate your unique story through the thoughtful choice of colors, carefully curated furniture, distinctive textures, and meaningful personal touches. Every home,

regardless of its size, shape, or location, has a story waiting to be told—and you, my dear reader, are the author. Together, we'll uncover the narrative your space has always wanted to share.

Perhaps you've often admired beautifully decorated homes on Instagram or Pinterest, saving countless photos and dreaming about bringing that same charm into your own rooms. Or maybe you've binge-watched countless episodes of popular home renovation shows, inspired by transformations that seem almost magical. No matter how daunting or unreachable these looks may have felt, I'm here to tell you that not only are they achievable—they're attainable by you. Yes, you!

My name is [Author Name], and I've spent decades designing dream homes for clients around the globe. Throughout my journey, I've learned that beautiful interior design is far less about spending enormous sums of money or hiring renowned designers, and far more about understanding the fundamentals, developing a keen eye for detail, and confidently trusting your intuition. Interior design is an art form accessible to anyone with the desire and determination to learn. This book is your personal mentor, your companion, and your source of endless inspiration.

Within these pages, I've distilled my extensive professional experience, industry knowledge, and creative insights into a single, comprehensive guide. Consider this your ultimate roadmap—a tool you'll reference again and again as you craft the home you've always envisioned. Regardless of whether you're a complete novice with no prior experience or a passionate decor enthusiast eager to refine your skills, you'll find precisely what you need here.

Together, we will demystify the seemingly complex principles of interior design. From the elegant simplicity of minimalist spaces to the rich, personality-filled rooms of maximalism, you'll explore an extensive array of styles and trends. You'll learn to harness the transformative power of color, master the essential rules of layout and spacing, select furniture that perfectly suits your lifestyle, and

uncover how even the smallest details can dramatically elevate the ambiance of a room.

Most importantly, you will gain the confidence necessary to bring your vision to life. Confidence is truly the hidden key in interior design. It allows you to make decisions without fear, to experiment boldly, and to build spaces that authentically reflect your personality and lifestyle.

WHAT MAKES THIS JOURNEY DIFFERENT?

This isn't a passive reading experience. Instead, think of this book as a deeply interactive manual—one designed not just to be read, but to be actively engaged with and applied. Throughout each chapter, you'll find practical advice, clearly explained principles, hands-on exercises, insightful tips, and creative challenges to help you apply each lesson directly to your home.

Moreover, I've carefully integrated a range of custom illustrations and diagrams. Each image is thoughtfully chosen and handcrafted to clearly illustrate key concepts, layouts, and design ideas, ensuring even complex principles become crystal clear.

From interactive quizzes that help you pinpoint your unique style to checklists that guide your shopping and decision-making, this book is your indispensable ally, providing clear, structured guidance every step of the way. No detail has been overlooked, and no question is left unanswered.

Additionally, you'll learn to overcome common obstacles that might have stopped you in the past: limited budgets, small or challenging spaces, rental restrictions, or simply a lack of clarity regarding your personal tastes. These hurdles will no longer stand between you and your ideal home. In fact, you might soon find yourself embracing them as exciting challenges that enhance your creativity.

THE MINDSET OF A DESIGNER

Before you dive deep into the upcoming chapters, it's important to briefly touch upon the mindset required for successful interior design. Great spaces don't just happen—they're thoughtfully created. Approach this journey with curiosity, patience, and openness to experimentation. Don't be afraid to challenge conventional wisdom or embrace your own distinctive tastes. Remember: there is no universally "correct" way to design a space—there is only the way that feels most authentic, comfortable, and joyful for you and those you love.

As you progress through this journey, remember that even the most celebrated interior designers once stood exactly where you stand today: excited, slightly uncertain, and eager to begin. The difference between them and everyone else lies simply in their willingness to learn, to experiment boldly, and, most importantly, to start.

LET'S BEGIN

Now it's your turn. Together, we'll take this blank canvas—your home—and transform it into a masterpiece filled with life, personality, and warmth. You are embarking on more than just a design project; you're stepping into a rewarding, personal journey toward a home you deeply love. Whether you're planning a full home renovation or just a simple refresh of your favorite room, every journey begins with the first step, and you've already taken it.

Welcome, wholeheartedly, to your design journey. Your dream home is waiting—let's create it together.

HOW TO USE THIS BOOK
Effectively

Now that you've officially begun your interior design journey, it's essential to understand how best to navigate this comprehensive guide. Just as a painter needs to know how to use brushes and palettes, you'll get the most from your design experience by knowing exactly how to utilize this book. Let's dive into how you can effectively engage with each section to ensure your journey is both seamless and transformative.

YOUR PERSONAL REFERENCE GUIDE

First and foremost, this book is crafted as an all-encompassing reference manual. It's not intended merely for a single read-through, but rather as a companion you'll return to frequently. Feel free to use it in ways that suit your specific needs, whether you're embarking on a complete home renovation, designing one particular space, or seeking inspiration for future projects.

Consider marking pages, highlighting key concepts, jotting down notes in the margins, or even adding sticky tabs to quickly reference important sections later on. This kind of active engagement will significantly enhance your learning experience.

NAVIGATING THE CONTENT

The Interior Design Bible is structured intentionally to take you progressively deeper into the world of design. Here's a brief outline of how each part serves your overall journey:

Introduction
This section sets the stage, familiarizing you with the basic approach, the book structure, and your personal design goals. Make sure to engage thoroughly with the interactive quiz to pinpoint your unique style clearly.

Part I: Interior Design Fundamentals
Before diving into specific room transformations, you'll first master foundational principles. Absorbing these fundamental concepts early

ensures your design decisions are purposeful and cohesive.

Part II: Room-by-Room Guide
This section guides you through practical applications, breaking down design techniques tailored explicitly to each area of your home. Ideal as a reference whenever you embark on a new room project.

Part III: Design Elements & Materials
Gain detailed insight into essential materials and elements such as lighting, furniture, textiles, wall treatments, and flooring. This part is particularly valuable when selecting materials or shopping for new home decor.

Part IV: Real-Life Design Solutions
This section is dedicated to overcoming practical design challenges, including budget limitations, small-space living, and pet or family-friendly design considerations.

Part V: Advanced Design Skills & Tips
Perfect for when you're feeling confident and ready to tackle more substantial projects like renovations or sustainable design. It also teaches timeless design principles to ensure your home remains stylish for years to come.

Part VI: Social & Community Engagement
Here you'll learn how to proudly showcase your finished projects, connect with like-minded individuals, and celebrate your creativity within a supportive community.

MAXIMIZING THE FEATURES OF THIS BOOK

To optimize your use of this guide, here are several recommended strategies:

Interactive Exercises & Quizzes
Throughout the book, you'll encounter interactive exercises and quizzes. Engage actively with these— grab a pencil, notebook, or digital device and fully

immerse yourself in the activities. This hands-on approach significantly strengthens your design intuition.

Visual & Graphic Illustrations
Key concepts are accompanied by detailed hand-drawn illustrations to clarify intricate ideas visually. Whenever you see a visual reference, pause to study it carefully. Often, these visuals can communicate principles even more effectively than text alone.

Checklists & Templates
Scattered throughout this book, you'll find helpful checklists and templates designed to simplify your shopping, planning, and decision-making processes. Feel free to photocopy or scan these resources, using them repeatedly as needed.

Step-by-Step Tutorials
Certain projects or concepts are explained using detailed step-by-step tutorials. Following these instructions closely will build your confidence and skill level dramatically. Don't rush through them; instead, give each step adequate attention.

CREATING YOUR PERSONAL WORKBOOK
Turning this guide into your personalized workbook is highly encouraged. Here's how you can do it effectively:

- **Design Journal**: Keep a dedicated notebook alongside this book to track ideas, inspirations, measurements, color swatches, and fabric samples. Document your progress—before and after pictures can significantly boost your motivation.

- **Inspiration Boards**: Regularly collect images, textures, or colors that resonate with your style and vision. Creating physical or digital inspiration boards provides visual clarity and ensures consistency in your projects.

- **Interactive Notes**: Actively annotate margins, underline essential tips, or jot down questions directly in the book. Personal annotations make your experience richer and serve as quick references later on.

SUGGESTED READING & PROGRESSION ORDER
Depending on your experience level or current project, you might find different approaches beneficial:

Situation	Suggested Approach
Brand-new to interior design	Follow chapters sequentially, mastering fundamentals first
Planning specific room transformations	Start with "Room-by-Room Guide" and refer back to fundamentals as needed
Limited budget or small space concerns	Prioritize "Real-Life Design Solutions" and refer to fundamentals for support
Renovation or major home overhaul	Engage deeply with "Advanced Design Skills & Tips" alongside room-specific chapters

RECOMMENDED PACE & MINDSET

Design is personal and should never feel rushed. Take your time with each section. If something doesn't immediately resonate or seems challenging, pause, reflect, or even step away briefly. Inspiration often strikes when you least expect it—over a cup of tea, a walk, or while flipping through unrelated visuals.

Maintain an open, curious mindset throughout your journey. Be prepared to pivot or change your mind entirely as you learn more about your preferences and uncover new ideas. Remember, interior design thrives on experimentation and evolution.

MEASURING YOUR PROGRESS

Regularly reflect on your progress by reviewing your design journal and before-after photos. Celebrate even small milestones along the way, whether it's finally settling on the perfect color palette or rearranging your furniture to create better flow.

LET'S START DESIGNING!

Now you understand precisely how this book is designed to serve you best. You're not simply holding a guide; you're holding a trusted companion, designed specifically to empower and guide you through every stage of creating your ideal home. Approach each page with enthusiasm, curiosity, and an open heart, and you'll find this journey more rewarding than you ever imagined.

It's time to confidently dive in—your beautifully designed home awaits!

DISCOVERING YOUR
Unique Style

Interior design, above all else, is deeply personal. Every great design journey begins by exploring and pinpointing your unique style—something inherently reflective of who you are, what you value, and how you want to feel in your own home. But uncovering that personal aesthetic can often feel daunting. With endless sources of inspiration, from Instagram feeds bursting with ideas to Pinterest boards overflowing with beautifully styled rooms, it's easy to feel overwhelmed. That's why we've carefully designed this interactive quiz. Think of it as your personal style compass, guiding you confidently toward the style that feels perfectly you.

This quiz isn't just a fun exercise—it's a fundamental starting point for your interior design journey. By clarifying your style preferences now, you'll approach each chapter with more precision, confidence, and clarity. So, grab a notebook or your design journal, a pen, and your favorite beverage, and let's dive into this engaging exploration of your inner designer.

INTERACTIVE STYLE QUIZ

Below you'll find a series of thoughtfully crafted questions designed to help identify the style or combination of styles most aligned with your personality and preferences. For each question, jot down your chosen letter (A, B, C, D, etc.) in your notebook or design journal.

Ready? Let's begin!

1. When imagining your dream living space, what feeling do you most wish to evoke?

A. Calm, serene, and uncluttered
B. Cozy, warm, and inviting
C. Eclectic, lively, and expressive
D. Timeless, refined, and classic
E. Bright, breezy, and relaxed
F. Bold, dramatic, and vibrant

2. Which color palette most resonates with your ideal home?

A. Neutral tones: whites, creams, greys
B. Earthy hues: olive green, rich browns, muted blues
C. Bright, vibrant colors mixed freely
D. Classic tones: navy, cream, gold accents
E. Soft pastels, whites, and light blues
F. Rich jewel tones and daring contrasts

3. When choosing furniture, you tend to prioritize:

A. Clean lines, minimal ornamentation
B. Distressed finishes, comfort, and rustic charm
C. Unique finds, vintage pieces, and eclectic combinations
D. Symmetry, elegance, and traditional craftsmanship
E. Natural textures, rattan, and light wood
F. Unusual shapes, bold fabrics, and striking visual impact

4. Your ideal weekend afternoon at home involves:

A. Relaxing in a minimalist, clutter-free space
B. Enjoying a cozy afternoon wrapped in soft blankets by the fireplace
C. Curating your latest vintage or flea market finds
D. Hosting a sophisticated dinner or tea party
E. Reading or lounging near an open window, feeling a gentle breeze
F. Experimenting creatively with bold DIY home decor projects

5. Which of these décor elements most appeals to you?

A. Sleek, streamlined furniture and open spaces
B. Farmhouse sink, rustic wood accents, exposed beams
C. Macramé wall hangings, colorful rugs, eclectic art
D. Antique mirrors, crystal chandeliers, elegant moldings
E. Coastal art, nautical accents, linen textures
F. Wallpaper with vivid patterns, maximalist gallery walls

6. How do you approach accessorizing shelves or coffee tables?

A. Keep it minimal—less is always more
B. Arrange vintage books, candles, and family heirlooms
C. Mix diverse objects, each with a personal story
D. Symmetrically arrange polished decor items
E. Incorporate seashells, driftwood, and airy décor
F. Display striking, bold accessories with bright accent.

7. Your favorite materials or finishes typically include:

A. Metal, glass, and polished concrete
B. Reclaimed wood, natural stone, and matte finishes
C. Bold textiles, mixed metals, and patterned ceramics
D. Marble, velvet, brass, and refined woods
E. Woven textures, whitewashed wood, and soft linens
F. Glossy finishes, lacquered furniture, and luxurious fabrics

INTERPRETING YOUR RESULTS

Now, tally up your answers. Which letter did you choose most frequently?

Use the guide below to discover your primary design style (or blend of styles):

	Your Primary Style	Description
A	**Modern & Minimalist**	Clean, uncluttered spaces emphasizing simplicity and function
B	**Farmhouse & Rustic Charm**	Warm, welcoming environments rich with character and texture
C	**Eclectic & Bohemian**	Vibrant spaces blending diverse cultural elements and vintage treasures
D	**Traditional & Classic**	Timeless elegance with refined symmetry and sophistication
E	**Coastal & Nautical**	Light-filled rooms evoking relaxation and seaside tranquility
F	**Maximalism & Dopamine Decor**	Bold, lively interiors filled with expressive color and abundant patterns

MIXING STYLES

Don't worry if your results don't fall neatly into one category! Many beautiful spaces emerge from blending two or even three styles. For instance:

- A mix of Modern & Minimalist with Coastal & Nautical can create sleek yet relaxed spaces.
- Eclectic & Bohemian with Maximalism can result in wonderfully vibrant and personalized interiors.

MOVING FORWARD WITH CONFIDENCE

You've now taken a critical step in clarifying your unique style or style combination. As you continue through the chapters of this book, consistently refer back to your quiz results. Allow them to serve as your design foundation, ensuring every choice you make contributes authentically to spaces that truly represent your aesthetic vision.

Remember, great design is never static—your style will continue evolving with your life experiences, inspirations, and evolving tastes. This quiz isn't meant to restrict you, but rather to give you clarity and confidence to experiment and evolve naturally.

So, are you ready to dive deeper into your style discovery? With this newfound awareness, you're now fully prepared to journey confidently into the next chapters of your personal design story.

Let's create something extraordinary together!

PART I

INTERIOR DESIGN FUNDAMENTALS

UNDERSTANDING
Interior Design Basics

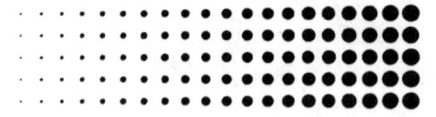

CHAPTER 1

PRINCIPLES OF
Interior Design

Designing your home may initially seem like a mystifying process—something reserved exclusively for seasoned professionals. However, by simply mastering some fundamental design principles, you'll quickly find yourself capable of creating beautiful, cohesive, and functional spaces that reflect your personality. Much like the foundational rules artists use to craft compelling paintings, these six core interior design principles—Balance, Harmony, Contrast, Scale, Proportion, and Rhythm—are your essential toolkit for creating extraordinary interiors. Let's explore each principle thoroughly to equip you with a solid foundation from which to confidently build.

01
BALANCE

In interior design, balance refers to the visual equilibrium within a space. Imagine your room as a scale: to achieve balance, visual weight must be evenly distributed, creating a pleasing and stable appearance. There are three primary types of balance:

Symmetrical Balance: Also known as formal balance, symmetrical balance occurs when objects on either side of an imaginary central axis mirror each other. This creates a classic and orderly feel.

Ideal For: Traditional spaces, formal living rooms, elegant dining rooms.

SYMMETRICAL BALANCE

Tip: Use pairs of matching furniture, lamps, or accessories to enhance symmetry.

ASYMMETRICAL BALANCE

Asymmetrical Balance: Known as informal balance, asymmetry involves different elements of equal visual weight that balance each other out without exact duplication. This creates a dynamic yet harmonious effect.

Ideal For: Modern, eclectic, and casual spaces.

Tip: Combine a large sofa on one side with a group of smaller furniture or decorative items on the opposite side.

Radial Balance: Elements radiate outwards from a central focal point, creating circular harmony.

Ideal For: Entryways, round dining tables, or rooms with chandeliers as centerpieces.

RADIAL BALANCE

02
HARMONY

Harmony ensures that all components in your space blend seamlessly to create a unified and cohesive look. When elements—colors, patterns, textures, and styles—work well together, they form a pleasing visual flow. Achieving harmony involves:

- Selecting colors from complementary or analogous palettes.
- Repeating shapes or textures throughout the space.
- Maintaining consistency in style and thematic elements.

Tip: Create a mood board or inspiration board to ensure every decision contributes harmoniously to the overall aesthetic.

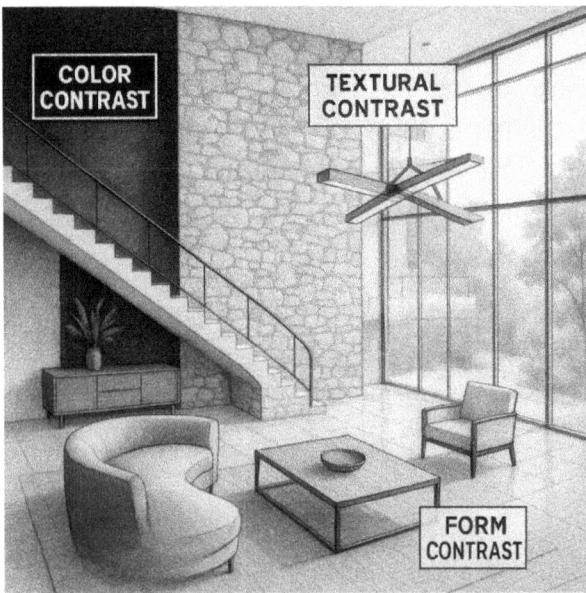

03
CONTRAST

Contrast adds depth, interest, and excitement to interiors by juxtaposing different elements. Thoughtful contrast keeps your room lively, preventing monotony and elevating visual engagement.

Here's how you can incorporate contrast effectively:

Contrast Type	Examples & Application
Color Contrast	Black-and-white color schemes; pairing bold colors against neutral backgrounds.
Textural Contrast	Smooth polished surfaces beside rough, rustic materials.
Form Contrast	Round furniture combined with angular, geometric pieces.
Scale Contrast	A large artwork next to smaller decorative objects.

Tip: Use contrast sparingly but intentionally; too much can cause visual chaos.

04
SCALE

Scale refers to the size of one object in relation to the overall space or other objects within that space. Correct scaling ensures that furniture and decor neither overwhelm nor appear insignificant within a room.

Consider these guidelines:
- Large rooms require substantial pieces to avoid looking sparse.
- Small rooms demand scaled-down furniture to prevent overcrowding.
- Adjust scale according to ceiling height, floor area, and architectural features.

Tip: Always measure your space before purchasing furniture. Create floor plans to visualize scale effectively.

05
PROPORTION

Proportion specifically refers to the relationship between individual elements within your interior —such as the size of a coffee table compared to the sofa or the height of a lamp in relation to a side table. Good proportion creates harmony, enhancing aesthetic appeal and comfort.

A common guide in design is the Golden Ratio (approximately 1.618), a natural proportion pleasing to the human eye.

- Ideal furniture groupings often follow ratios approximating the Golden Ratio.
- Artwork is frequently placed using this ratio, achieving visually balanced compositions.

06
RHYTHM

Rhythm in interior design refers to the flow created by the thoughtful repetition and progression of design elements such as colors, shapes, and patterns. It guides the viewer's eyes through the space, enhancing visual continuity and cohesion.

Ways to establish rhythm:
- **Repetition**: Echoing elements like colors, patterns, or textures throughout the space.
- **Transition**: Using subtle gradations in size, shape, or color to create a smooth flow.
- **Progression**: Creating visual rhythm through a gradual increase or decrease in size or intensity of elements.

Tip: Use similar patterns or colors across adjoining rooms to establish visual continuity throughout your home.

APPLYING THESE PRINCIPLES TOGETHER

To truly excel in interior design, remember that these principles don't operate independently. Instead, they should be thoughtfully combined, adapted, and balanced to achieve truly exceptional spaces. Practice by observing your favorite interior designs—magazines, websites, or physical spaces—and identifying how each principle is effectively applied.

For instance, notice how a professionally decorated living room balances furniture symmetrically, achieves harmony through color consistency, adds excitement with contrasting textures, and guides your eyes effortlessly through rhythmic repetition of certain elements.

YOUR DESIGNER'S MINDSET

Mastering these foundational principles is your first major step toward professional-quality interiors. Embrace each project with curiosity and an eagerness to experiment, and you'll naturally internalize these fundamentals, guiding every design decision you make moving forward.

Remember, creativity flourishes within structure. By grounding your designs firmly in these six core principles—Balance, Harmony, Contrast, Scale, Proportion, and Rhythm—you empower yourself with the clarity, confidence, and competence necessary to create beautifully designed spaces that uniquely reflect you.

Let's carry these lessons forward, building upon this strong foundation as we explore more about essential design terminology, concepts, and common myths in the next sections.

DESIGN MYTHS DEBUNKED: **ANYONE**
Can Learn to Decorate

If I had a dollar for every time someone told me, "I just don't have an eye for design," or "Decorating just isn't my thing," I'd probably be sitting comfortably in one of my beautifully designed beach homes sipping a margarita right now. The reality is that these common beliefs are simply myths that can unnecessarily hold people back from unleashing their full creative potential. Trust me when I say this: anyone—and yes, I mean absolutely anyone—can learn to decorate and create stunning interiors that feel personally fulfilling.

In this chapter, we'll dissect and debunk the most prevalent myths surrounding interior design, empowering you with clarity, confidence, and a fresh perspective. Let's banish those misconceptions once and for all, replacing hesitation with inspiration, and doubt with determination.

MYTH #1: YOU MUST BE BORN WITH A "DESIGN GENE"

THE TRUTH: DESIGN IS A LEARNED SKILL, NOT AN INHERITED TRAIT

One of the most persistent myths is the belief that great interior design skills are innate—you're either born with them or you're not. While some individuals naturally have a more intuitive visual sense, successful decorating is largely about mastering specific principles and techniques, combined with practical experience and experimentation.

Just like cooking or painting, interior design is a skill that improves dramatically through practice, patience, and persistence. The more you experiment and practice applying design fundamentals, the more confidently and effectively you'll design spaces that reflect your unique tastes.

Tip: Commit to small decorating projects first, gradually building your confidence and expertise.

MYTH #2: GOOD DESIGN REQUIRES A LARGE BUDGET

THE TRUTH: CREATIVITY OUTWEIGHS EXPENSE

Another widespread misconception is that stylish interiors require significant financial investment. This myth often discourages people from attempting to decorate altogether, mistakenly believing great style is beyond their financial reach. The truth is entirely different: outstanding design is about creativity and ingenuity rather than just spending power. Here are a few affordable ideas to elevate your space instantly:

- **Upcycling & DIY**: Transform inexpensive thrifted furniture into custom masterpieces.
- **Strategic Purchases**: Invest only in a few quality "anchor pieces," complementing them with budget-friendly accents.
- **Use of Paint**: Dramatically transform spaces inexpensively using bold paint colors or interesting paint techniques.

MYTH #3: SMALLER SPACES CAN'T BE BEAUTIFUL

THE TRUTH: THOUGHTFUL DESIGN CAN TRANSFORM ANY SPACE

Many believe beautiful interiors require spacious rooms, high ceilings, or grand proportions. The reality is that thoughtfully designed small spaces can be exceptionally charming, stylish, and functional.

Strategies for smaller spaces include:
- **Scale and Proportion**: Select appropriately sized furniture to enhance space rather than overwhelm it.
- **Multifunctional Furniture**: Opt for pieces that can serve multiple purposes—such as storage ottomans, foldable tables, or sleeper sofas.
- **Vertical Space**: Maximize your walls with shelves, hooks, and vertical storage options.

MYTH #4: DECORATING MEANS FOLLOWING TRENDS

THE TRUTH: TIMELESS, PERSONAL DESIGN IS ALWAYS IN STYLE

Design trends can be incredibly inspiring. However, becoming overly reliant on passing trends can result in interiors that quickly feel dated or impersonal. The true magic in decorating lies in creating spaces that resonate deeply with your personal taste and lifestyle—spaces that bring joy and comfort for years.

To design timeless interiors:
- Focus on classic, quality foundational pieces.
- Add trend-driven accents sparingly, allowing them to evolve over time.
- Trust your intuition—if a trend doesn't resonate, simply skip it.

Tip: Limit trend-following to easily changeable elements like accessories, pillows, and artwork.

MYTH #5: YOU MUST STICK TO ONE STYLE

THE TRUTH: MIXING STYLES CREATES AUTHENTICITY AND DEPTH

Many novice decorators fear mixing different styles, believing that successful interiors must rigidly adhere to a singular style category. Yet, the richest, most intriguing spaces are often those combining multiple styles cohesively, reflecting diverse influences and personal history.

Successful style mixing involves:
- Identifying common threads such as color palettes, materials, or shapes.
- Maintaining balance by ensuring each style has a clear purpose within the space.
- Starting slowly, adding layers and mixing styles deliberately rather than randomly.

MYTH #3: YOU NEED TO DECORATE EVERYTHING ALL AT ONCE

THE TRUTH: GREAT INTERIORS EVOLVE OVER TIME

Another common myth is the feeling that decorating is a single, all-or-nothing event—that you must have every element perfectly coordinated from day one. In reality, truly compelling interiors develop naturally over time, layer by thoughtful layer.

Great spaces come together gradually through experiences, travels, and collected treasures. It's perfectly acceptable—indeed preferable—to allow your interiors to evolve organically.

Here's how to approach decorating gradually:

STEP	APPROACH
Prioritize	Begin with essential furniture items and key functional elements.
Build Gradually	Slowly add accessories, art, and accents as you discover pieces that truly resonate.
Enjoy the Process	View decorating as a joyful journey rather than a stressful task.

MYTH #3: PROFESSIONAL RESULTS REQUIRE A PROFESSIONAL DESIGNER

THE TRUTH: DIY CAN ACHIEVE PROFESSIONAL-LEVEL RESULTS

While professional interior designers bring extensive experience and vision to projects, the belief that professional-quality results can't be achieved independently is untrue. With access to resources, guides (like this one!), tutorials, and a willingness to learn, anyone can achieve professional-caliber design.

Equip yourself with foundational design principles, familiarize yourself with essential terminology, and confidently embrace creative experimentation. Your resulting spaces will reflect your individuality, passion, and determination, rivaling professional designs.

EMPOWERING YOUR INNER DESIGNER

Now that we've thoroughly debunked these widespread myths, you can see clearly: anyone can absolutely learn to decorate beautifully. Interior design is a skillset accessible to everyone, requiring simply curiosity, patience, and practice.

Your decorating journey is unique, personal, and richly rewarding. Never let misconceptions hold you back again. Approach each project with enthusiasm, courageously experiment, and trust your intuition to create interiors that genuinely reflect your personality and lifestyle.

The next chapters of this book will give you detailed knowledge, powerful tools, and inspired ideas to further develop your decorating skills. Together, we'll ensure your home beautifully tells your unique story.

CHAPTER 2

Styles and Themes

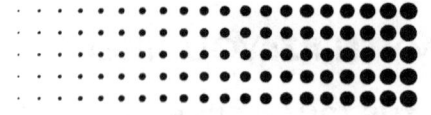

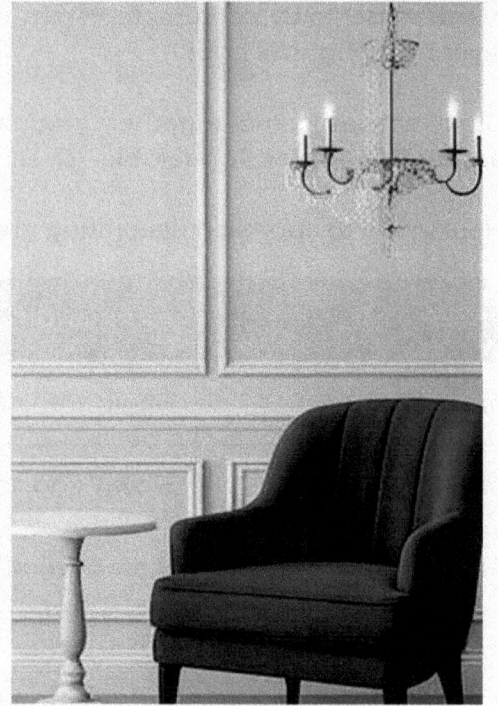

MODERN &
Minimalist

The modern and minimalist interior design style isn't merely an aesthetic preference; it's an entire philosophy—one that emphasizes simplicity, clarity, functionality, and intentional living. Rooted deeply in the concept of "less is more," this style challenges conventional ideas that more objects mean greater luxury or comfort. Instead, minimalism showcases beauty through restraint and careful selection, crafting spaces that are not only visually striking but also emotionally calming.

Whether you're drawn to sleek modern aesthetics or find peace in uncluttered minimalist spaces, mastering the essentials of Modern & Minimalist design will empower you to create interiors that are both sophisticated and serene. Let's dive deeply into

what defines this style, its history, core characteristics, essential components, practical tips, and how you can implement it effectively into your own home.

HISTORY AND EVOLUTION

Modern Design Roots

Modern design emerged around the early to mid-20th century as a reaction against ornate, overly decorative styles that preceded it. Influenced heavily by movements like Bauhaus and Scandinavian functionalism, modern design focuses strongly on practicality and simplicity. Iconic architects and designers such as Ludwig Mies van der Rohe,

Le Corbusier, and Eero Saarinen pioneered this style, emphasizing clean lines, geometric forms, and functional layouts.

Rise of Minimalism
Minimalism gained prominence during the late 20th century, largely inspired by Japanese Zen philosophies and minimalist art movements emphasizing simplicity, harmony, and clarity. Minimalist interiors strip away excess decoration, leaving only essentials, thereby emphasizing the beauty of empty space and intentional living.

CORE CHARACTERISTICS

To clearly identify a modern and minimalist space, look for these definitive features:

- **Clean Lines and Shapes**: Furniture and architectural features are sleek, straightforward, and uncluttered, emphasizing simplicity and clarity.

- **Limited Color Palettes**: Neutral tones—white, black, grays, beige—with carefully chosen pops of color.

- **Functionality Above All**: Each item has a clear purpose, highlighting practicality and usefulness over ornamentation.

- **Ample Negative Space**: Embracing empty or "negative" space to create calm, orderly environments.

- **Absence of Clutter**: Carefully curated interiors with only meaningful, useful, or beautiful items on display.

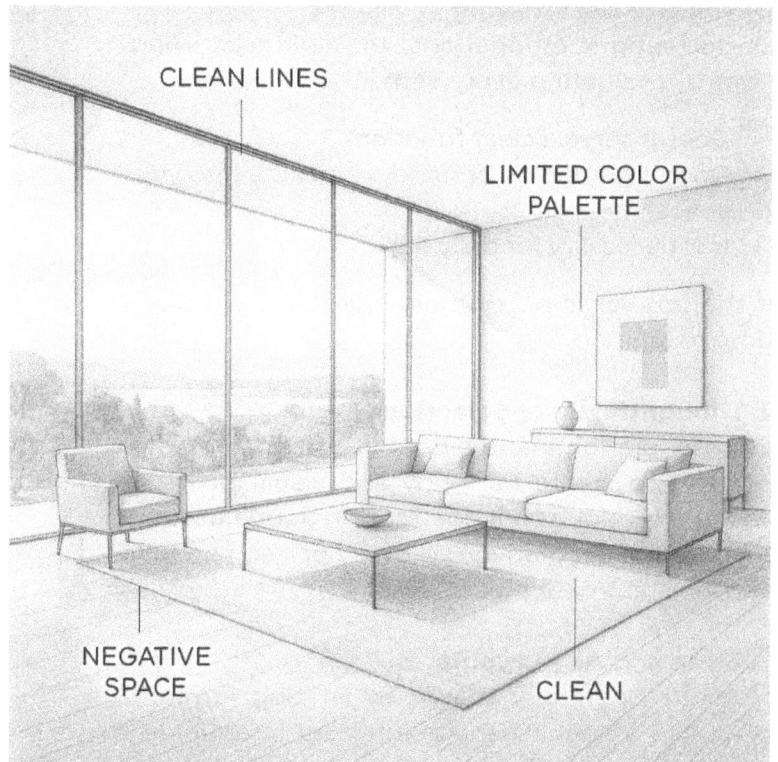

ESSENTIAL ELEMENTS & MATERIALS

The following are staple components and materials typically associated with Modern & Minimalist design:

ELEMENTS & MATERIALS	DESCRIPTION & USAGE
Glass & Metal	Often used in minimalist furniture, emphasizing sleekness and transparency.
Natural Wood	Provides warmth and textural interest against minimalistic neutral backdrops.
Concrete & Stone	Popular for flooring, countertops, or accent walls, offering a sleek, contemporary vibe.
Monochromatic Textiles	Curtains, upholstery, and rugs in neutral, muted colors to maintain calm simplicity.
Lighting as Art	Statement lighting fixtures often act as sculptural art pieces, adding visual interest without clutter.

PRACTICAL TIPS FOR CREATING MODERN & MINIMALIST INTERIORS

Achieving a successful modern minimalist interior isn't about having stark, sterile spaces—it's about thoughtful reduction and intentional choices. Follow these actionable guidelines to transform your interiors effectively:

1. Prioritize Decluttering

Decluttering is foundational to minimalist living. Start by evaluating every item in your space:

- Does it serve a clear function?
- Does it genuinely bring joy or beauty into your space?
- Is it necessary for daily life?

If the answer is no to these questions, it's likely time to let it go.

2. Thoughtful Color Selections

Choose predominantly neutral, monochromatic palettes to create harmony and visual peace. If you crave color, use it sparingly in subtle accents—artwork, decorative pillows, or a carefully chosen statement piece.

3. Open and Airy Layouts

Maintain open, airy spaces by limiting furniture pieces to essentials. Place furniture intentionally to enhance the feeling of openness, optimize traffic flow, and maximize natural light.

4. Texture as Interest

When your palette is minimalistic, texture becomes your primary tool for visual interest. Incorporate subtle yet contrasting textures such as natural fibers, smooth leather, sleek metal, or rough stone surfaces.

5. Furniture with Purpose

Invest in fewer, high-quality pieces of furniture that emphasize functionality and form over quantity. Opt for items that serve multiple purposes—such as storage ottomans or beds with built-in drawers.

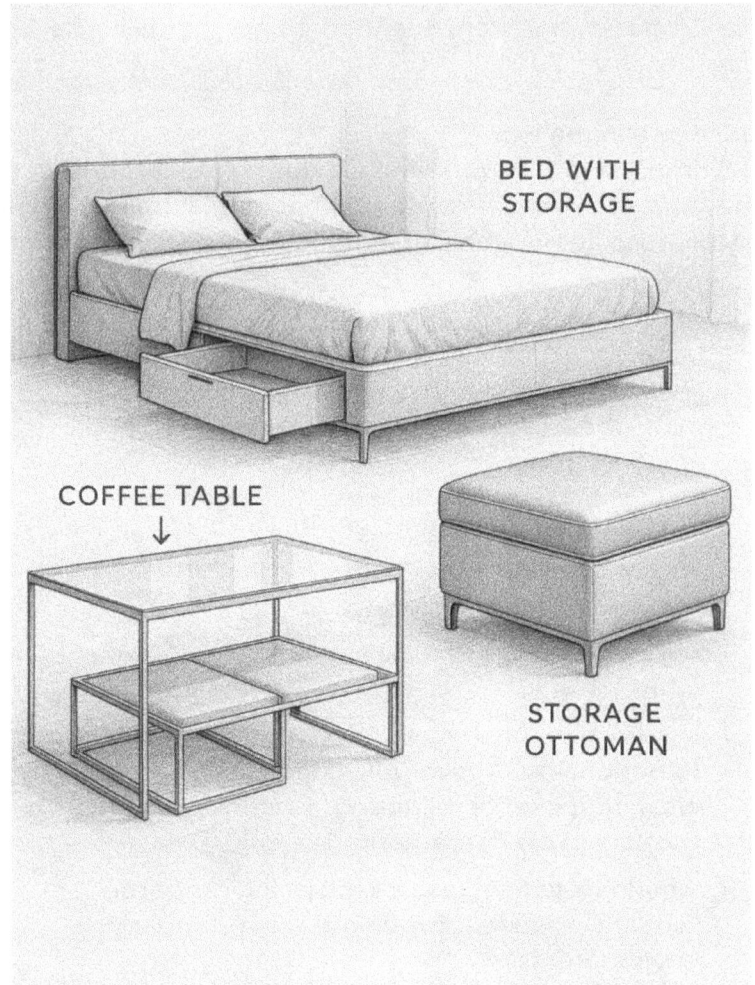

BED WITH STORAGE

COFFEE TABLE

STORAGE OTTOMAN

COMMON MISCONCEPTIONS AND PITFALLS TO AVOID

Myth: Minimalist interiors must be entirely white and devoid of personality.

- **Truth**: Personality shines brightest when decoration is thoughtful and limited. Minimalism doesn't exclude color or character—it emphasizes intentional selection.

Pitfall: Mistaking minimalism for empty spaces without comfort.

- **Solution**: Prioritize comfort through quality materials, soft textures, and ergonomic designs to achieve warmth alongside simplicity.

MODERN VS. MINIMALIST: UNDERSTANDING THE NUANCES

Though frequently used interchangeably, Modern and Minimalist styles have distinct nuances:

Aspect	Modern	Minimalist
Historical Roots	Early 20th-century movements; Bauhaus, mid-century modernism	Japanese Zen philosophy, minimal art
Color Palette	Neutral with bold contrasts	Primarily neutral, soft, muted
Visual Complexity	Moderate, allowing limited decor	Extremely restrained, few decorative elements
Furniture & Decor	Sleek, geometric forms, iconic mid-century pieces	Ultra-streamlined, functional, and highly curated

MODERN

- Bold Contrast
- Stylish mid-century modern furniture
- Carefully curated decor
- Distinct geometric patterns

MINIMALIST

- Ultra-streamlined, calming extremely refined room
- Intentionally limited, abundant open space and tranquility

CASE STUDY: DESIGNING A MODERN & MINIMALIST LIVING ROOM

To put these concepts into action, let's briefly walk through creating a modern minimalist living room:

Furniture: Choose a streamlined sofa with geometric lines in neutral fabric. Complement it with minimalist metal and glass coffee tables.

Lighting: Incorporate sculptural floor lamps or understated recessed ceiling lights.

Decor: Display a carefully selected piece of abstract artwork or a singular sculptural vase.

Color Scheme: Maintain a base of white or gray walls, complemented by warm wood flooring and carefully chosen textile accents.

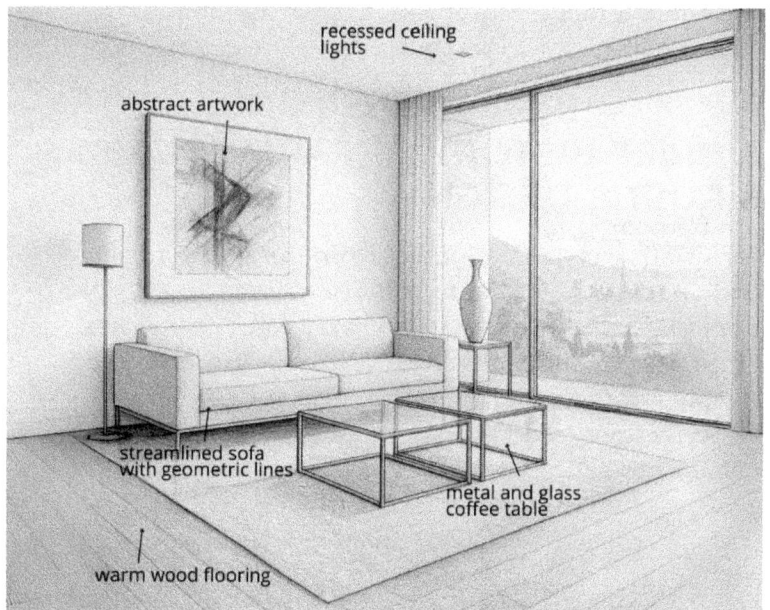

ACHIEVING HARMONY AND LONGEVITY

To create modern minimalist spaces that feel both timeless and genuinely livable, consistently reflect upon the "why" behind each choice. Each piece, each color, each texture should have a clear reason for its presence—whether functionality, beauty, or comfort.

As you cultivate this intentional approach, your interiors will organically develop into environments that support your lifestyle, reflect your personality, and offer enduring visual and emotional satisfaction.

Embrace the art of intentional simplicity, and allow Modern & Minimalist design to become not just an aesthetic choice, but a way of living beautifully and authentically.

FARMHOUSE &
Rustic Charm

Farmhouse and rustic charm is more than a design trend—it's a comforting embrace, a return to authenticity, and an invitation to slow down and savor life's simple pleasures. Rooted deeply in tradition, warmth, and practicality, farmhouse interiors evoke images of cozy gatherings, family dinners around an inviting table, and the timeless beauty of well-loved spaces.

Whether you're inspired by picturesque country cottages or modern farmhouse aesthetics popularized by design icons such as Joanna Gaines, this chapter will guide you step-by-step through the principles and techniques needed to master the farmhouse and rustic style. Together, we'll explore its rich history, key characteristics, essential elements, materials, practical guidelines, and the thoughtful nuances that make this style uniquely inviting.

A BRIEF HISTORY OF FARMHOUSE & RUSTIC DESIGN

Farmhouse style originated from rural practicality and necessity. Early farmhouses were built for durability, using readily available materials, emphasizing simplicity and function. Rustic charm, deeply intertwined with farmhouse style, celebrates imperfections and organic beauty, inspired by nature and simpler times.

In recent years, farmhouse design experienced a significant revival, influenced heavily by popular media, DIY movements, and an increased desire for comfort, authenticity, and heritage in contemporary living spaces.

KEY CHARACTERISTICS OF FARMHOUSE & RUSTIC INTERIORS

A successful farmhouse space seamlessly blends warmth, simplicity, and practicality. To clearly identify and cultivate farmhouse interiors, look for these hallmark characteristics:

- **Warm, Welcoming Atmosphere:** Prioritize cozy elements that immediately invite relaxation and comfort.
- **Natural and Distressed Materials**: Wood, stone, and reclaimed materials with visible wear, imperfections, and patina.
- **Neutral, Earthy Color Palette**: Whites, creams, tans, muted greens, soft blues, and gentle pastels.
- **Vintage or Antique Pieces**: Furnishings and décor reflecting history, nostalgia, and personal stories.
- **Practical and Functional Layouts**: Spaces designed for daily living, family gatherings, and communal activities.
- **Soft Textiles and Layers**: Comfortably layered with soft, natural textiles—cotton, linen, wool—that enhance warmth.

ESSENTIAL ELEMENTS & MATERIALS

Mastering farmhouse and rustic charm begins with carefully selecting elements that reflect tradition, authenticity, and warmth. Here's a comprehensive guide to essential materials and components:

Elements & Materials	How to Use Effectively
Reclaimed Wood	Flooring, exposed beams, furniture pieces, accent walls.
Vintage Furniture	Antique tables, chairs, cabinets, or benches with visible age and character.
Natural Stone	Fireplaces, flooring, kitchen backsplashes, accent walls.
Wrought Iron & Metal Accents	Lighting fixtures, handles, hinges, decorative hardware, adding rustic character.

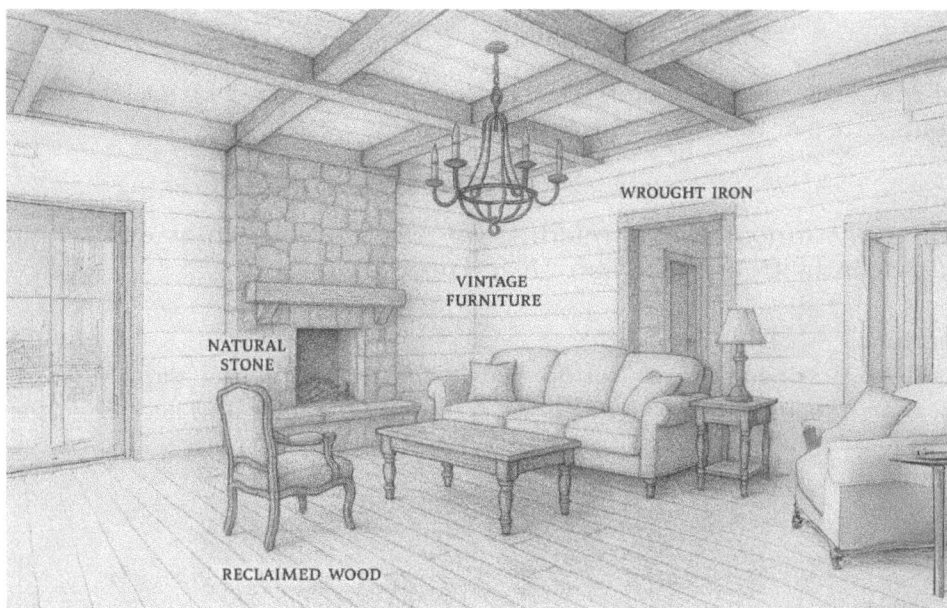

FARMHOUSE COLOR PALETTE GUIDE

Creating farmhouse interiors starts with a soothing, harmonious color palette that feels welcoming and timeless. Use this palette guide as a foundation:

Primary Neutrals	WARM WHITES · CREAMY BEIGES · SOFT GRAYS
Accent Colors	SAGE GREENS · MUTED BLUES · DUSTY ROSE · PALE YELLOWS
Material Colors	NATURAL WOOD TONES · AGED METAL · MATTE BLACK

PALETTE CATEGORY	RECOMMENDED COLORS
Walls	White Dove, Alabaster, Swiss Coffee
Cabinets	Soft Gray, Natural Wood, Sage Green
Accents	Muted Navy, Charcoal, Soft Mustard
Textiles	Linen, Soft Ivory, Earthy Taupe

PRACTICAL TIPS FOR ACHIEVING FARMHOUSE & RUSTIC CHARM

Transform your interiors into farmhouse havens by embracing these practical strategies:

1. Blend Old and New

Create depth by blending contemporary functionality with vintage charm. Combine new upholstered seating with antique wooden tables, modern appliances alongside vintage cabinetry, or sleek lighting fixtures above reclaimed wood islands.

2. Prioritize Natural Elements

Use plenty of natural materials such as wood, wicker, stone, and plants. Opt for live-edge wooden furniture, woven baskets, and terracotta planters filled with lush greenery.

3. Cozy Textural Layers

Farmhouse interiors are synonymous with comfort. Layer soft textiles such as quilts, knitted blankets, fluffy pillows, and natural rugs to instantly enhance warmth and texture.

4. Authentic Imperfections

Rustic charm comes alive in imperfections—rough textures, patina finishes, slightly worn surfaces. Embrace these elements rather than concealing them; they bring genuine character and lived-in appeal.

FARMHOUSE ROOM-BY-ROOM QUICK GUIDE

Tailor your farmhouse style beautifully room-by-room using this quick reference table:

Room	Essential Elements & Decor Suggestions
Kitchen	Open shelving, farmhouse sink, wooden countertops, pendant lighting, subway tile backsplash
Living Room	Comfortable seating, distressed coffee table, shiplap walls, stone fireplace, soft rugs

KITCHEN   LIVING ROOM

Room	Essential Elements & Decor Suggestions
Bedroom	Iron bed frame, linen bedding, vintage nightstands, reclaimed wood headboard, layered textiles
Dining Room	Long wooden farmhouse table, mismatched antique chairs, vintage sideboard, wrought iron chandelier
Bathroom	Freestanding claw-foot tub, rustic wooden shelves, vintage mirrors, matte black hardware

BEDROOM   DINING ROOM   BATHROOM

COMMON MISTAKES TO AVOID

Avoid common pitfalls that may dilute or confuse your farmhouse style:

- **Over-Decoration**: Farmhouse style should feel naturally curated, not cluttered. Edit décor thoughtfully, avoiding excessive accessories.
- **Ignoring Practicality**: Farmhouse is fundamentally about function and comfort. Avoid prioritizing aesthetics over livability.
- **Lack of Authenticity**: Avoid excessive new items that lack character. Balance contemporary pieces with vintage, authentic elements.

MODERN VS. CLASSIC FARMHOUSE: KEY DIFFERENCES

While farmhouse style traditionally celebrates rustic charm, there's a growing distinction between classic and modern farmhouse interpretations:

Elements	Classic Farmhouse	Modern Farmhouse
Color Palette	Warm creams, earthy hues	Predominantly white, grays, subtle black accents
Furniture Style	Vintage, traditional, visibly worn	Contemporary shapes, cleaner lines mixed with vintage
Decorative Elements	More ornate, eclectic and nostalgic	Minimal, curated, simpler accents
Materials	Deeply rustic, heavily distressed	Lightly distressed, balanced modern materials

Classic Farmhouse

Modern Farmhouse

CASE STUDY: CREATING A COZY FARMHOUSE DINING ROOM

Imagine designing a dining room that radiates warmth, heritage, and charm:

- **Table & Chairs**: Choose a long reclaimed wood farmhouse table paired with mismatched vintage chairs.
- **Lighting**: Hang a wrought-iron chandelier with subtle rust finish.
- **Storage**: Vintage sideboard with patina finish for practicality and aesthetics.
- **Decor**: Include handmade pottery, woven textiles, and simple greenery as centerpieces.
- **Color Scheme**: Soft cream walls, exposed wooden beams, natural wood tones, muted textiles.

WROUGHT-IRON CHANDELIER

RECLAIMEND WOOD TABLE

VINTAGE CHAIRS

VINTAGE SIDEBOARD

FINAL THOUGHTS ON FARMHOUSE & RUSTIC CHARM

Farmhouse interiors are beloved because they create immediate feelings of comfort, nostalgia, and authenticity. By embracing practicality, natural materials, vintage charm, and thoughtfully curated details, your spaces will become warm retreats that invite both family and guests alike to slow down, relax, and savor life's precious moments.

As you continue to explore this enduringly popular style, remember—true farmhouse design is never pretentious. It's deeply personal, perfectly imperfect, and authentically welcoming.

Embrace the simplicity and charm, and you'll create spaces filled with warmth and genuine heart.

ECLECTIC &
Bohemian

Eclectic and Bohemian interiors are a vibrant celebration of freedom, creativity, and personality. They defy rigid rules and formal constraints, instead inviting you to weave a tapestry rich with global influences, personal stories, diverse textures, and bold colors. Unlike any other design style, eclectic and bohemian spaces flourish precisely because of their imaginative spontaneity, artistic flair, and confident expression of individuality.

If you're someone who finds beauty in blending diverse eras, cultures, and visual elements, this chapter is your guide to mastering the delightful art of eclectic and bohemian design. Together, we'll explore the origins, identify essential elements, discuss key characteristics, and provide practical strategies to help you create spaces that authentically reflect your unique spirit.

UNDERSTANDING ECLECTIC & BOHEMIAN ORIGINS

The eclectic style emerged in the 19th century when interior designers began blending different historical styles into cohesive interiors. Rather than sticking to a single aesthetic, designers combined furniture, art, and decorative objects from varied periods and cultures to craft visually dynamic spaces.

Bohemian style (often called "boho"), closely intertwined with eclecticism, originated in Paris in the late 19th century, influenced by artistic communities and nomadic lifestyles. It celebrates creativity, freedom, and unconventional living, frequently incorporating cultural artifacts, vintage finds, and rich textiles.

KEY CHARACTERISTICS OF ECLECTIC & BOHEMIAN INTERIORS

To clearly capture eclectic and bohemian aesthetics, consider these definitive characteristics:

- **Personal Expression**: Spaces uniquely reflective of the owner's personality, interests, and adventures.
- **Vibrant Colors and Patterns**: Bold, lively combinations that create dynamic visual interest.
- **Cultural Influence**: Incorporation of global artifacts, travel mementos, and ethnic textiles.
- **Layered Textures**: Richly textured fabrics and surfaces—rugs, throws, tapestries, and more.
- **Artistic & Vintage Finds**: Unique vintage furniture, antiques, and original artwork.
- **Relaxed, Casual Atmosphere**: Comfortably informal, encouraging relaxation and creative expression.

ESSENTIAL ELEMENTS & MATERIALS

Here's a detailed guide to the key materials and elements essential to creating authentic eclectic and bohemian spaces:

Elements & Materials	Best Uses & Suggestions
Vintage Furniture	Sofas, armchairs, tables with character, mixing eras and styles.
Global Textiles	Kilim rugs, Moroccan cushions, Indian kantha quilts, Mexican embroidery.
Woven & Natural Fibers	Rattan chairs, macramé wall hangings, wicker baskets, jute rugs.

Artwork & Collections	Original art, personal collections, framed travel photography.
Plants & Greenery	Hanging plants, succulents, lush tropical foliage to enliven spaces.

Personal Art and Collections

Abundant Greenery

Vintage Furniture

Global Textiles

COLOR PALETTE FOR ECLECTIC & BOHEMIAN INTERIORS

Eclectic and bohemian spaces thrive on rich, saturated palettes balanced by natural, earthy hues. Consider these color recommendations:

Primary Neutrals		JEWEL TONES LIKE EMERALD GREEN · SAPPHIRE BLUE · RUBY RED · MUSTARD YELLOW
Accent Colors		WARM BEIGE · IVORY, SOFT GRAY · RICH BROWNS
Material Colors		METALLIC GOLD · BRASS · COPPER FOR REFLECTIVE WARMTH AND DEPTH

PALETTE CATEGORY	RECOMMENDED COLORS
Walls	Warm whites, soft taupe, or deep, saturated jewel tones
Textiles & Fabrics	Vibrant patterns, multi-colored, global-inspired prints
Furniture	Rich wood tones, painted finishes, eclectic upholstery
Accessories & Decor	Bold metallic accents, textured ceramics, vibrant artwork

PRACTICAL TIPS FOR MASTERING ECLECTIC & BOHEMIAN DESIGN

Creating eclectic and bohemian interiors requires a careful yet confident balance. Follow these practical strategies:

1. Curate Meaningfully
While eclectic design celebrates mixing, successful interiors are thoughtfully curated. Ensure each piece feels intentional, holding personal significance, aesthetic beauty, or functional value.

2. Embrace Layers
Layering is key to achieving the cozy, visually rich essence of bohemian style. Mix patterned rugs, layered cushions, and cozy throws to craft welcoming spaces.

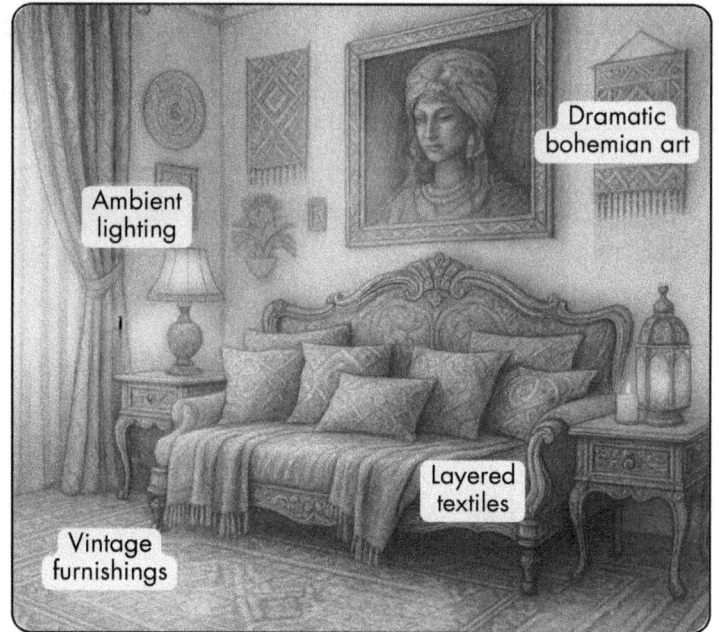

3. Balance Cohesion and Variety
While mixing diverse styles, maintain some elements of cohesion—such as repeating a particular color, shape, or texture throughout your space. This subtle repetition creates unity amidst diversity.

4. Celebrate Global Influence
Integrate elements from various cultures—Moroccan lanterns, African masks, Indian textiles—to enrich visual interest and reflect global inspiration.

ECLECTIC & BOHEMIAN ROOM-BY-ROOM INSPIRATION GUIDE

Use this table as a quick reference guide to inspire authentic eclectic and bohemian rooms:

Room	Key Elements & Styling Suggestions
Living Room	Vintage velvet sofa, patterned rugs, global cushions, gallery wall of eclectic art, statement plants
Bedroom	Patterned textiles, layered bedding, vintage side tables, rattan headboard, cozy seating nook

LIVING ROOM | BEDROOM

Dining Room	Mismatched chairs, vintage dining table, ethnic-inspired tableware, dramatic chandelier or pendant
Home Office	Antique desk, eclectic gallery wall, shelves displaying personal collections, comfortable upholstered chair
Outdoor Spaces	Woven hammock, outdoor rugs, global-inspired lanterns, lush container plants, bohemian textiles

DINING ROOM   OUTDOOR SPACE

COMMON MISTAKES AND HOW TO AVOID THEM

MISTAKE: OVERWHELMING CLUTTER.

- **Solution**: Practice intentional curation; periodically edit and reorganize your collections.

MISTAKE: LACK OF COHESION.

- **Solution**: Incorporate common threads—repeated colors, materials, or shapes—to unify the space.

MISTAKE: NEGLECTING COMFORT FOR AESTHETICS.

- **Solution**: Ensure spaces are as comfortable and functional as they are visually compelling.

ECLECTIC VS. BOHEMIAN: UNDERSTANDING SUBTLE DIFFERENCES

While closely related, eclectic and bohemian styles hold distinct nuances:

Feature	Eclectic Interiors	Bohemian Interiors
Color Usage	Diverse but can be more restrained	Richly saturated, bold, often maximalist
Decor Approach	Thoughtful, curated mixes	More spontaneous, free-spirited collections

Global Influence	Can be subtle, more varied	Strongly emphasized, vibrant cultural textures
Atmosphere	Visually dynamic yet balanced	Informal, relaxed, creatively energetic

CASE STUDY: DESIGNING A VIBRANT ECLECTIC & BOHEMIAN LIVING SPACE

Envision creating a lively, inviting living area filled with artistic charm and global inspiration:

- Furniture: Velvet vintage sofa, antique coffee table, eclectic side chairs.
- Textiles: Layered rugs with global patterns, richly embroidered cushions, cozy throws.
- Lighting: Moroccan-style pendant lamps, vintage table lamps, candles.
- Decor: Personal collection displays, abundant greenery, diverse artwork.
- Color Scheme: Jewel tones paired with neutrals, accented by metallic accessories.

Eclectic Interior   Bohemian Interior

FINAL THOUGHTS ON ECLECTIC & BOHEMIAN DESIGN

Eclectic and bohemian interiors free you from rigid design rules, inviting bold expression and genuine individuality. These styles thrive on contrast, texture, and personality—welcoming global accents, handmade items, and meaningful collections that speak to your story.

When thoughtfully curated, these interiors become more than just decorated rooms—they become soulful reflections of your identity, interests, and travels. The magic lies not in randomness, but in the intentional layering of elements that feel authentic and lived-in.

True eclectic and bohemian spaces are visually rich, emotionally warm, and endlessly inspiring. Don't aim for perfection—aim for feeling. Let your space evolve with you, honoring both memory and spontaneity. Trust your instincts, embrace creative freedom, and design a home that feels undeniably yours.

TRADITIONAL &
Classic

Stepping into a traditional and classic interior evokes an immediate sense of timeless elegance, grace, and sophistication. This enduring style, deeply rooted in history and refined taste, conveys a profound respect for craftsmanship, attention to detail, and harmonious balance. Traditional design has the remarkable ability to feel simultaneously luxurious and comfortable, reflecting decades—if not centuries—of refinement and cultural influence.

If you're drawn to spaces that exude classic charm, subtle sophistication, and tasteful formality, this chapter provides an essential roadmap. You'll learn about the rich heritage, defining characteristics, fundamental elements, and practical guidelines necessary for creating exquisite traditional and classic interiors that age gracefully and never go out of style.

HISTORICAL BACKGROUND AND EVOLUTION

Traditional and classic interiors trace their origins to 18th and 19th-century European homes, influenced by British, French, and American colonial design aesthetics. Styles such as Georgian, Victorian, Federal, and Colonial Revival heavily influenced today's traditional design vocabulary, celebrating proportion, symmetry, and finely crafted details.

Historically, traditional interiors symbolized status and refinement, often featuring furniture and decorative arts of superior craftsmanship and artistic value. Today, these timeless qualities endure, providing lasting appeal and continued inspiration.

DEFINING CHARACTERISTICS OF TRADITIONAL & CLASSIC INTERIORS

To effortlessly identify or create a traditional interior, look for these distinctive characteristics:

- **Symmetry and Order**: Furniture arrangements and decorative elements carefully balanced to create visual harmony.

- **Rich, Muted Color Palette**: Neutral and muted colors such as creams, taupe, beige, burgundy, navy, and deep green.

- **Classic Furniture Lines**: Curved, elegant shapes, and detailed ornamentation reflective of historical periods.

- **Refined Patterns and Textures**: Subtle florals, damasks, paisleys, and classic stripes that offer sophistication without overwhelming.

- **Detailed Architectural Elements**: Crown moldings, wainscoting, paneling, columns, and fireplaces providing depth and structure.

- **Timeless Accessories**: Antiques, fine artwork, porcelain, crystal, silver, and heirloom-quality items.

ESSENTIAL ELEMENTS & MATERIALS

A traditional interior is distinctly characterized by specific materials and elements, chosen for their historical authenticity, quality, and elegance:

Elements & Materials	Ideal Applications & Recommendations
Rich Woods	Dark-stained oak, mahogany, cherry for furniture, flooring, cabinetry
Ornate Fabrics	Velvet, silk, linen, brocade for upholstery, curtains, pillows
Classic Furniture	Wingback chairs, Chesterfield sofas, pedestal tables, sideboards
Decorative Moldings	Crown moldings, ceiling medallions, intricate baseboards and trim
Metals & Finishes	Polished brass, antique gold, silver finishes for hardware and lighting fixtures

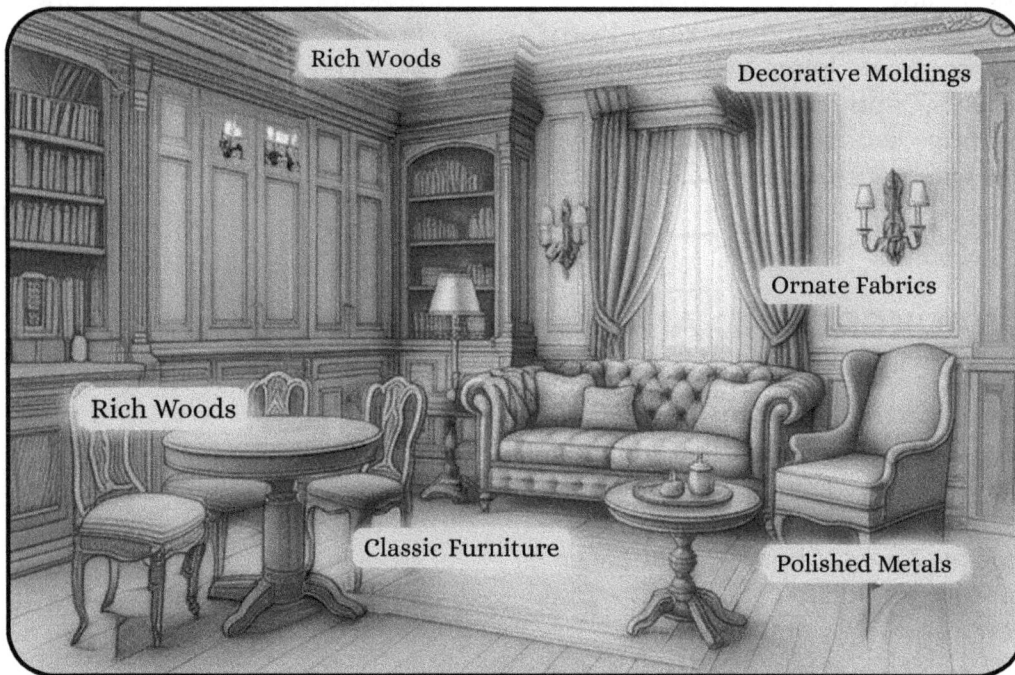

TRADITIONAL & CLASSIC COLOR PALETTE

Classic interiors favor palettes that feel rich yet restrained, sophisticated yet welcoming:

Foundation Colors		CREAM · BEIGE · IVORY · TAUPE
Primary Coastal Colors		DEEP JEWEL TONES—BURGUNDY · NAVY · EMERALD · PLUM
Accent Colors		METALLIC GOLD · BRASS · ANTIQUE SILVER · MUTED FLORAL SHADES

PALETTE CATEGORY	RECOMMENDED COLORS
Walls	Soft creams, warm grays, neutral taupe
Upholstery	Rich velvets, neutral linens, subtle patterning
Wood Tones	Deep mahogany, rich cherry, walnut
Accents	Jewel tones in small doses, gold/brass metallics

PRACTICAL GUIDELINES FOR DESIGNING TRADITIONAL INTERIORS

Creating timeless, traditional spaces involves intentional and informed decision-making. Here are practical strategies to guide your approach:

1. Emphasize Symmetry and Balance
Arrange furniture symmetrically around a clear focal point, such as a fireplace or grand window, reinforcing visual harmony and order.

2. Prioritize Architectural Details
Invest in refined architectural features—detailed moldings, built-in bookshelves, paneled walls—to lend structure and historical authenticity.

3. Select Classic Furniture
Opt for timeless pieces with elegant lines—wingback chairs, rolled-arm sofas, and carved wooden tables—that remain relevant and stylish through generations.

4. Incorporate Luxurious Textiles
Choose luxurious, high-quality fabrics—velvets, silks, damasks—for curtains, upholstery, and soft furnishings to add sophisticated texture and comfort.

TRADITIONAL & CLASSIC ROOM-BY-ROOM INSPIRATION GUIDE

Use this room-by-room guide as inspiration for crafting traditional interiors:

ROOM	KEY ELEMENTS & STYLING SUGGESTIONS
Living Room	Symmetrical seating arrangements, upholstered sofas, carved wood tables, elegant draperies, antique rugs
Dining Room	Formal dining set with upholstered chairs, crystal chandelier, sideboard with silver or porcelain accents

Living Room

Dining Room

Bedroom	Four-poster or upholstered bed, refined bedding, classic nightstands, subtle patterned wallpaper
Home Office	Traditional desk, tufted leather chair, built-in bookshelves, framed artwork
Entryway	Console table, classic mirror, table lamps, carefully chosen decorative accessories

Bedroom

Home Office

COMMON MISTAKES AND HOW TO AVOID THEM

MISTAKE: OVERLY FORMAL SPACES THAT FEEL UNAPPROACHABLE.

- **Solution**: Balance elegance with comfort by incorporating plush textiles, comfortable seating, and warm lighting.

MISTAKE: EXCESSIVE CLUTTER FROM TOO MANY DECORATIVE ELEMENTS.

- **Solution**: Thoughtfully curate accessories; showcase fewer, higher-quality items.

MISTAKE: INCONSISTENCY IN DESIGN ELEMENTS AND MATERIALS.

- **Solution**: Maintain visual cohesion through repeated color schemes, textures, and finishes.

TRADITIONAL VS. CLASSIC: UNDERSTANDING SUBTLE DIFFERENCES

Though often interchangeable, subtle differences define traditional and classic design:

FEATURE	TRADITIONAL INTERIORS	CLASSIC INTERIORS
Design Influence	More ornate, historically detailed	Simpler, refined elegance
Furniture Style	Curved, intricately carved, ornamented	Symmetrical, restrained ornamentation
Textiles & Patterns	More elaborate floral, damask patterns	Subtler patterns, solid colors
Overall Ambiance	Formal, rich, deeply historic	Refined, elegant, timelessly simple

TRADITIONAL INTERIOR

CLASSIC INTERIOR

CASE STUDY: DESIGNING A SOPHISTICATED TRADITIONAL LIVING ROOM

To effectively illustrate traditional design principles, envision creating a classic living room:

- **Furniture**: Rolled-arm sofa with velvet upholstery, pair of matching wingback chairs.
- **Architectural Elements**: Crown moldings, fireplace with detailed mantel, built-in bookcases.
- **Textiles**: Luxurious velvet curtains, Persian-style rug, decorative pillows with subtle patterns.
- **Lighting**: Brass floor lamps, classic chandelier or sconces, elegant table lamps.
- **Decor**: Framed artwork, crystal vases, antique silver trays or porcelain collectibles.

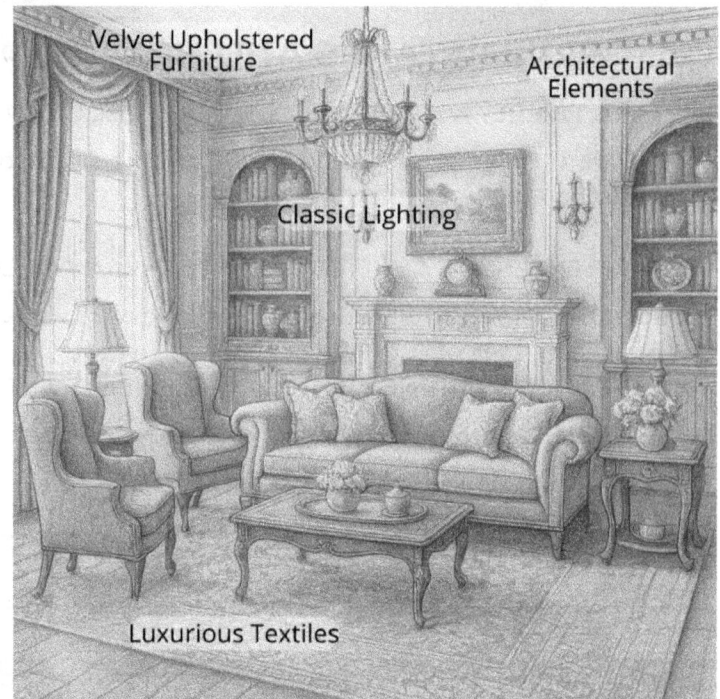

FINAL THOUGHTS ON TRADITIONAL & CLASSIC DESIGN

Traditional and classic interiors remain profoundly relevant because they are rooted in principles that transcend trend cycles. These spaces are anchored in symmetry, scale, proportion, and a deep respect for craftsmanship. What makes them timeless is not nostalgia, but their enduring ability to offer structure, clarity, and quiet elegance in a world that often leans toward the ephemeral and chaotic. In a design culture that frequently celebrates disruption, the consistency and calm of traditional interiors provide a necessary counterbalance.

This design language speaks softly but confidently—never shouting for attention, yet never unnoticed. Mouldings, woodwork, and heirloom furnishings are not just decorative, but intentional; they echo a lineage of design history that rewards those who look closely and value detail. A classic space doesn't compete—it endures. It doesn't demand—it welcomes. This is design with memory, weight, and grace—where every piece has purpose, and every corner is considered.

In a culture constantly drawn to novelty, there's something quietly radical about restraint. Traditional interiors, when thoughtfully composed, offer a sense of permanence. They age with dignity and invite continuity. Instead of constant reinvention, they allow for subtle evolution—introducing updated textiles, contemporary lighting, or modern art without disrupting the room's architectural integrity or emotional atmosphere. This is where classic design becomes personal: a canvas where your own heritage and experiences breathe life into a framework of timeless beauty and thoughtful intention.

To design in this language is to resist the disposable. It requires discipline, yes—but also empathy and a long view. Choose quality that lasts, materials that feel lived in, and silhouettes that have proven their worth. Think of rooms not as isolated moments, but as part of a continuum—spaces that reflect where you've come from, where you are, and where you're going.

The success of a traditional or classic interior lies not in replication, but interpretation. It's not about recreating the past—it's about honoring its wisdom while living fully in the present. Let your spaces carry warmth and structure, invitation and refinement.

Done well, traditional design offers something rare today: beauty with depth, permanence with soul.

COASTAL &
Nautical

Imagine stepping into your home and instantly feeling the serene breeze of the ocean, hearing the gentle whisper of waves, and sensing the warmth of sunlight on your skin. Coastal and nautical interiors bring this blissful seaside tranquility indoors, creating spaces that feel fresh, relaxed, and deeply connected to nature. This style captures the essence of the coast—whether it's the rugged shores of New England, the sunlit beaches of California, or the charming tranquility of the Mediterranean coast—through soothing palettes, organic textures, and maritime-inspired accents.

In this detailed exploration, you'll discover how to authentically embrace coastal and nautical design. We'll dive into the historical inspirations, essential features, practical guidance, and subtle distinctions that make this style uniquely captivating. By the end, you'll confidently bring the refreshing charm of the coast into your own interiors.

HISTORICAL ROOTS AND INSPIRATIONS

Coastal and nautical interiors draw their inspiration from seaside lifestyles around the world. Originating in the sun-washed cottages of New England and the breezy beach homes of the Mediterranean coast, coastal style emphasizes laid-back comfort, abundant natural light, and effortless simplicity. It celebrates airiness, relaxed textures, and a connection to the outdoors. Rooms often feel open, with pale tones, woven materials, and sheer fabrics that evoke the ease of coastal living without becoming overly thematic.

Nautical style, on the other hand, is shaped more directly by maritime history. Influenced by the precision and romance of sailing culture, it draws on classic naval palettes—deep navy, bright white, touches of brass—and details like rope, stripes, and weathered woods. It's more structured than coastal design, but just as evocative. Nautical interiors can feel like a gentle nod to life at sea: elegant, tailored, and full of character without being theatrical.

Both styles have evolved over time, adapting to different regions and personal preferences, but they maintain a lasting appeal because of their emotional roots. They are not just aesthetics—they're atmospheres. Whether it's the sense of freedom evoked by open water or the grounding calm of a shoreline retreat, these styles invite the outside in and offer a rhythm of living that feels both timeless and restorative.

KEY CHARACTERISTICS OF COASTAL & NAUTICAL INTERIORS

To create inviting coastal or nautical spaces, consider these foundational characteristics:

- **Light & Breezy Ambiance**: Bright interiors with ample natural light, open windows, and airy layouts.
- **Fresh, Nature-Inspired Colors**: Shades of white, sand, sky blue, navy, and ocean-inspired tones.
- **Natural Textures**: Organic materials like linen, cotton, seagrass, jute, weathered wood.
- **Subtle Maritime Accents**: Elements like ropes, anchors, stripes, shells, driftwood.
- **Relaxed, Comfortable Furniture**: Casual, inviting seating arrangements and cozy textiles.

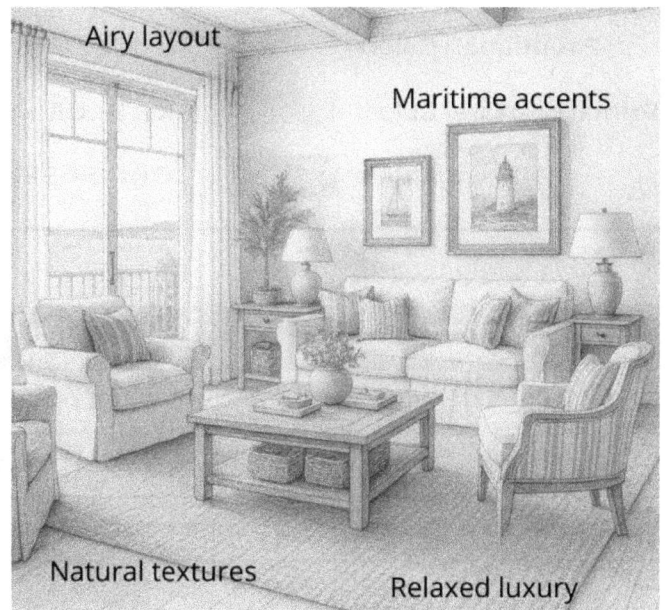
Airy layout

Maritime accents

Natural textures

Relaxed luxury

ESSENTIAL ELEMENTS & MATERIALS

Mastering coastal and nautical interiors begins by thoughtfully choosing materials and elements that echo seaside living:

Elements & Materials	Ideal Usage and Recommendations
Natural Woods	Weathered oak, driftwood finishes, reclaimed wood for furniture, flooring
Maritime Motifs	Stripes, anchors, ropes, maritime flags for subtle accents in textiles and decor
Organic Textiles	Linen upholstery, cotton slipcovers, seagrass rugs, woven jute baskets
Light Colors	Crisp whites, soft blues, sandy neutrals for walls, fabrics, furniture
Glass & Reflective Surfaces	Mirrors, glass vases, lanterns, to reflect natural light and evoke ocean sparkle

Weathered Wood   Maritime Motifs   Organic Textiles   Reflective Surfaces

COASTAL & NAUTICAL COLOR PALETTE GUIDE

An authentic coastal ambiance begins with a soothing, nature-inspired palette:

Foundation Colors		WHITES • SANDY BEIGES • SOFT GRAYS
Primary Coastal Colors		SKY BLUE • AQUA • TURQUOISE • NAVY
Accent Colors		CORAL • SEA GREEN • SUNSET HUES • MUTED PASTELS

PALETTE CATEGORY	RECOMMENDED COLORS
Walls & Ceilings	Bright whites, pale blues, light sandy neutrals
Furniture & Textiles	Whites, muted blues, navy stripes, neutral linens
Accents & Decor	Subtle coral, soft turquoise, metallic silver, driftwood gray

PRACTICAL GUIDELINES FOR ACHIEVING COASTAL & NAUTICAL STYLE

Create spaces that embody coastal ease by following these practical, actionable steps:

1. Prioritize Natural Light
Keep window treatments minimal—sheer curtains or simple blinds—to maximize natural light, enhancing the fresh, airy coastal feel.

2. Embrace Natural Textures
Incorporate natural fibers—linen sofas, cotton bedding, woven baskets—to evoke casual comfort and visual warmth.

3. Integrate Subtle Maritime Accents
Rather than obvious seaside clichés, choose understated maritime elements like striped cushions, rope accents, or vintage nautical artwork.

4. Maintain Open, Airy Layouts
Design spacious, open floor plans to replicate seaside openness. Arrange furniture to encourage conversation, relaxation, and views toward windows or outdoor areas.

COASTAL & NAUTICAL ROOM-BY-ROOM INSPIRATION GUIDE

Use this detailed room-specific guide for perfect coastal charm throughout your home:

ROOM	STYLING SUGGESTIONS & KEY ELEMENTS
Living Room	White slipcovered sofas, weathered wood coffee tables, woven rugs, nautical art
Bedroom	Crisp white linens, upholstered headboards, maritime striped pillows, natural textures
Dining Room	Driftwood dining tables, woven chairs, nautical lighting fixtures, simple table settings
Bathroom	Whitewashed wood cabinetry, coastal-inspired tiles, maritime-themed accessories, polished chrome fixtures
Outdoor Areas	Adirondack chairs, weather-resistant striped textiles, lanterns, nautical rope accents

COMMON MISTAKES AND HOW TO AVOID THEM

MISTAKE: EXCESSIVE NAUTICAL CLICHÉS CREATING THEME-LIKE SPACES.

- **Solution**: Incorporate nautical elements sparingly, maintaining subtlety and sophistication.

MISTAKE: OVERWHELMING CLUTTER OR ACCESSORIES THAT DETRACT FROM OPENNESS.

- **Solution**: Choose fewer, meaningful decor items; prioritize a clean, airy feel.

MISTAKE: IGNORING FUNCTIONALITY FOR AESTHETICS.

- **Solution**: Ensure every coastal-inspired space is practical, comfortable, and livable, not just visually appealing.

COASTAL VS. NAUTICAL: UNDERSTANDING SUBTLE DIFFERENCES

Though often grouped together, coastal and nautical styles differ subtly:

ASPECT	COASTAL STYLE	NAUTICAL STYLE
Color Scheme	Soft, relaxed tones, muted colors	Crisp contrast of navy, white, bold stripes
Materials & Textures	Natural, organic, relaxed	Structured, polished, maritime-inspired
Decorative Elements	Subtle seaside references	Direct maritime motifs (ropes, anchors)
Overall Feel	Relaxed, casual, airy	Structured, classic maritime elegance

COASTAL INTERIOR

NAUTICAL INTERIOR

CASE STUDY: DESIGNING A COASTAL-INSPIRED BEDROOM

Envision creating a bedroom retreat that embodies serene coastal charm:

- **Furniture**: Upholstered bed frame, weathered wood side tables.
- **Textiles**: White linen bedding, subtle blue-and-white striped pillows, woven throw blankets.
- **Lighting**: Glass pendant lamps or lantern-style bedside lamps.
- **Decor**: Framed coastal photography, driftwood mirrors, woven baskets.
- **Color Scheme**: Soft white walls, natural textures, accents of ocean-inspired blues and sandy beige.

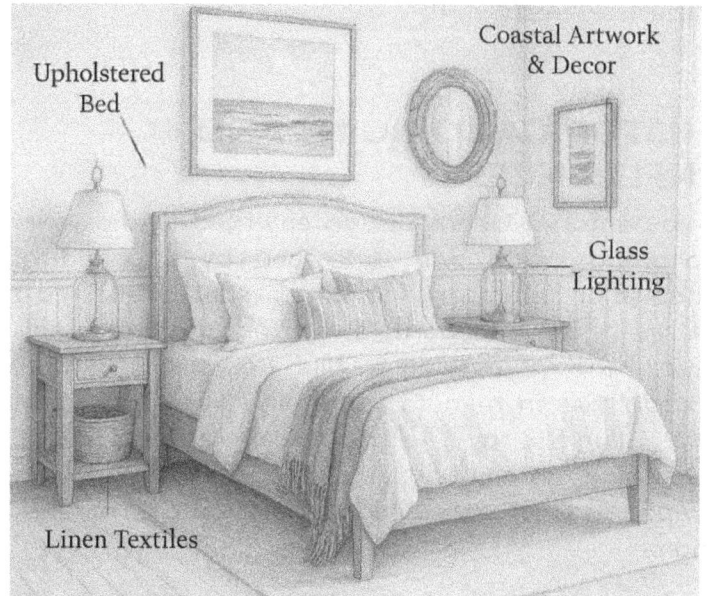

Upholstered Bed
Coastal Artwork & Decor
Glass Lighting
Linen Textiles

FINAL THOUGHTS ON COASTAL & NAUTICAL DESIGN

The enduring popularity of coastal and nautical interiors lies in their capacity to transport us mentally and emotionally to tranquil seaside retreats. By thoughtfully combining natural textures, soft palettes, ample light, and carefully chosen maritime elements, you can effortlessly recreate the relaxing ambiance of the coast within your home.

Keep in mind that the magic of coastal design lies in restraint, subtlety, and authenticity. The goal is not to recreate a literal beachfront, but rather to evoke its serene essence. Focus on comfort, simplicity, and meaningful details, and your interiors will naturally reflect the timeless charm and rejuvenating tranquility of coastal living.

Mid-Century
MODERN

Mid-Century Modern isn't just a design style—it's a lifestyle and cultural phenomenon that defined an entire era. Emerging prominently from the 1940s through the 1960s, Mid-Century Modern captured the optimism and innovation of post-war America, embodying sleek functionality, clean simplicity, and a celebration of form and materials. Its enduring popularity lies in its timeless elegance, subtle sophistication, and seamless integration with contemporary interiors.

In this comprehensive exploration, we'll delve deeply into the roots, core characteristics, essential elements, and practical guidelines for mastering Mid-Century Modern design. You'll learn how to authentically recreate its distinctive aesthetic, creating spaces that feel simultaneously vintage and timelessly fresh.

HISTORICAL ORIGINS AND INFLUENCES

Mid-Century Modern design emerged in the years following World War II, shaped by a period of innovation, optimism, and cultural shift. It reflected a desire to move forward—away from the ornate and into the functional—while embracing new possibilities in manufacturing and living. The style was fueled by technological advancements, changing family dynamics, and the growing importance of accessible design for the modern home.

Key figures such as Charles and Ray Eames, Eero Saarinen, Arne Jacobsen, and George Nelson redefined how people interacted with their spaces. Their creations were not only visually clean but thoughtfully engineered, offering beauty through purpose. Materials like molded plywood, fiberglass, bent wire, and plastics were used not for novelty, but to solve real design challenges in elegant ways.

Mid-Century Modern wasn't just a trend—it was a philosophy. It stood for clarity, openness, and democratic ideals, bringing well-designed pieces into the reach of ordinary people. At its core, it represented a belief that good design could improve daily life. This enduring legacy explains why the style continues to resonate, feeling just as relevant today as it did then.

CORE CHARACTERISTICS OF MID-CENTURY MODERN INTERIORS

To successfully achieve a genuine Mid-Century Modern interior, focus on these definitive characteristics:

- **Clean, Simple Lines**: Uncluttered furniture and architectural forms emphasizing geometric simplicity.
- **Organic & Geometric Shapes**: Gentle curves combined with sleek straight lines.
- **Integration with Nature**: Large windows, natural materials, and indoor-outdoor harmony.
- **Iconic Furniture Pieces**: Recognizable designer chairs, tables, lighting fixtures.
- **Bold, Contrasting Colors**: Rich wood tones contrasted with vibrant or muted hues.
- **Open, Functional Layouts**: Spaces designed with comfort, function, and ease of living in mind.

ESSENTIAL ELEMENTS & MATERIALS

Mastering Mid-Century Modern interiors involves choosing authentic elements and materials synonymous with this period:

Elements & Materials	Ideal Usage and Recommendations
Rich Woods	Teak, walnut, rosewood furniture and cabinetry.
Plywood & Molded Plastics	Iconic chairs, tables, accessories with organic shapes.
Metal Accents	Chrome, brass, black iron for furniture legs and lighting fixtures.
Bold Fabrics & Textiles	Wool, tweed, leather upholstery, bold graphic prints, geometric patterns.
Glass & Open Shelving	Glass coffee tables, open display shelves maintaining airy feel.

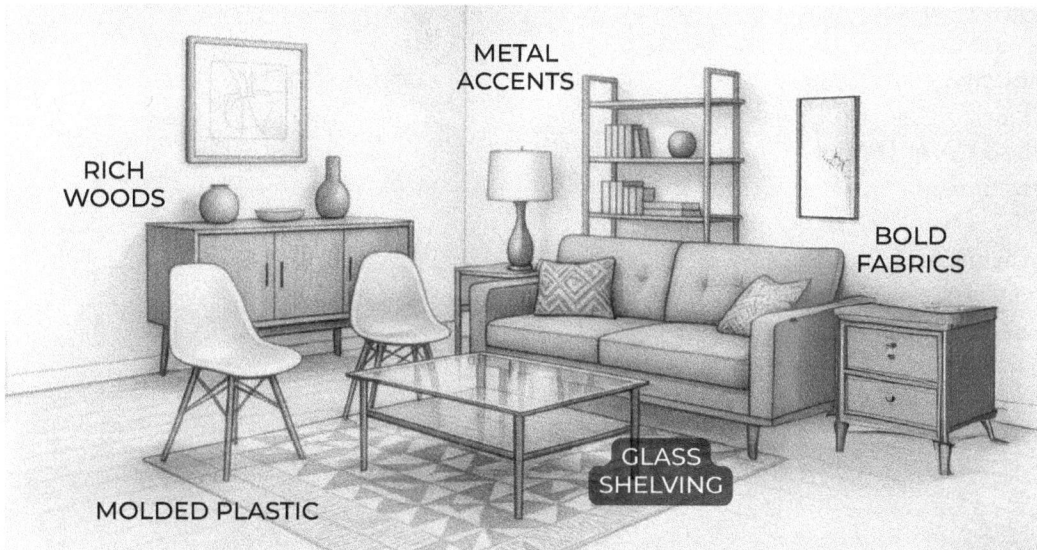

MID-CENTURY MODERN COLOR PALETTE GUIDE

Mid-Century Modern design favors palettes that balance warmth, vibrancy, and subtlety:

Foundation Colors	WARM WOODS • IVORY • BEIGE • SOFT GRAY
Primary Coastal Colors	MUSTARD YELLOW • BURNT ORANGE • OLIVE GREEN • DEEP TEAL
Accent Colors	RICH NAVY • CORAL • MUTED PASTELS • BRASS OR COPPER

PALETTE CATEGORY	RECOMMENDED COLORS
Walls	Warm whites, subtle neutrals, muted pastels
Furniture & Fabrics	Rich wood tones, bold solids (mustard, teal, orange), geometric patterns
Accessories	Brass metallics, ceramics in earthy hues, vibrant artwork

PRACTICAL GUIDELINES FOR ACHIEVING MID-CENTURY MODERN STYLE

To authentically capture Mid-Century Modern, follow these detailed and practical guidelines:

1. Invest in Iconic Furniture Pieces
Select at least one iconic Mid-Century item—Eames lounge chair, Saarinen tulip table, or Noguchi coffee table—to anchor your design and provide instant authenticity.

2. Embrace Clean Lines & Organic Forms
Favor furniture with streamlined, uncluttered designs and gently curved forms that reflect this era's fascination with organic shapes and functional simplicity.

3. Bold, Balanced Color Usage
Balance neutrals and natural wood tones with intentional splashes of bold colors—textiles, accent walls, or artwork.

4. Foster Indoor-Outdoor Flow
Highlight Mid-Century architecture's harmony with nature by maximizing natural light, incorporating plants, and creating smooth transitions to outdoor living spaces.

Eames Lounge Chair

Noguchi Table

Saarinen Tulip Table

MID-CENTURY MODERN ROOM-BY-ROOM INSPIRATION GUIDE

Use this inspiration table to capture authentic Mid-Century Modern charm throughout your home:

ROOM	KEY ELEMENTS & STYLING RECOMMENDATIONS
Living Room	Iconic lounge chairs, clean-lined sofas, geometric rugs, statement lighting, abstract artwork
Dining Room	Saarinen tulip dining table, molded plastic chairs, brass chandelier, streamlined sideboard
Bedroom	Platform bed, wood-paneled accent wall, graphic textiles, minimalist bedside tables
Home Office	Mid-Century desk, ergonomic designer chair, open shelving, streamlined lighting fixtures
Entryway	Console with tapered legs, abstract mirror, geometric patterned runner, sculptural decor

COMMON MISTAKES AND HOW TO AVOID THEM

MISTAKE: OVERLY THEMATIC, MUSEUM-LIKE INTERIORS.

- **Solution**: Balance vintage and contemporary pieces for livability.

MISTAKE: CLUTTER AND OVERLY COMPLEX ACCESSORIES.

- **Solution**: Embrace minimalism; showcase fewer, impactful items.

MISTAKE: MISMATCHED COLOR SCHEMES.

- **Solution**: Stick to consistent palettes grounded in natural woods and selective bold hues.

MID-CENTURY MODERN VS. CONTEMPORARY: UNDERSTANDING SUBTLE DIFFERENCES

Mid-Century Modern shares certain traits with contemporary design, but distinct differences exist:

ASPECT	MID-CENTURY MODERN	CONTEMPORARY
Furniture Style	Iconic vintage pieces, organic shapes	Sleek, current trends, neutral tones
Color Usage	Bold, vibrant contrasts	More muted, restrained, neutral
Decorative Elements	Authentic mid-century art, collectibles	Minimalist decor, fewer vintage items
Atmosphere	Warm vintage charm	Cooler, modern simplicity

MID-CENTURY MODERN INTERIOR

CONTEMPORARY INTERIOR

CASE STUDY: DESIGNING AN ICONIC MID-CENTURY MODERN LIVING ROOM

To practically illustrate Mid-Century Modern style, imagine designing a welcoming, authentic living room:

- Furniture: Eames lounge chair with ottoman, sleek leather or fabric sofa with tapered legs.
- Color Scheme: Warm wood tones, ivory walls, pops of mustard yellow, teal, or burnt orange.
- Textiles: Geometric patterned area rug, bold-colored pillows, wool or tweed upholstery.
- Lighting: Iconic floor lamps (e.g., Arco lamp), globe-shaped or sputnik-style chandelier.
- Decor: Abstract art, sculptural ceramics, brass accents, strategically placed houseplants.

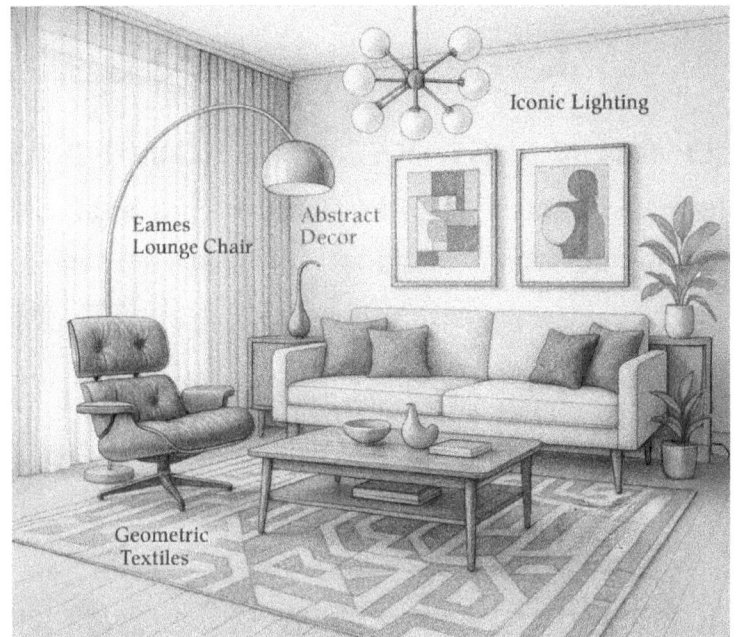

FINAL THOUGHTS ON MID-CENTURY MODERN DESIGN

The enduring popularity of Mid-Century Modern lies in its masterful blend of nostalgia, function, and elegant simplicity. By thoughtfully selecting iconic furniture, balancing bold colors with natural elements, and integrating interiors seamlessly with nature, you'll create spaces that celebrate this timeless aesthetic while perfectly complementing modern living.

As you embrace Mid-Century Modern, remember: authenticity is key. Focus on genuine materials, classic forms, and intentional minimalism. In doing so, you'll effortlessly create interiors that remain stylish, comfortable, and truly timeless.

Scandinavian
& HYGGE

Imagine arriving home on a cold winter day, stepping into an environment that instantly wraps you in warmth, comfort, and tranquility. That's precisely what Scandinavian design and the Danish concept of hygge (pronounced "hoo-ga") are all about. More than just an interior style, Scandinavian design coupled with hygge represents a holistic philosophy celebrating simplicity, natural beauty, functionality, and heartfelt coziness.

Throughout this comprehensive chapter, we'll explore the fascinating history, defining characteristics, essential elements, and practical guidelines necessary to authentically embrace Scandinavian design and hygge in your own home.

HISTORICAL ORIGINS AND PHILOSOPHY

Scandinavian design began taking shape in the early 20th century throughout Denmark, Sweden, Norway, Finland, and Iceland. These northern countries, shaped by long winters, limited natural light, and a need for practicality, developed a design philosophy rooted in simplicity, warmth, and function. Interiors reflect these conditions by focusing on clean lines, purposeful furnishings, and natural textures. Pale wood floors, soft textiles, and a neutral palette help maximize light and create a calming atmosphere.

This approach is not purely aesthetic—it's deeply tied to values of balance, modesty, and livability. Spaces are meant to be used, appreciated, and maintained with ease. Scandinavian interiors resist excess, offering instead a sense of grounded clarity and quiet refinement.

A vital element within this philosophy is hygge, a Danish concept that centers on comfort, connection, and small joys. It's not just about candles or warm blankets—it's about cultivating emotional well-being through your environment. Hygge is a mindset, encouraging the creation of homes that feel safe, inviting, and genuinely restorative amid daily life.

KEY CHARACTERISTICS OF SCANDINAVIAN & HYGGE INTERIORS

To create authentic Scandinavian spaces that embody hygge, focus on these essential characteristics:

- **Minimalist Simplicity**: Clear spaces with minimal clutter, emphasizing functionality and intentionality.
- **Soft, Neutral Color Palette**: Whites, grays, beige, muted pastels inspired by natural surroundings.
- **Natural Light & Warmth**: Maximizing daylight through windows, soft lighting with candles, fireplaces, and lamps.
- **Organic Textures & Materials**: Natural woods, wool, cotton, linen, fur for warmth and visual comfort.
- **Functional Beauty**: Everyday items chosen for both practical utility and aesthetic charm.
- **Cozy Atmosphere** (Hygge): Candles, blankets, soft rugs, comfortable seating arrangements encouraging relaxation and intimacy.

MINIMALIST

NATURAL LIGHTING

NEUTRAL ELEGANCE

HYGGE COMFORT

ORGANIC MATERIALS

ESSENTIAL ELEMENTS & MATERIALS

Scandinavian & Hygge design is distinctly characterized by specific materials and components:

ELEMENTS & MATERIALS	USAGE AND RECOMMENDATIONS
Natural Wood	Light oak, ash, birch for flooring, furniture, accents.
Soft Textiles	Wool blankets, knitted throws, cotton or linen bedding.
Candles & Soft Lighting	Candles, lanterns, simple pendant lamps, table lamps.
Neutral & Pastel Colors	Soft whites, muted grays, beige, pale blues, blush tones.
Minimalist Furniture	Clean lines, functional, comfortable sofas, chairs, tables.

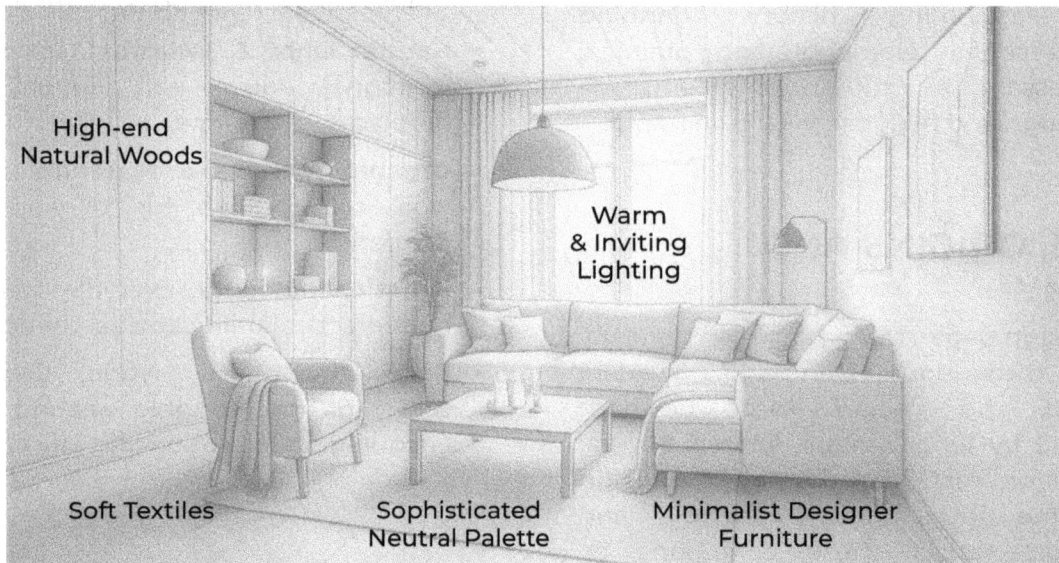

High-end Natural Woods

Warm & Inviting Lighting

Soft Textiles

Sophisticated Neutral Palette

Minimalist Designer Furniture

SCANDINAVIAN & HYGGE COLOR PALETTE GUIDE

Embracing Scandinavian style starts with a soothing, tranquil palette inspired by Nordic landscapes.

Primary Colors	WHITE • IVORY • PALE GRAY • BEIGE
Supporting Colors	SOFT PASTELS—BLUES • BLUSH • SAGE GREENS • DUSTY LAVENDER
Accent Colors	WARM WOOD TONES • MATTE BLACK/CHARCOAL • SUBTLE METALLIC

PALETTE CATEGORY	RECOMMENDED COLORS
Walls	Soft white, pale gray, creamy beige
Furniture	Natural wood tones, muted upholstery, pastel textiles
Decor & Accents	Subtle pastels, matte black frames, brass or copper accents

PRACTICAL GUIDELINES FOR ACHIEVING SCANDINAVIAN & HYGGE INTERIORS

Authentically capture the essence of Scandinavian & hygge by following these practical tips:

1. Emphasize Natural Light
Maximize daylight with minimal window coverings, using reflective whites and mirrors to amplify natural brightness.

2. Curate for Comfort
Layer cozy textiles like blankets, rugs, and plush cushions, creating inviting corners and seating areas designed for relaxation.

3. Prioritize Functional Minimalism
Choose furniture and decor items thoughtfully for their combined aesthetic beauty and practical use, avoiding unnecessary clutter.

4. Celebrate Warm Lighting
Incorporate candles, lanterns, and soft glowing lamps to cultivate a warm, inviting hygge ambiance, especially during darker months.

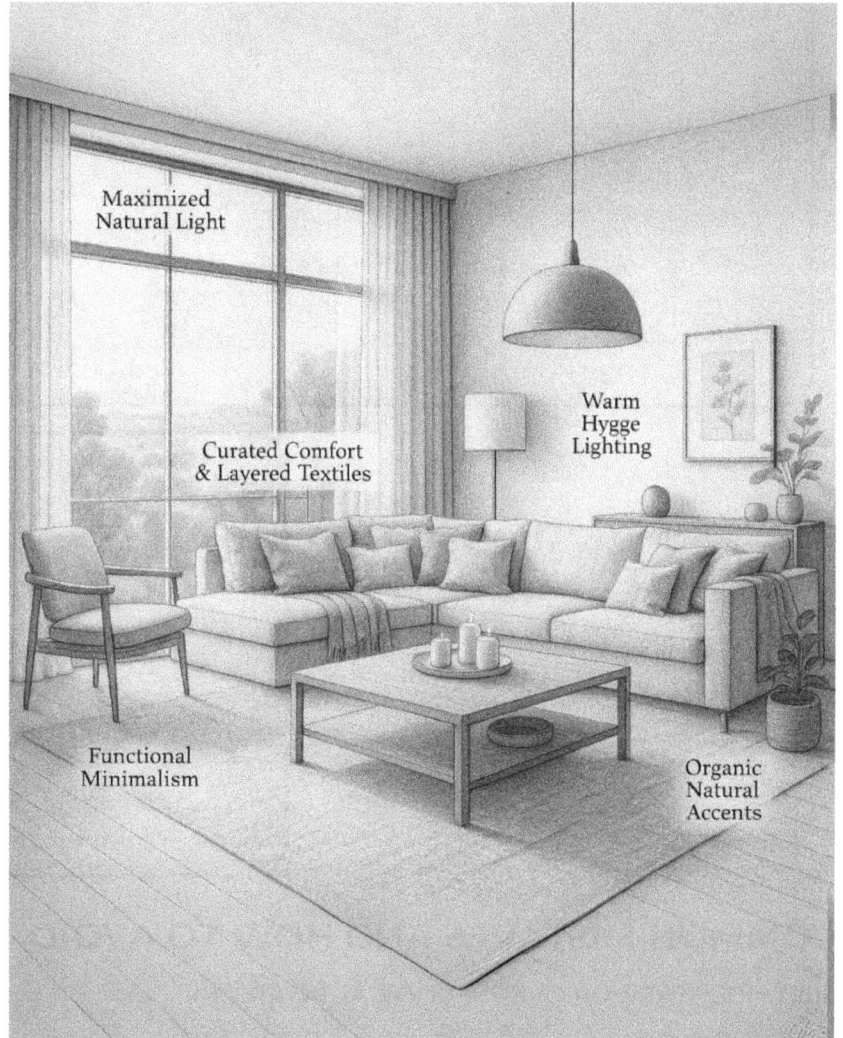

SCANDINAVIAN & HYGGE ROOM-BY-ROOM INSPIRATION GUIDE

Use this guide for crafting beautifully harmonious Scandinavian & hygge interiors:

ROOM	ESSENTIAL ELEMENTS & HYGGE SUGGESTIONS
Living Room	Minimalist sofa, cozy throw blankets, natural wood coffee tables, soft area rugs, candles, pendant lighting
Bedroom	Neutral bedding, wool throws, natural wooden furniture, bedside candles, simple decor
Dining Area	Natural wood table, upholstered chairs, simple pendant lamps, subtle table linens, ceramics
Bathroom	Clean, neutral colors, simple cabinetry, soft towels, candles, minimalistic decor accents
Home Office	Functional wood desk, comfortable chair, soft area rug, cozy lighting, minimal clutter

COMMON MISTAKES AND HOW TO AVOID THEM

MISTAKE: STARK OR OVERLY CLINICAL INTERIORS.

- **Solution**: Introduce warm textures—soft textiles, natural wood—to create warmth and comfort.

MISTAKE: OVERLY DECORATED OR CLUTTERED SPACES.

- **Solution**: Edit decor thoughtfully; prioritize functionality and simplicity.

MISTAKE: NEGLECTING EMOTIONAL COMFORT.

- **Solution**: Embrace hygge through soft lighting, comfortable seating, and intimate spaces encouraging relaxation.

SCANDINAVIAN VS. HYGGE: UNDERSTANDING SUBTLE DIFFERENCES

While closely related, subtle distinctions differentiate Scandinavian design and hygge philosophy:

ASPECT	SCANDINAVIAN STYLE	HYGGE PHILOSOPHY
Design Focus	Minimalism, functionality, clarity	Emotional warmth, coziness, comfort
Decor Approach	Functional, aesthetically simple	Intentionally cozy, layered textures
Color Usage	Soft neutrals, muted tones	Warm, comforting neutrals, inviting lighting
Overall Atmosphere	Clean simplicity, structured comfort	Deeply comforting, intimate relaxation

SCANDINAVIAN INTERIOR

CONTEMPORARY INTERIOR

CASE STUDY: DESIGNING A COZY SCANDINAVIAN & HYGGE LIVING ROOM

Consider creating a living space that embodies true Scandinavian charm infused with hygge warmth:

- **Furniture**: Simple, upholstered sofa, wooden coffee table, minimalist shelving.

- **Textiles**: Layered wool throws, plush pillows, soft rugs underfoot.

- **Lighting**: Multiple candle groupings, pendant lamps, soft-glowing floor lamps.

- **Decor**: Subtle botanical artwork, woven baskets, minimalist ceramics.

- **Color Scheme**: Soft whites, muted pastels, warm wood tones, subtle grays.

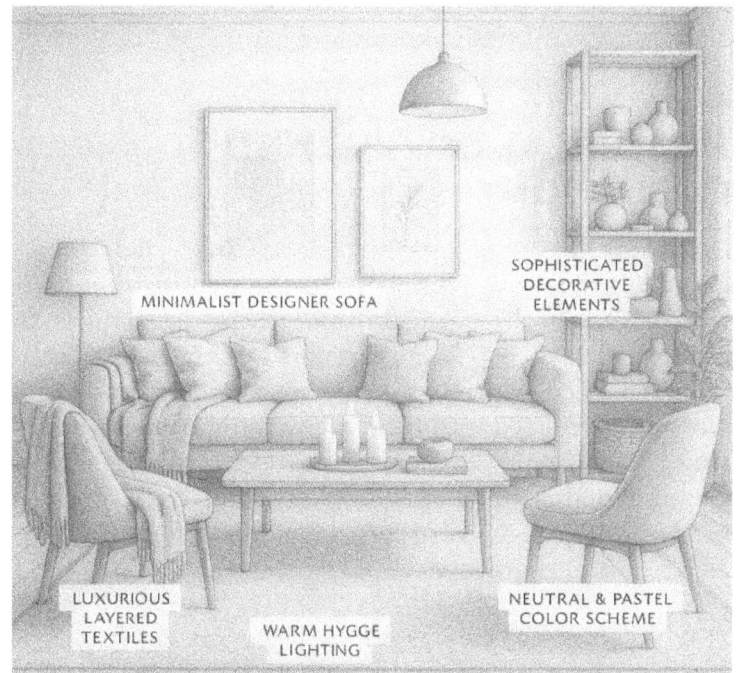

FINAL THOUGHTS ON SCANDINAVIAN & HYGGE DESIGN

The profound appeal of Scandinavian interiors and the comforting allure of hygge lie in their sincere emphasis on simplicity, warmth, and genuine comfort. By carefully blending minimalist aesthetics with intentional coziness, you create interiors that nourish not just the eyes but the soul itself.

Remember, the beauty of Scandinavian & hygge isn't mere decoration—it's cultivating spaces that deeply enrich daily life, fostering serenity, emotional connection, and meaningful moments shared with loved ones.

Industrial
& URBAN

Picture the allure of city lofts, converted warehouses, and stylish urban apartments—spaces defined by raw authenticity, bold character, and sophisticated ruggedness. Industrial and urban interiors proudly showcase their history through exposed materials, structural details, and a powerful sense of practicality. This style transforms the industrial past of urban environments into spaces with dramatic appeal, modern sensibility, and timeless charm.

In this comprehensive chapter, we'll unravel the distinctive characteristics, historical influences, essential elements, and practical guidelines required to master industrial and urban design in your own space. You'll discover how to achieve a sophisticated balance between rugged textures, minimalist elegance, and functional comfort.

HISTORICAL ORIGINS AND EVOLUTION

Industrial interiors originated in the mid-20th century as creative responses to the adaptive reuse of warehouses, factories, and other utilitarian buildings. With housing shortages in cities like New York, Chicago, and London, these vacant spaces were transformed into livable environments. Rather than concealing imperfections, industrial design embraced them—highlighting exposed brick, steel beams, ductwork, and concrete floors as visual assets rather than flaws.

This aesthetic wasn't about ornamentation; it was about honesty in materials and construction. Clean lines, open layouts, and repurposed elements gave these spaces a sense of purpose and individuality.

Over time, industrial and urban styles moved beyond converted lofts. Today, they influence residential homes, boutique hotels, coffee shops, and commercial spaces alike. Their continued appeal lies in the raw elegance they offer—spaces that feel grounded, unpretentious, and connected to the structure's history and utility.

KEY CHARACTERISTICS OF INDUSTRIAL & URBAN INTERIORS

Successfully creating industrial and urban interiors involves embracing these defining characteristics:

- **Exposed Structural Elements**: Visible brick, concrete walls, pipes, beams, ductwork, and unfinished surfaces.
- **Open & Spacious Layouts**: Emphasizing large, unobstructed spaces with minimal partitions.
- **Raw, Rugged Textures**: Concrete, metal, distressed wood, leather, glass elements with visible imperfections.
- **Neutral & Muted Palette**: Dominated by grays, blacks, browns, metallic finishes, and earthy hues.
- **Functional Furniture**: Minimalist designs, metal and wood combinations, sturdy and practical.
- **Vintage & Repurposed Accents**: Salvaged furniture, industrial lighting fixtures, reclaimed materials.

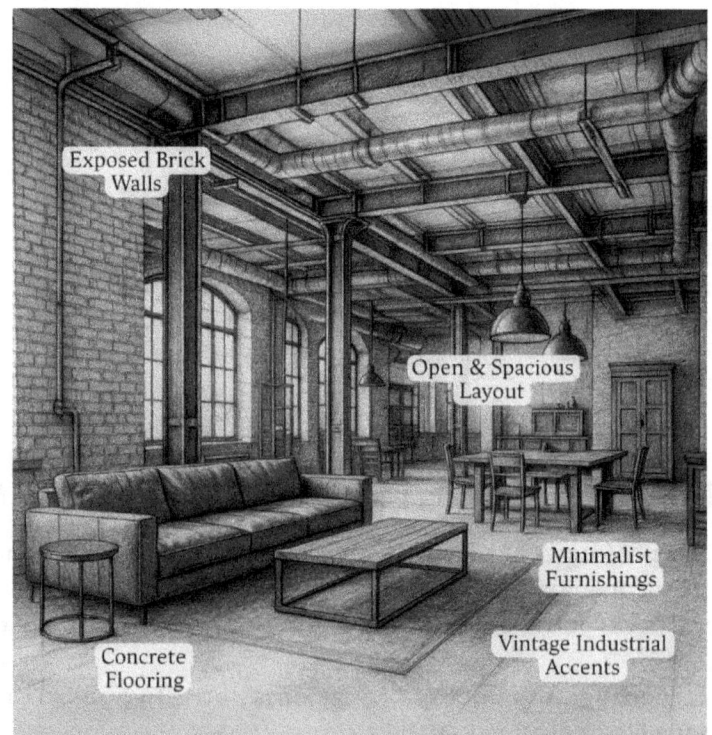

Exposed Brick Walls

Open & Spacious Layout

Minimalist Furnishings

Vintage Industrial Accents

Concrete Flooring

ESSENTIAL ELEMENTS & MATERIALS

For authentic industrial-urban style, carefully select these foundational elements and materials:

ELEMENTS & MATERIALS	USAGE AND RECOMMENDATIONS
Exposed Brick & Concrete	Walls, floors, structural features highlighting raw textures.
Metals (Steel, Iron)	Structural elements, furniture legs, lighting fixtures.
Distressed Wood	Reclaimed or weathered furniture, flooring, shelving.
Glass & Reflective Surfaces	Industrial-style windows, minimalist partitions, mirrors.
Leather & Textiles	Leather sofas, canvas or burlap textiles, minimal decor.

INDUSTRIAL & URBAN COLOR PALETTE GUIDE

Industrial interiors are anchored by neutral, earthy tones complemented by stark contrasts:

Primary Colors	CHARCOAL GRAY • BLACK • CONCRETE GRAY • STEEL METALLICS
Secondary Colors	EARTHY BROWNS • RUST TONES • NATURAL WOOD HUES
Accent Colors	MUTED NAVY • DEEP GREENS • BURNT ORANGE • VINTAGE METALLIC FINISHES

PALETTE CATEGORY	RECOMMENDED COLORS
Walls & Surfaces	Exposed brick reds, concrete grays, deep charcoal, whites
Furniture	Dark woods, black metals, brown leather, muted textiles
Accents & Decor	Metallic finishes, vintage rust tones, industrial blacks

PRACTICAL GUIDELINES FOR ACHIEVING INDUSTRIAL & URBAN STYLE

Use these detailed practical steps to authentically capture industrial-urban interiors:

1. Embrace Structural Authenticity
Showcase existing architectural elements—exposed beams, brick walls, concrete floors—rather than concealing them.

2. Select Functional Furnishings
Choose minimalist, durable furniture combining metal frames and wooden surfaces. Industrial carts, metal shelving units, and reclaimed wood tables embody this practicality perfectly.

3. Curate Vintage & Salvaged Pieces
Incorporate reclaimed furniture or vintage industrial items—factory lamps, storage lockers, vintage signs—to add authentic character.

4. Use Lighting to Accentuate Raw Details
Employ industrial-style lighting such as metal pendant lights, filament bulbs, and factory-inspired sconces to highlight structural textures.

Metal-and-Wood Industrial Dining Table

Minimalist Industrial Seating

Open Metal Shelving Unit

Industrial Cart Coffee Table

Vintage Storage Locker or Cabinet

INDUSTRIAL & URBAN ROOM-BY-ROOM INSPIRATION GUIDE

Create genuine industrial charm with this comprehensive room-by-room guide:

ROOM	ESSENTIAL ELEMENTS & STYLING RECOMMENDATIONS
Living Room	Leather sofa, metal coffee table, exposed brick wall, metal lighting fixtures, industrial-style rug
Bedroom	Simple metal bed frame, exposed concrete walls, reclaimed wood nightstands, minimalist lighting
Dining Area	Reclaimed wood dining table, metal chairs, industrial pendant lighting, open shelving
Kitchen	Stainless steel appliances, open shelving, concrete or butcher-block countertops, metal stools
Bathroom	Concrete sink or countertop, exposed pipes, metal framed mirrors, industrial lighting fixtures

Dining Area

Bathroom

Living Room

Bedroom

COMMON MISTAKES AND HOW TO AVOID THEM

MISTAKE: OVERUSING INDUSTRIAL CLICHÉS OR MAKING SPACES FEEL COLD.

- **Solution**: Balance raw materials with warm elements—wood, leather, soft lighting—to create inviting spaces.

MISTAKE: IGNORING FUNCTIONALITY FOR AESTHETICS.

- **Solution**: Select durable, practical furniture and layouts promoting usability and comfort.

MISTAKE: OVERCROWDING SPACES.

- **Solution**: Maintain open, minimalist arrangements to highlight architectural authenticity.

INDUSTRIAL VS. URBAN: UNDERSTANDING SUBTLE DIFFERENCES

Industrial and urban styles overlap but have distinct nuances:

ASPECT	INDUSTRIAL STYLE	URBAN STYLE
Material Focus	Raw, rugged textures (brick, concrete)	Slightly polished, contemporary finishes
Color Usage	Deep earthy neutrals, raw finishes	Slightly broader palette, modern neutrals
Decor Approach	Salvaged, authentically vintage	Contemporary art, streamlined minimalism
Overall Feel	Boldly rugged, historic authenticity	Sleek, metropolitan sophistication

INDUSTRIAL INTERIOR

URBAN INTERIOR

CASE STUDY: DESIGNING AN AUTHENTIC INDUSTRIAL LIVING SPACE

Visualize creating a genuinely inviting industrial living area:

- **Furniture**: Leather sofa, metal coffee table with reclaimed wood surface, open metal shelving.

- **Structural Elements**: Exposed brick walls, concrete floors, visible metal beams or ducts.

- **Textiles**: Rug in earthy tones, leather cushions, minimalist window treatments.

- **Lighting**: Factory-inspired pendant lights, vintage floor lamps, filament bulbs.

- **Decor**: Vintage industrial signs, metal or wood-framed mirrors, carefully curated art.

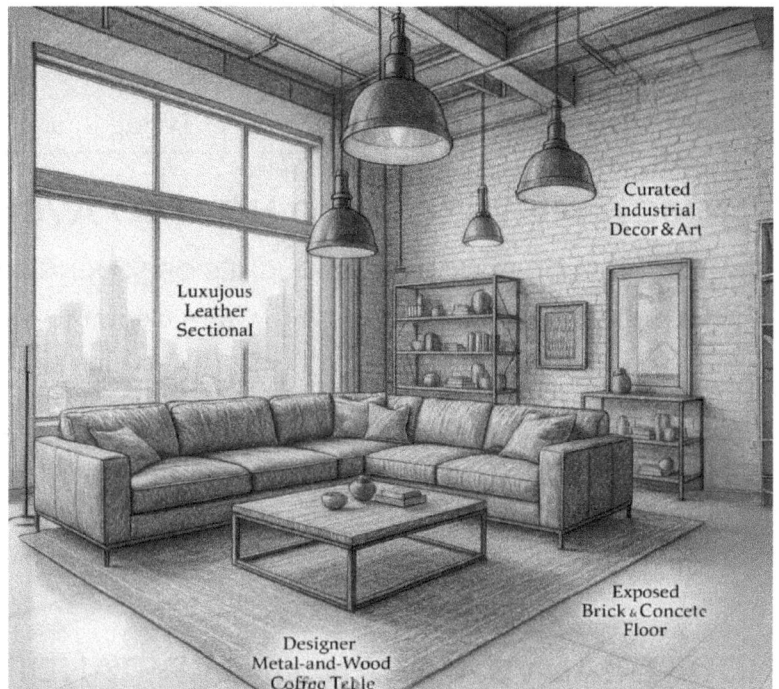

FINAL THOUGHTS ON INDUSTRIAL & URBAN DESIGN

The powerful appeal of industrial and urban interiors lies in their authentic celebration of raw materials, functional simplicity, and historic character. Rather than hiding structural elements, industrial design boldly embraces them, turning ordinary textures into extraordinary visual focal points.

Remember, achieving authenticity in industrial interiors involves intentional restraint and thoughtful balance. Combine rugged materials with warmer, softer elements; curate spaces carefully; and allow historical authenticity to shine through. In doing so, you create interiors rich in personality, timeless in charm, and endlessly captivating.

JAPANESE &
Zen Garden

Picture stepping into a sanctuary—an environment meticulously designed to soothe your senses, ease your mind, and reconnect you with nature and tranquility. Japanese and Zen-inspired interiors embody precisely this—an elegant philosophy of simplicity, mindfulness, and serene beauty. Rooted deeply in Japanese culture, Zen interiors are more than a style; they are an intentional way of life, emphasizing harmony, balance, and meaningful simplicity.

In this extensive chapter, we will delve into the rich history, essential characteristics, foundational elements, and practical guidelines to authentically incorporate Japanese and Zen-inspired design into your space. You'll gain clarity on creating interiors that exude tranquility, elegance, and mindful purpose.

HISTORICAL ORIGINS AND PHILOSOPHY

Japanese interior design traces its roots back thousands of years, drawing from Zen Buddhism, Shinto beliefs, and enduring aesthetic principles like Wabi-Sabi—the appreciation of imperfection—and Ma—the intentional use of empty space. These philosophies emerged through traditional architecture, especially in Zen temples and tea houses, where structure and spirit were intimately connected.

The focus is not on decoration but on balance, stillness, and the subtle dialogue between light, shadow, and material. Natural elements—wood, paper, stone, and bamboo—create a quiet elegance, linking the interior to the rhythms of the outside world.

Zen interiors go beyond visual appeal. They are designed to cultivate awareness, calm, and introspection. Every object has intention. Every space allows for breath. This mindful approach transforms the home into a place of reflection and serenity—an antidote to the speed and stimulation of modern life.

KEY CHARACTERISTICS OF JAPANESE & ZEN INTERIORS

To successfully capture authentic Japanese and Zen-inspired spaces, embody these core characteristics:

- **Minimalism & Simplicity**: Carefully curated, clutter-free spaces emphasizing intentional selection.
- **Natural Harmony**: Seamless integration with nature—natural materials, indoor greenery, harmonious views.
- **Neutral & Earthy Palette**: Muted colors inspired by nature—soft whites, beiges, earthy browns, gentle greens.
- **Functional & Mindful Furniture**: Low-profile, purposefully designed pieces emphasizing comfort, simplicity, and utility.
- **Balanced Lighting & Ambiance**: Natural light complemented by soft artificial lighting, fostering calm and relaxation.
- **Open, Flowing Layouts**: Spaces thoughtfully arranged, encouraging mindfulness and unobstructed movement.

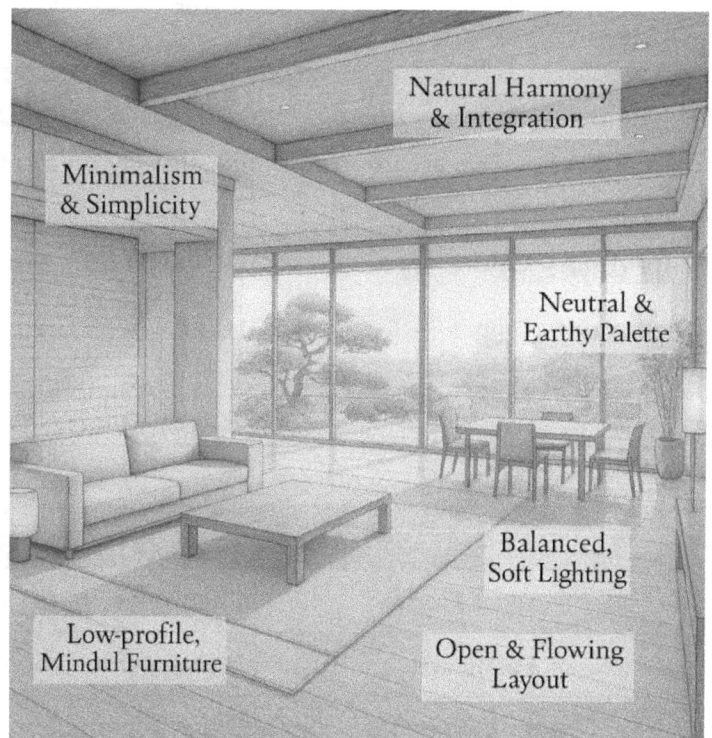

Natural Harmony & Integration

Minimalism & Simplicity

Neutral & Earthy Palette

Balanced, Soft Lighting

Low-profile, Mindul Furniture

Open & Flowing Layout

ESSENTIAL ELEMENTS & MATERIALS

For an authentic Zen ambiance, carefully choose these foundational elements and materials:

ELEMENTS & MATERIALS	USAGE AND RECOMMENDATIONS
Natural Woods	Cedar, cypress, bamboo for furniture, flooring, architectural elements
Shoji Screens	Translucent rice paper screens as room dividers, window coverings, soft diffusers of natural light
Tatami Mats	Traditional woven mats for flooring or meditation areas
Stone & Ceramics	Stone flooring, minimalist ceramics for decor, natural accents
Indoor Plants	Bonsai, bamboo, and minimalist greenery to emphasize natural harmony

Zen Inspired Low Wooden Tab

Tatami-Inspired Seating Area

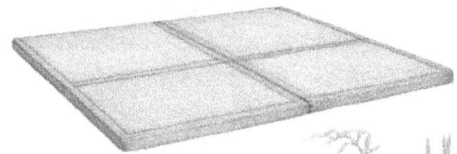

Minimalist Low-Profile Sofa

Indoor Zen Water Feature

Natural Stone
Decor

Soft Lighting
(Paper Lanterns, Foo Lamps)

Indoor Plants (Bonsai & Bamboo)

JAPANESE & ZEN COLOR PALETTE GUIDE

An authentic Zen environment relies heavily on a calming, nature-inspired palette:

Primary Colors   SOFT WHITES · MUTED CREAMS · EARTHY BROWNS · PALE GRAYS

Secondary Colors   GENTLE GREENS · SUBTLE BLUES · DELICATE PASTELS

Accent Colors   BLACK (AS IN CALLIGRAPHY AND ACCENTS) · STONE GRAY · NATURAL WOOD TONES

PALETTE CATEGORY	RECOMMENDED COLORS
Walls & Floors	Pale beige, warm whites, soft gray, earthy neutrals
Furniture	Natural wood tones, muted upholstery, neutral fabrics
Decor & Accents	Black accents, muted greens, stone-inspired grays

PRACTICAL GUIDELINES FOR ACHIEVING JAPANESE & ZEN INTERIORS

Apply these practical tips thoughtfully to achieve serene, authentic Zen-inspired interiors:

1. Prioritize Minimalism & Intentionality
Curate each space carefully, ensuring every item serves a purpose—visual clutter detracts from mindfulness.

2. Create Harmony with Nature
Include indoor plants, water features, or natural elements like stones or bamboo, seamlessly connecting indoor spaces to the natural world.

3. Optimize Lighting for Serenity
Use natural daylight enhanced by soft artificial lights—paper lanterns, floor lamps, candles—to foster calm and warmth.

4. Balance & Flow in Layout
Design open, uncluttered layouts allowing intuitive movement, enhancing mindfulness, and creating a harmonious spatial flow.

Indoor Plants (Bonsai, Bamboo)

Natural Daylight & Soft Lighting

Natural Stone Water Feature

Minimalist & Intentional Layout

Tranquil Zen Water Feature

Open, Harmonious Spatial Flow

JAPANESE & ZEN ROOM-BY-ROOM INSPIRATION GUIDE

Incorporate Zen tranquility into your home with this detailed room-by-room guide:

ROOM	ESSENTIAL ELEMENTS & ZEN SUGGESTIONS
Living Room	Low seating arrangements, tatami mats, minimalist tea table, shoji screens, simple greenery, muted lighting
Bedroom	Low-profile wooden bed or futon, soft bedding in neutral tones, minimal furnishings, subtle decorative art
Meditation Space	Tatami mat flooring, minimalistic altar, Zen garden elements (stones, bonsai), gentle lighting
Bathroom	Natural stone surfaces, minimalist bathtub, wooden elements, plants, soft ambient lighting
Dining Area	Low wooden dining table, floor cushions or low benches, minimalist ceramics, soft lighting, shoji screens

Living Room | Bedroom

Meditation Space | Bathroom | Dining Area

COMMON MISTAKES AND HOW TO AVOID THEM

MISTAKE: OVER-DECORATING SPACES.

- **Solution**: Prioritize intentional minimalism; every object should have purpose and significance.

MISTAKE: IGNORING NATURE INTEGRATION.

- **Solution**: Always include natural elements—plants, wood, stone—to reinforce harmony with nature.

MISTAKE: HARSH OR OVERLY BRIGHT LIGHTING.

- **Solution**: Opt for gentle, diffused lighting (e.g., paper lamps, candles, dimmable fixtures) to create calm environments.

JAPANESE VS. ZEN-INSPIRED: UNDERSTANDING SUBTLE DIFFERENCES

Though deeply interconnected, Japanese and Zen styles differ subtly:

ASPECT	JAPANESE STYLE	ZEN-INSPIRED STYLE
Design Influence	Traditional Japanese cultural elements, specific aesthetics like shoji screens and tatami mats	Broader minimalist philosophy emphasizing tranquility and mindfulness
Decorative Approach	Precise, culturally authentic items	More generalized minimalism inspired by Zen principles
Color Usage	Neutral tones plus specific traditional colors (like deep reds in certain decor)	Strictly neutral, calming earth tones
Overall Atmosphere	Cultural authenticity, traditional elegance	Universal tranquility, meditation-friendly

TRADITIONAL JAPANESE INTERIOR

ZEN-INSPIRED INTERIOR

CASE STUDY: DESIGNING A TRANQUIL ZEN-INSPIRED BEDROOM

Visualize creating an authentic Zen-inspired bedroom retreat:

- **Furniture**: Low wooden bed frame or futon platform, minimal bedside tables.
- **Textiles**: Natural cotton or linen bedding in neutral tones, muted pillows, simple window treatments.
- **Lighting**: Paper lanterns, floor lamps, dimmable bedside lighting, candles.
- **Decor**: Shoji screens, minimalist calligraphy or subtle botanical artwork, simple plants or bamboo accents.
- **Color Scheme**: Soft whites, warm neutrals, natural wood tones, subtle grays and greens.

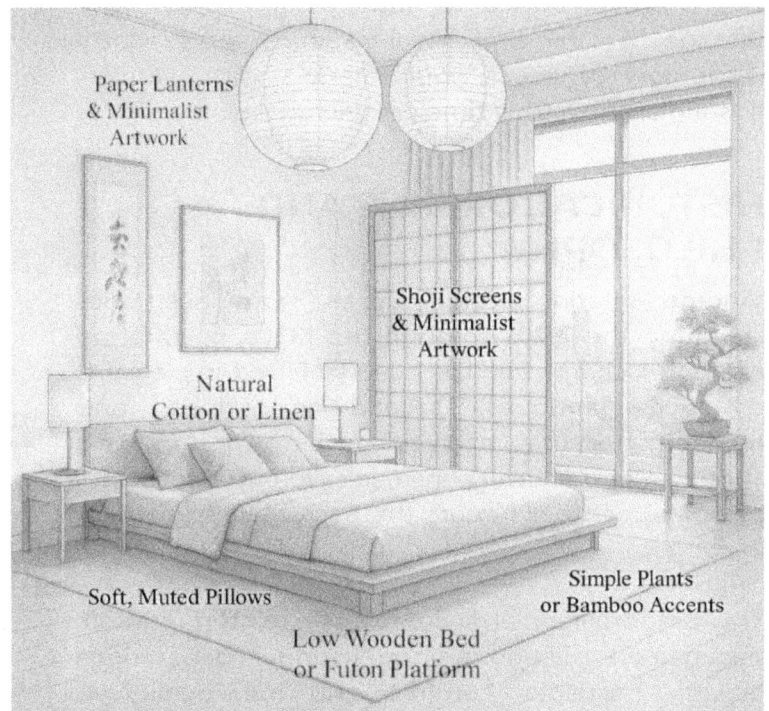

Paper Lanterns & Minimalist Artwork

Shoji Screens & Minimalist Artwork

Natural Cotton or Linen

Soft, Muted Pillows

Simple Plants or Bamboo Accents

Low Wooden Bed or Futon Platform

FINAL THOUGHTS ON JAPANESE & ZEN-INSPIRED DESIGN

Japanese and Zen-inspired interiors provide more than aesthetic beauty; they offer profound emotional calm, mental clarity, and spiritual nourishment. By meticulously curating minimalist spaces, carefully integrating nature, and mindfully crafting each detail, you'll create interiors that foster mindfulness, harmony, and serenity.

Remember: Zen is not just a style—it's a philosophy. Approach your home as a thoughtful sanctuary designed intentionally, compassionately, and harmoniously. Through simplicity and mindful arrangement, your spaces will reflect not merely visual elegance but deeper tranquility and profound peace.

VINTAGE &
Grandmillennial

Imagine stepping into a room brimming with charm, nostalgia, and personality—an enchanting blend of timeless treasures, heirloom pieces, and contemporary freshness. Vintage and Grandmillennial interiors celebrate individuality and tradition, rejecting stark minimalism in favor of cozy, personality-driven spaces filled with eclectic finds, heirloom furnishings, and whimsical touches. Embracing the charm of the past, this delightful style gracefully merges antique elements with youthful exuberance, resulting in interiors that feel deeply personal, inviting, and comforting.

In this comprehensive guide, we'll explore the rich origins, distinctive features, foundational elements, and practical advice to authentically curate your Vintage & Grandmillennial-inspired space. You'll learn how to infuse your interiors with warmth, nostalgia, and a truly timeless personality.

HISTORICAL ORIGINS AND PHILOSOPHY

Vintage interior design draws from aesthetics spanning the 1920s through the 1980s, celebrating character, charm, and the beauty of lived-in pieces. It embraces antiques, second-hand finds, and heirloom treasures, each telling its own story. This style resists uniformity, instead favoring a collected, personal feel that honors the past while remaining inviting.

The Grandmillennial style, a fresh reinterpretation, has gained traction among younger generations craving nostalgia, comfort, and individuality. It revives traditional elements like chintz, needlepoint, ruffles, and chinoiserie—adding playful color, layered textures, and modern sensibilities. It's less about strict preservation, more about thoughtful reinvention.

Both vintage and Grandmillennial designs value sustainability by reusing cherished objects and avoiding disposability. These styles offer depth and warmth, creating spaces that feel grounded, expressive, and emotionally rich—places that remember and reimagine all at once.

KEY CHARACTERISTICS OF VINTAGE & GRANDMILLENNIAL INTERIORS

To authentically achieve the Vintage & Grandmillennial look, focus on these key features:

- **Eclectic Elegance**: Thoughtful mixing of antique and contemporary furniture, accessories, and textiles.
- **Vibrant Patterns & Textiles**: Floral chintz, toile, embroidered linens, needlepoint cushions, ruffles, and lace.
- **Personal Collections & Heirlooms**: Cherished family heirlooms, antique collectibles, vintage accessories.
- **Warm, Inviting Palette**: Soft pastels, muted earth tones, vintage-inspired colors, gentle metallics.
- **Layered & Cozy Ambiance**: Plush upholstery, layered rugs, multiple textures creating warmth and coziness.
- **Whimsical, Nostalgic Accents**: Vintage china, brass fixtures, crystal chandeliers, botanical prints, and heirloom-quality items.

Eclectic Antique & Modern Furniture

Warm & Inviting Color Palette

Vibrant Patterns & Luxurious Textiles

Personal Collections & Heirlooms

Layered & Cozy Ambiance

Whimsical & Nostalgic Accents

ESSENTIAL ELEMENTS & MATERIALS

For a vintage charm and Grandmillennial flair, thoughtfully select these foundational materials and elements:

ELEMENTS & MATERIALS	IDEAL USAGE AND RECOMMENDATIONS
Vintage Furniture	Antique dressers, upholstered armchairs, ornate tables.
Patterned Textiles	Chintz curtains, embroidered pillows, vintage bedding.
Heirloom Accents	Antique china, silverware, vintage glassware.
Natural Woods & Metals	Polished mahogany, walnut furniture, brass fixtures, gilded mirrors.
Wallpaper & Wall Decor	Floral wallpaper, botanical prints, ornate framed art.

VINTAGE & GRANDMILLENNIAL COLOR PALETTE GUIDE

Capture authentic vintage charm through these carefully selected colors:

Primary Colors	SAGE GREEN · BLUSH PINK · PALE BLUE · CREAM · BEIGE · TAUPE
Secondary Colors	DEEP EMERALD · NAVY · BURGUNDY · RUST · OCHRE · OLIVE
Accent Colors	GOLD · BRASS · COPPER · SOFT WHITES · VINTAGE PATINAS

PALETTE CATEGORY	RECOMMENDED COLORS
Walls	Creamy whites, floral wallpapers, muted pastels, pale sage green
Furniture	Rich wood tones, pastel upholstery, antique finishes
Accents & Decor	Brass fixtures, jewel-tone cushions, vintage ceramics

PRACTICAL GUIDELINES FOR ACHIEVING VINTAGE & GRANDMILLENNIAL STYLE

Create inviting, personality-driven spaces with these actionable tips:

1. Curate a Meaningful Mix
Blend heirloom furniture with carefully chosen contemporary pieces for a fresh yet timeless feel. Eclecticism is encouraged but maintain cohesive color or pattern themes for harmony.

2. Embrace Bold Patterns & Textiles
Don't shy from vibrant florals, toiles, and needlepoint cushions. Use patterns confidently on upholstery, wallpaper, curtains, or rugs.

3. Prioritize Heirlooms & Antiques
Showcase family heirlooms and antique finds, using vintage decor intentionally to narrate personal stories and histories.

4. Layer for Comfort
Create coziness by layering rugs, cushions, throws, curtains, and upholstery, enhancing warmth, comfort, and visual interest.

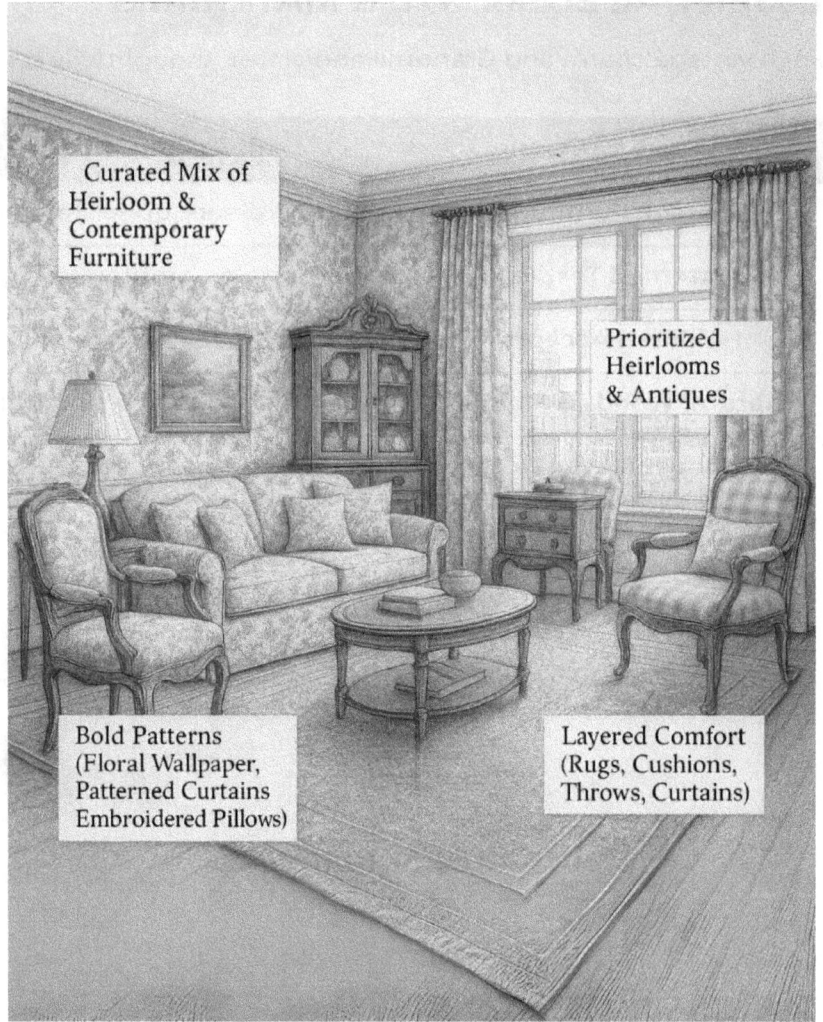

Curated Mix of Heirloom & Contemporary Furniture

Prioritized Heirlooms & Antiques

Bold Patterns (Floral Wallpaper, Patterned Curtains Embroidered Pillows)

Layered Comfort (Rugs, Cushions, Throws, Curtains)

VINTAGE & GRANDMILLENNIAL ROOM-BY-ROOM INSPIRATION GUIDE

Personalize your home with these detailed vintage styling recommendations:

ROOM	ESSENTIAL ELEMENTS & VINTAGE SUGGESTIONS
Living Room	Upholstered sofas with floral patterns, antique side tables, vintage rugs, brass lighting, framed art
Bedroom	Vintage four-poster bed, floral bedding, heirloom dressers, embroidered linens, soft pastel wallpaper
Dining Room	Antique dining set, vintage china, crystal chandelier, botanical wallpaper, embroidered table linens
Bathroom	Claw-foot tub, vintage brass fixtures, floral or pastel wall coverings, antique mirrors, cozy textiles
Kitchen	Vintage-inspired cabinetry, heirloom china display, brass hardware, retro accessories, floral curtains

COMMON MISTAKES AND HOW TO AVOID THEM

MISTAKE: OVER-DECORATING SPACES.

- **Solution**: Carefully edit collections; showcase fewer, meaningful pieces for maximum impact.

MISTAKE: MISMATCHED PATTERNS CLASHING EXCESSIVELY.

- **Solution**: Balance bold patterns with neutral backdrops, consistent color palettes to unify the space.

MISTAKE: OVERLY KITSCHY OR OUTDATED FEEL.

- **Solution**: Mix vintage with contemporary items to maintain freshness and relevance.

VINTAGE VS. GRANDMILLENNIAL: UNDERSTANDING SUBTLE DIFFERENCES

Although intertwined, subtle distinctions separate Vintage from Grandmillennial style:

ASPECT	VINTAGE STYLE	GRANDMILLENNIAL STYLE
Design Influence	Authentic antiques, broader vintage era range (1920s-1980s)	Specifically nostalgic, updated traditional elements from grandparents' homes
Decorative Approach	Genuine antiques, historically accurate pieces	Traditional decor revived in youthful contexts (chintz, embroidery, chinoiserie)
Color Usage	Rich vintage tones, broad color range	Predominantly pastels, fresh reinterpretations of traditional colors
Overall Atmosphere	Historical authenticity, broad nostalgia	Youthful freshness, intentional nostalgia

VINTAGE INTERIOR

GRANDMILLENNIAL INTERIOR

CASE STUDY: DESIGNING A GRANDMILLENNIAL-INSPIRED LIVING ROOM

Create a living space reflecting vibrant nostalgia and contemporary charm:

- **Furniture**: Upholstered floral sofa, antique wooden coffee table, vintage armchairs with contemporary cushions.
- **Patterns**: Floral wallpaper, embroidered throw pillows, vintage-style rugs layered over each other.
- **Lighting**: Brass table lamps, crystal chandelier, vintage sconces.
- **Decor**: Botanical artwork, heirloom ceramics, vintage books, brass accessories.
- **Color Scheme**: Soft pastels (sage green, blush pink), cream, brass metallic accents.

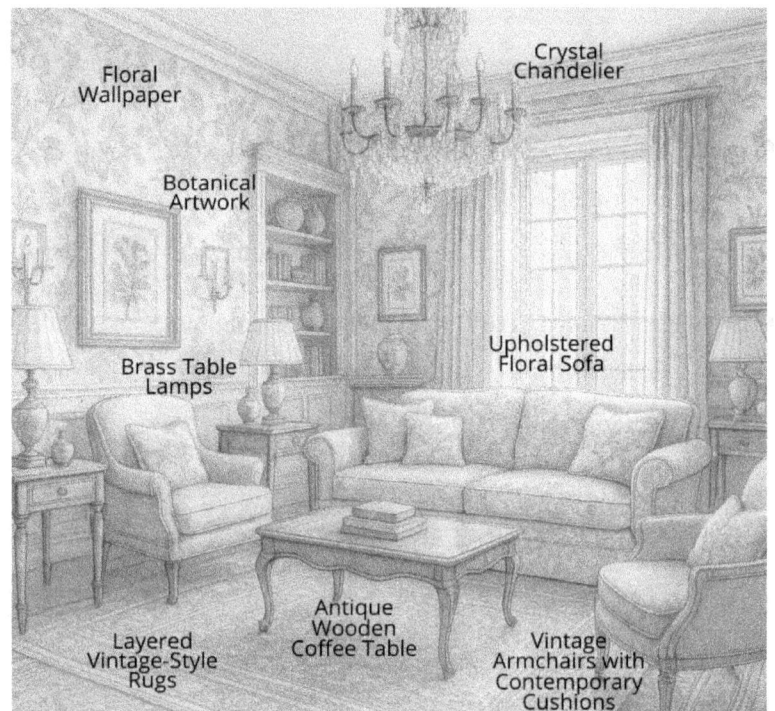

FINAL THOUGHTS ON VINTAGE & GRANDMILLENNIAL DESIGN

Vintage and Grandmillennial interiors celebrate authenticity, storytelling, and emotional resonance. Embracing these styles invites you to thoughtfully curate your spaces, mixing past and present, tradition and modernity, antiques and contemporary charm.

Remember, achieving a meaningful interior involves carefully selecting pieces that genuinely resonate with your personal history, tastes, and lifestyle. Through intentional layering, vibrant patterns, cherished heirlooms, and contemporary freshness, you'll craft warm, inviting interiors radiating timeless charm and endless comfort.

Maximalism
& DOPAMINE DECORE

Imagine stepping into a vibrant space bursting with energy, creativity, and fearless individuality—a room designed to uplift your spirits, inspire joy, and celebrate life's abundance. Maximalism and Dopamine Decor embody exactly this: exuberant, expressive interiors that boldly embrace vibrant colors, mixed patterns, and eclectic charm. In direct contrast to minimalist restraint, these styles invite you to express your personality fully, curate without constraint, and create spaces that energize, delight, and comfort.

This chapter thoroughly explores the bold history, defining characteristics, essential elements, and practical tips for authentically curating Maximalism and Dopamine Decor in your own home. You'll discover how to harness bold colors, playful patterns, and abundant textures, creating interiors that spark joy and nourish creativity.

HISTORICAL ORIGINS AND PHILOSOPHY

Maximalism emerged as a vibrant counter-response to minimalism's strict restraint, championing abundance, personality, and unapologetic self-expression. Historically rooted in rich design movements like Baroque, Victorian, and Art Deco, Maximalism celebrates detail, ornamentation, and layered storytelling through color, texture, and pattern. It resists the idea of stripping things down and instead embraces the emotional power of surrounding oneself with meaningful, expressive objects. In recent years, Dopamine Decor has grown from this tradition, drawing on psychological principles to use bold color, playful motifs, and sentimental items as tools for enhancing mood and fostering happiness. It's not just about aesthetics—it's about emotional resonance.

Both Maximalism and Dopamine Decor encourage creativity without limits. These styles invite people to make their homes deeply personal, emotionally fulfilling, and joyfully individual—spaces that radiate energy, memory, and delight with every corner and curated choice.

KEY CHARACTERISTICS OF MAXIMALISM & DOPAMINE DECOR INTERIORS

To authentically embrace Maximalism and Dopamine Decor, center your designs around these definitive features:

- **Bold & Vibrant Colors**: Rich jewel tones, bright primaries, neon accents, or a blend of saturated hues.
- **Layered Patterns & Textures**: Confidently mixing florals, stripes, geometrics, and abstract designs in textiles, wallpaper, and furnishings.
- **Eclectic Collections**: Curated but abundant displays of artwork, accessories, books, antiques, and meaningful personal items.
- **Whimsical & Playful Elements**: Unexpected decor, bold statement furniture, quirky art, vibrant wall treatments.
- **Abundant & Inviting Atmosphere**: Plush textiles, layered rugs, diverse seating, cozy corners encouraging relaxation and socializing.
- **Emotional Well-being & Joyful Expression (Dopamine Decor)**: Intentional use of colors, decor, and layout scientifically proven to boost mood, comfort, and positivity.

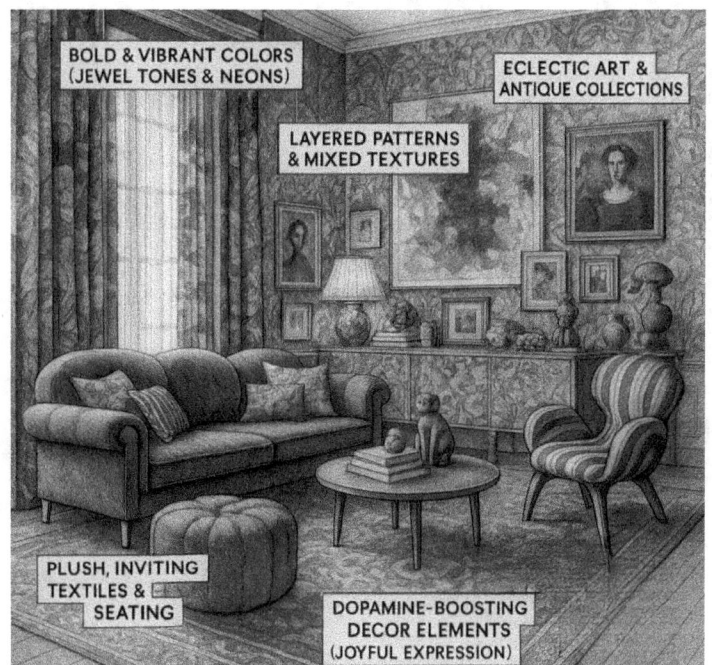

BOLD & VIBRANT COLORS (JEWEL TONES & NEONS)

ECLECTIC ART & ANTIQUE COLLECTIONS

LAYERED PATTERNS & MIXED TEXTURES

PLUSH, INVITING TEXTILES & SEATING

DOPAMINE-BOOSTING DECOR ELEMENTS (JOYFUL EXPRESSION)

ESSENTIAL ELEMENTS & MATERIALS

For authentic Maximalism & Dopamine-inspired spaces, integrate these foundational elements:

ELEMENTS & MATERIALS	USAGE AND RECOMMENDATIONS
Vibrant Wallpapers	Bold florals, graphic patterns, abstract designs.
Mixed Textiles	Velvet upholstery, patterned cushions, layered rugs.
Artistic Decor	Colorful paintings, quirky sculptures, vintage posters.
Bold Furniture	Statement sofas, unique chairs, vividly colored cabinetry.
Metallic & Reflective Accents	Gold, brass, mirrors, glossy finishes adding dimension.

Vibrant Wallpaper

Bold Furnitures
(Statement Sofas, Unique Chairs)

Artristic Decor
(Quirky Sculiptures, Colorful paintings)

Mixed Textiles
(Velvet, Patterned Cushions, Layered Rugs)

MAXIMALISM & DOPAMINE DECOR COLOR PALETTE GUIDE

Capturing authentic Maximalism & Dopamine-inspired interiors involves confident use of vibrant hues:

Primary Colors	EMERALD • SAPPHIRE • RUBY DEEP BLUES • BRIGHT YELLOWS • BOLD REDS
Secondary Colors	HOT PINK • ELECTRIC LIME • MINT • LILAC • CORAL
Accent Colors	GOLD · BRASS · BLACK OR WHITE CONTRASTS · PLAYFUL MULTICOLOR DETAILS

PALETTE CATEGORY	RECOMMENDED COLORS
Walls & Floors	Deep jewel tones, vivid wallpapers, bold painted accents
Furniture	Richly colored upholstery, statement pieces in bold hues
Accents & Decor	Bright accessories, metallic highlights, multicolored artwork

PRACTICAL GUIDELINES FOR ACHIEVING MAXIMALISM & DOPAMINE DECOR

Confidently embody these vibrant styles with the following practical tips:

1. Fearlessly Mix Patterns & Colors
Combine diverse patterns (florals, stripes, geometrics) and saturated colors intentionally. Balance with neutrals to avoid overwhelming spaces.

2. Curate Eclectic Displays
Thoughtfully showcase collections, meaningful objects, books, art, and vintage items, creating personality-driven vignettes.

3. Embrace Whimsy & Unexpected Elements
Integrate quirky artwork, unusual furnishings, or unexpected decor items to create playful surprises and joy.

4. Prioritize Comfort & Layering
Layer plush rugs, velvet upholstery, cushions, and throws to enhance coziness, warmth, and inviting atmosphere.

MAXIMALISM & DOPAMINE DECOR ROOM-BY-ROOM INSPIRATION GUIDE

Infuse vibrant joy into each room with this detailed inspiration guide:

ROOM	ESSENTIAL ELEMENTS & STYLING SUGGESTIONS
Living Room	Patterned sofas, eclectic gallery walls, vibrant rugs, whimsical coffee tables, bold curtains, plush seating
Bedroom	Bold headboards, vibrant bedding, colorful wallpaper, layered textiles, statement lighting
Dining Room	Statement chairs, patterned table linens, bold wall treatments, eclectic dinnerware, vibrant lighting fixtures
Bathroom	Vibrant tiles, patterned wallpaper, bold-colored cabinetry, unique mirrors, metallic accents
Home Office	Colorful shelving, bold wallpaper, artistic desk accessories, vibrant seating, playful lighting

Living Room

Bedroom

Dining Room

Bathroom

Home Office

COMMON MISTAKES AND HOW TO AVOID THEM

MISTAKE: CHAOTIC OR CLUTTERED APPEARANCE.

- **Solution**: Use consistent color themes or motifs to maintain visual harmony amidst abundant decor.

MISTAKE: PATTERN OVERLOAD WITHOUT BALANCE.

- **Solution**: Mix large-scale patterns with smaller-scale motifs, punctuating them with solid-color elements for clarity.

MISTAKE: NEGLECTING COMFORT IN PURSUIT OF AESTHETICS.

- **Solution**: Ensure ample seating, cozy textiles, and inviting arrangements prioritize comfort and livability.

MAXIMALISM VS. DOPAMINE DECOR: UNDERSTANDING SUBTLE DIFFERENCES

Maximalism and Dopamine Decor overlap closely, but subtle differences define each:

ASPECT	MAXIMALISM	DOPAMINE DECOR
Design Philosophy	Bold extravagance, abundant visual interest	Purposeful emotional uplift through color and decor
Pattern & Color Approach	Unrestricted maximal combinations	Intentionally vibrant colors scientifically linked to mood improvement
Decorative Intent	Artistic eclecticism, personal storytelling	Joyful, mood-enhancing curation
Overall Atmosphere	Lavishly expressive, eclectic charm	Energizing, mood-boosting, emotionally uplifting

MAXIMALISM

DOPAMINE DECOR

CASE STUDY: DESIGNING A JOYFUL MAXIMALIST LIVING SPACE

Imagine crafting a joyful, energized maximalist living room:

- Furniture: Bold velvet sofa, patterned armchairs, whimsical coffee table.

- Patterns & Textiles: Floral wallpaper, geometric rugs, colorful cushions.

- Color Scheme: Rich jewel tones (emerald, sapphire), neon accents (pink, yellow).

- Decor & Accents: Eclectic gallery wall, quirky sculptures, metallic mirrors, vibrant ceramics.

- Lighting: Playful chandeliers, statement lamps, neon accents.

FINAL THOUGHTS ON MAXIMALISM & DOPAMINE DECOR

Maximalism and Dopamine Decor empower you to embrace boldness, creativity, and joy in your interiors fully. Rather than restricting expression, these styles encourage personal storytelling, emotional uplift, and vibrant individuality.

Remember, successful Maximalism and Dopamine Decor require intentionality despite abundant decoration. Curate thoughtfully, balance color and pattern strategically, and prioritize comfort alongside aesthetics. By doing so, you create not just visually captivating interiors, but genuinely joyful, emotionally nourishing spaces uniquely tailored to your personality.

CHAPTER 3

Color Mastery

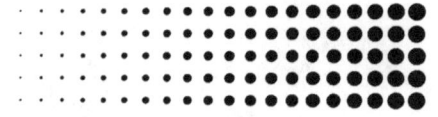

Color Theory
ESSENTIALS

The emotional weight of a space is often determined before a single word is spoken—through color. Whether it's the quiet calm of muted earth tones or the vibrant pulse of jewel-toned contrasts, color directs how we experience and remember interiors. More than surface treatment, it is an architectural language in its own right—capable of energizing, grounding, soothing, or awakening. Understanding the fundamentals of color theory is indispensable for those shaping spatial experiences, from professional designers to homeowners with a keen eye. This guide unpacks the foundational principles behind hue relationships, tonal balance, and chromatic context. When applied with intention, color becomes a masterful tool—one that invites cohesion, communicates narrative, and transforms ordinary rooms into atmospheres of meaning. Great design begins with the confident application of this often-underestimated force

UNDERSTANDING THE COLOR WHEEL

The color wheel is the fundamental tool designers use to navigate color relationships. At its core, the color wheel visually represents color relationships, offering clarity and direction when selecting harmonious palettes.

PRIMARY COLORS

These fundamental colors can't be created by mixing others, yet form the basis for all other hues:

- Red
- Yellow
- Blue

SECONDARY COLORS

Formed by mixing primary colors:

- Orange (Red + Yellow)
- Green (Blue + Yellow)
- Purple (Red + Blue)

TERTIARY COLORS

Created by mixing primary and secondary colors:

- Yellow-orange
- Red-orange
- Red-purple
- Blue-purple
- Blue-green
- Yellow-green

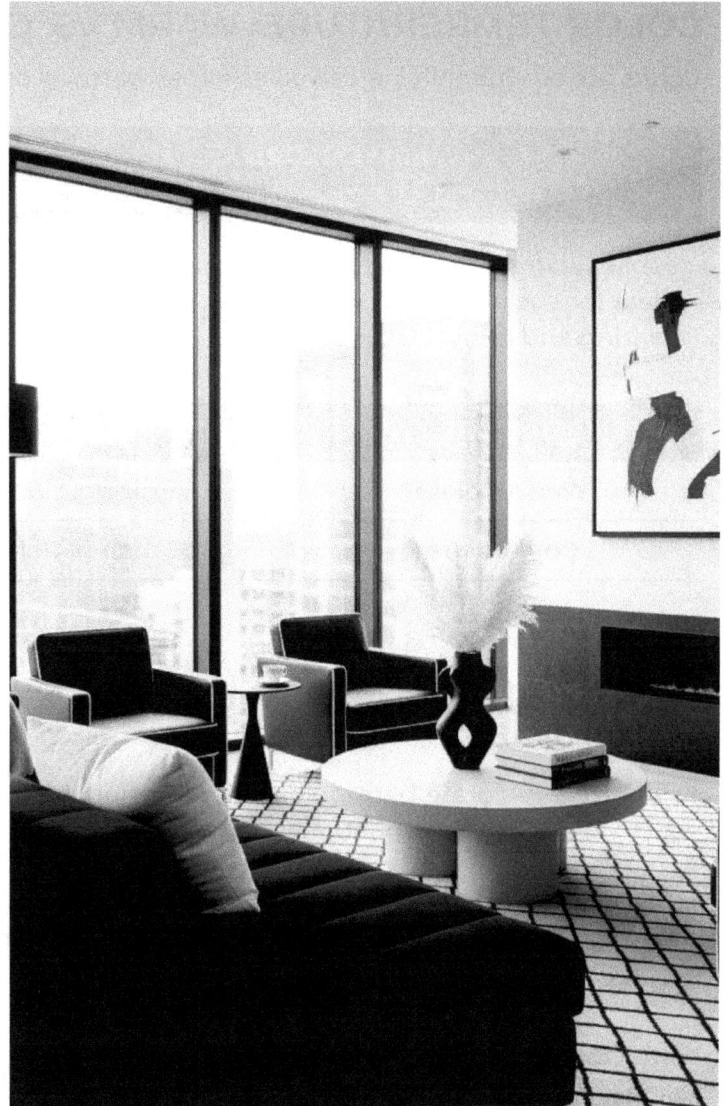

COLOR PROPERTIES EXPLAINED

Mastering color involves understanding three crucial properties: hue, saturation, and value.

HUE • The purest form of a color (e.g., pure red or blue).

SATURATION • Intensity/purity of a color; vibrant colors have high saturation, muted colors have low saturation.

VALUE • Lightness or darkness of a color; adjusted by adding white (tint), black (shade), or gray (tone).

COLOR ADJUSTMENT	METHOD	EXAMPLE	EFFECT ON INTERIORS
Tint	Adding white to lighten	Red → Pink	Airy, delicate, spacious
Shade	Adding black to darken	Red → Burgundy	Intimate, dramatic, sophisticated
Tone	Adding gray to soften	Red → Muted Mauve	Calm, refined, versatile

COLOR TEMPERATURE: WARM VS. COOL COLORS

Colors are emotionally perceived as either warm or cool, significantly impacting the mood of interiors.

WARM COLORS (Red, Orange, Yellow)	COOL COLORS (Blue, Green, Purple)
Evoke warmth, coziness, energy, and intimacy. Ideal for social spaces or rooms designed to feel inviting and lively.	Foster calmness, serenity, freshness, and relaxation. Excellent for bedrooms, bathrooms, or spaces dedicated to tranquility.

TEMPERATURE TYPE	EMOTIONAL IMPACT	IDEAL ROOMS
Warm Colors	Energizing, Welcoming	Living rooms, dining areas, kitchens
Cool Colors	Calming, Relaxing	Bedrooms, bathrooms, meditation areas

ESSENTIAL COLOR SCHEMES & HARMONIES

To effortlessly curate harmonious interiors, familiarize yourself with these foundational color schemes:

MONOCHROMATIC SCHEME
Using various tints, shades, and tones of a single color.
- **Effect**: Calming, cohesive, sophisticated interiors.

ANALOGOUS SCHEME
Using colors adjacent on the color wheel (e.g., blue, blue-green, green).
- **Effect**: Harmonious, natural, relaxing spaces.

COMPLEMENTARY SCHEME
Colors directly opposite each other (e.g., blue and orange).
- **Effect**: Bold, vibrant, energetic contrast.

TRIADIC SCHEME
Using three colors evenly spaced on the color wheel (e.g., purple, orange, green).
- **Effect**: Balanced, dynamic, lively spaces.

SPLIT-COMPLEMENTARY SCHEME
One base color combined with two colors adjacent to its complement (e.g., blue with yellow-orange and red-orange).
- **Effect**: Balanced contrast, visually stimulating yet harmonious.

PRACTICAL APPLICATION: SELECTING AND BALANCING COLORS

Applying color theory practically requires thoughtful consideration of your room's purpose, lighting, size, and desired emotional impact:

- **Lighting**: Natural daylight brightens colors, while artificial lighting (warm or cool) significantly influences perception. Test colors in various lighting conditions before finalizing your choice.
- **Room Size**: Use lighter, cooler colors to visually expand smaller spaces; darker, warmer shades create intimacy in larger areas.
- **Purpose & Mood**: Align your color choices to the room's function and emotional intent—vibrant, energizing colors in social areas, tranquil palettes in private spaces.

ROOM TYPE	RECOMMENDED COLORS & SCHEMES	EMOTIONAL GOAL
LIVING ROOM	Warm, complementary or analogous colors	Welcoming, vibrant, socializing
BEDROOM	Cool, monochromatic or analogous colors	Calm, restful, tranquil
KITCHEN	Warm, energetic hues, complementary contrasts	Inviting, lively, stimulating
HOME OFFICE	Balanced triadic or split-complementary	Creative, focused, energizing

COMMON MISTAKES AND HOW TO AVOID THEM

MISTAKE: OVERWHELMING ROOMS WITH TOO MANY COLORS.

- **Solution**: Limit your palette to 2–4 main colors; use neutrals for balance.

MISTAKE: IGNORING UNDERTONES.

- **Solution**: Always test colors in the room's lighting conditions; identify and align undertones carefully.

MISTAKE: FORGETTING TO BALANCE SATURATION LEVELS.

- **Solution**: Mix saturated hues with neutral tones or subtler shades for visual harmony.

EXPERT TIPS FOR MASTERING COLOR

SWATCH TESTING: Paint large swatches directly on walls to accurately test colors in different lighting conditions.

START SMALL: If uncertain, introduce bold or bright colors through accessories or accent walls before fully committing.

COLOR JOURNALS: Keep a journal of color combinations and inspirations—collect fabric swatches, paint chips, and magazine clippings to inspire cohesive schemes.

FINAL THOUGHTS ON COLOR THEORY ESSENTIALS

Mastery of colour theory is the silent signature that separates competent interiors from inspiring architecture. When hue, value, and chroma converse fluently, rooms shift from static enclosures to orchestrated experiences. A cultivated palette establishes rhythm, guides circulation, and frames the rituals that unfold across timber, stone, and fabric. Approach each commission as a composition: study undertones, temper saturation, and honour the daylight that drapes every surface. Such discipline recasts the designer as curator, composing atmospheres that linger in memory. Yet colour's influence stretches far beyond the eye. Pigment modulates emotion, encourages repose, sparks dialogue, even refines perceived function. A quiet neutral steadies the breath; a calibrated accent draws attention; a nuanced gradient invites contemplation. Trust instinct, but anchor decisions in the principles honed by painters and architects through centuries of observation. Apply them with measured confidence, observe the elegant alchemy they unleash, and watch your interiors mature into living canvases that enrich daily life immeasurably.

HOW TO CREATE A COHESIVE
Color Schemes

When you enter a beautifully designed space, one of the first things you notice—consciously or subconsciously—is the harmonious color palette. Cohesive color schemes are essential in making rooms feel connected, intentional, and visually pleasing. A carefully planned palette can seamlessly guide your eye throughout the space, creating a unified and polished appearance that feels effortless yet captivating. In this section, you'll discover the practical steps, expert techniques, and detailed guidelines necessary to create harmonious color schemes, empowering you to confidently design interiors with professional-grade appeal.

01 STEP — DEFINE YOUR VISION AND MOOD

Before selecting colors, clearly articulate the mood and atmosphere you wish to create:

Relaxed & Serene: Consider cool colors (soft blues, muted greens, gentle grays).

Vibrant & Energizing: Opt for bright, warm hues (oranges, yellows, reds).

Sophisticated & Elegant: Favor rich jewel tones (emerald, navy, burgundy).

Neutral & Timeless: Stick with whites, creams, taupes, and grays accented sparingly.

Clearly defining your desired atmosphere ensures your palette aligns perfectly with your design intent.

02 STEP — SELECTING YOUR BASE COLOR

Begin by choosing a foundational color, which typically covers the largest surface area (walls, large furniture). The base color sets the tone for the entire room:

Neutral Base: Versatile, accommodating multiple accents (creams, grays, whites).

Bold Base: Makes a powerful statement (deep teal, bold navy, vivid terracotta).

Pastel Base: Creates softness and subtlety (blush pink, powder blue, pale sage).

03 STEP — BUILDING YOUR PALETTE (THE 60-30-10 RULE)

The widely-adopted 60-30-10 rule ensures balanced, visually appealing interiors:

60% Dominant Color: Typically your chosen base color; covering walls, floors, major furniture.

30% Secondary Color: Supports and complements the dominant color; appears on upholstery, curtains, rugs.

10% Accent Color: Adds contrast and personality; introduced through accessories, artwork, cushions.

PRACTICAL EXAMPLE
The 60-30-10 rule is a classic design principle that helps you create balanced and visually appealing spaces.

- The dominant color (60%) typically covers the largest areas like walls, sofa upholstery, and flooring, providing a calm backdrop. A good suggestion for this is a soft gray.

- The secondary color (30%) is used for significant elements such as draperies, area rugs, and side chairs, adding depth. Consider a muted navy blue for this proportion.

- The accent color (10%) adds impactful pops of interest through items like throw pillows, artwork, and decorative accents, drawing the eye. Burnt orange works well as an accent.

04
STEP
HARMONIZE YOUR COLORS

Understanding and effectively applying color harmonies ensure visual cohesion:

Monochromatic Harmony
Different shades and tones of a single hue create a calming and elegant atmosphere. Ideal for bedrooms, bathrooms, or tranquil spaces.

Analogous Harmony
Adjacent colors on the color wheel blend naturally, creating comfortable, visually pleasing interiors (blue-green, green, yellow-green).

Complementary Harmony
Colors opposite each other on the wheel produce vibrant contrast and energy. Balance intensity by varying saturation levels (deep navy with muted gold).

Triadic Harmony
Equally spaced colors on the color wheel provide dynamic visual interest without overwhelming (purple, orange, green).

05
STEP
CONSIDER UNDERTONES AND LIGHTING

Lighting conditions dramatically influence how colors appear. A color that looks soft beige under natural daylight might turn overly warm or yellow under incandescent bulbs.

Natural Daylight: Highlights true colors; softens and brightens hues.

Warm Artificial Light: Adds yellow or golden tones; intensifies warmth.

Cool Artificial Light: Adds blue tones; makes colors appear cooler or duller.

Always test swatches in your specific lighting conditions throughout different times of day.

06
STEP
CONNECTING SPACES COHESIVELY

Create color continuity between adjoining spaces for harmonious transitions:

Common Neutral: Use one neutral consistently throughout various spaces.

Gradual Variation: Slightly adjust color intensity from one room to the next (lighter shades to darker tones).

Repeated Accent: Use a recurring accent color, subtly linking spaces through decorative accessories or details.

EXAMPLE FLOW BETWEEN ROOMS
Creating a harmonious flow between rooms can really make a house feel cohesive. Here's how colors can connect different spaces:

- **Living Room**: The **soft beige** dominant color truly grounds the space, while **navy blue** and **rust orange** serve as striking secondary and accent colors. The **beige** then acts as a subtle linking color that can be carried into adjacent areas, creating unity.

- **Dining Room**: A **muted navy blue** takes center stage here as the dominant color, beautifully complemented by **beige** and **warm gold accents**. The **navy blue** itself becomes the strong linking color, perhaps appearing in smaller, thoughtful touches in the next room.

- **Kitchen**: In the kitchen, a **warm white** creates a bright, inviting dominant backdrop, reflecting ample light. This is perfectly paired with **navy cabinetry** and **brass hardware** for sophisticated depth. The **navy blue** from the cabinets then serves as a strong linking color, providing continuity to other rooms, even subtly.

This strategic repetition fosters seamless visual connections.

COMMON MISTAKES AND HOW TO AVOID THEM

MISTAKE: TOO MANY COMPETING COLORS.

- **Solution**: Limit primary palette to 2-4 complementary shades; keep additional colors minimal.

MISTAKE: NEGLECTING ROOM FUNCTIONALITY.

- **Solution**: Match palettes to room usage; calming colors in restful areas, vibrant shades in active spaces.

MISTAKE: FORGETTING CONSISTENCY ACROSS OPEN SPACES.

- **Solution**: o Maintain consistent undertones and repeated colors across connected rooms for harmony.

EXPERT TIPS FOR COHESIVE COLOR SUCCESS

SWATCH TESTING: Compile paint chips, fabric swatches, images, and textures for clear visual direction.

START SMALL: ·Choose rugs, curtains, or upholstery first; pull complementary paint colors afterward.

COLOR JOURNALS: Always test large paint samples directly in spaces; observe them throughout day and night.

FINAL THOUGHTS ON COHESIVE COLOR SCHEMES

Cohesive color schemes are the visual architecture of a well-designed home. They provide a unifying thread that allows individual rooms to express their own character while still feeling undeniably connected. Crafting a palette that flows gracefully from one space to the next isn't about adhering to trends or rigid formulas—it's about making deliberate, informed choices that support the identity and purpose of each room. Whether your style leans soft and understated or bold and expressive, color is your most powerful tool for storytelling through design.

Harmony doesn't mean uniformity. A cohesive scheme may feature variation, contrast, and complexity—as long as every shade has a reason for being there. Begin by selecting a foundational hue that anchors your palette and serves as a common reference point throughout the home. Layering with complementary tones, subtle undertones, or rhythmic accents can then introduce interest without disrupting the overall continuity. This approach builds sophistication and depth into your interiors while maintaining a visual through-line.

Color should not confine creativity—it should refine it. When used intentionally, color offers both structure and freedom: structure to guide your decisions and freedom to explore nuances within a cohesive framework. The art lies in balancing familiarity with surprise—allowing certain elements to repeat or echo while introducing variation in material, texture, and light. This interplay keeps the design visually engaging and emotionally resonant.

Above all, let intuition play a role. While theory provides the foundation, the best interiors are those that feel personal and alive. If a color speaks to you—evokes warmth, calm, joy, or intrigue—honor that instinct. A successful color story doesn't just look beautiful; it feels right. By trusting your sensibility, refining your palette, and thinking holistically, you transform your home into an environment of coherence, elegance, and expressive intention—one where every room feels thoughtfully curated and effortlessly connected.

PSYCHOLOGY OF COLOR:
Influence Mood with Colors

Have you ever wondered why certain spaces immediately evoke specific feelings—calmness, excitement, warmth, or even anxiety? It's no coincidence. The secret lies in the powerful psychology of color. As an interior designer, understanding the emotional impact of color is like possessing a hidden superpower, enabling you to intentionally shape the moods, behaviors, and experiences within any space.

In this essential chapter, we'll dive deep into how various colors impact our emotions, behaviors, and overall psychological state. By mastering color psychology, you can intentionally and skillfully design interiors that precisely reflect the desired emotional atmosphere, making your home not just visually appealing but emotionally nourishing and supportive.

THE SCIENCE BEHIND COLOR PSYCHOLOGY

Far beyond mere ornament, colour operates as a quiet engine of spatial emotion. Neurological studies reveal that pigment wavelengths register in the limbic system in milliseconds, modulating pulse, cortisol, and even circadian rhythm. Architects, therefore, treat hue as a structural element: smoky greys temper restless corridors; celadon greens soften the glare of northern light; deep terracotta steadies communal tables, amplifying conviviality. When sapphire slips across a bedroom wall, it cools mental noise, encouraging unbroken REM cycles, while a burst of turmeric beside a skylight nudges morning alertness like sunshine held in suspension.

Cultural memory refines these instincts—scarlet signals festivity in Manila yet calm restraint in Copenhagen—inviting designers to choreograph palettes that honour context as much as aesthetics. Curated with intention, colour becomes not decoration but a calibrated experience, aligning physiology, history, and habitation with subtle, enduring resonance for everyone inside.

EMOTIONAL & PSYCHOLOGICAL IMPACT OF COLORS

Explore how common interior design colors affect mood, emotion, and behavior:

WARM COLORS: ENERGIZING AND INVITING

- **Red**: Energetic, passionate, stimulating.
  - **Ideal for**: Dining rooms, kitchens, social spaces.
- **Orange**: Optimistic, friendly, confident.
  - **Ideal for**: Kitchens, creative spaces, social areas.
- **Yellow**: Cheerful, uplifting, energizing.
  - **Ideal for**: Breakfast nooks, hallways, home offices.

COOL COLORS: CALMING AND RESTORATIVE

- **Blue**: Calming, serene, trustworthy.
  - **Ideal for**: Bedrooms, bathrooms, study rooms.
- **Green**: Balanced, restorative, peaceful.
  - **Ideal for**: Bedrooms, living rooms, wellness areas.
- **Purple**: Luxurious, creative, introspective.
  - **Ideal for**: Bedrooms, meditation spaces, creative studios.

NEUTRAL COLORS: BALANCED AND VERSATILE

- **White**: Pure, clean, airy.
  - **Ideal for**: Kitchens, bathrooms, small spaces.
- **Gray**: Elegant, balanced, sophisticated.
  - **Ideal for**: Living rooms, offices, contemporary spaces.
- **Beige/Tan**: Warm, comforting, approachable.
  - **Ideal for**: Open-plan rooms, family spaces, hallways.

ADVANCED COLOR ASSOCIATIONS & EFFECTS

Colors affect us beyond the basic emotional responses, influencing various specific reactions and behaviors:

COLOR	PSYCHOLOGICAL EFFECTS	PRACTICAL INTERIOR APPLICATION
RED	Enhances appetite, stimulates conversation.	Dining areas, restaurants, kitchens
BLUE	Lowers heart rate, promotes relaxation.	Bedrooms, bathrooms, meditation spaces
GREEN	Reduces anxiety, encourages creativity.	Workspaces, studios, relaxation rooms
YELLOW	Improves mood, stimulates memory and attention.	Home offices, learning spaces, kids' rooms
ORANGE	Stimulates activity, fosters social interaction.	Family rooms, creative studios, play areas
PURPLE	Encourages imagination, inspires reflection.	Creative spaces, libraries, meditation rooms

TAILORING COLOR PSYCHOLOGY TO YOUR INTERIOR GOALS

Align your color choices strategically to meet specific emotional and functional goals within different spaces:

RELAXATION & REST
- **Ideal Colors**: Soft blues, muted greens, pale lavender.
- **Recommended Areas**: Bedrooms, bathrooms, reading nooks.

SOCIAL ENGAGEMENT & CONVERSATION
- **Ideal Colors**: Warm oranges, vibrant reds, cheerful yellows.
- **Recommended Areas**: Living rooms, dining spaces, kitchens.

CREATIVITY & PRODUCTIVITY
- **Ideal Colors**: Stimulating yellow, balanced green, inspiring purple.
- **Recommended Areas**: Home offices, studios, children's rooms.

CULTURAL & PERSONAL COLOR ASSOCIATIONS

Remember that personal experiences and cultural backgrounds heavily influence individual reactions to color. These deeply ingrained associations can significantly impact how a design is perceived.

Cultural Differences

Color meanings are far from universal and often vary greatly. For instance, in Western cultures, white typically symbolizes purity, innocence, and joyous weddings. Conversely, in many Eastern cultures, particularly in Asia, white is often directly associated with mourning, somber funerals, and unfortunate death. Similarly, red symbolizes good luck, prosperity, and vibrant celebration in many Asian cultures, frequently seen during Lunar New Year festivities. In stark contrast, red in Western societies often symbolizes danger, urgent warning, passionate love, or even anger. Understanding these crucial nuances is absolutely essential.

Personal Memories & Associations

Beyond broad cultural strokes, individual experiences profoundly impact personal color perceptions. A specific color might evoke a strong positive or even negative emotion based on a cherished childhood memory or a significant life event. Therefore, always consider and thoughtfully prioritize personal preferences and unique associations alongside general psychological guidelines or accepted cultural norms.

When designing for diverse or international clients, it's essential to sensitively research and discuss color choices. This ensures not only emotional alignment with the user but also crucial cultural appropriateness, leading to a more impactful and well-received design.

COMMON MISTAKES AND HOW TO AVOID THEM

MISTAKE: SELECTING COLORS SOLELY BASED ON TRENDS.

- **Solution**: Prioritize emotional intent and room function above trends, creating timeless spaces.

MISTAKE: IGNORING INDIVIDUAL OR CULTURAL SENSITIVITIES.

- **Solution**: Engage in conversations to understand personal histories, preferences, and cultural influences before finalizing palettes.

MISTAKE: OVERLOOKING ROOM-SPECIFIC COLOR SUITABILITY.

- **Solution**: Always align your color selection directly with each room's intended use and desired emotional impact.

PRACTICAL EXERCISE: EMOTIONAL COLOR AUDIT

Perform a quick, practical audit of your current home spaces to determine how color impacts your mood:

Step 1: Identify each room's current colors.

Step 2: Note your immediate emotional reaction upon entering each room (calm, energized, anxious, indifferent).

Step 3: Analyze whether colors align with your intended emotional experience for that space.

ROOM	CURRENT COLORS	IMMEDIATE EMOTIONAL REACTION	DESIRED EMOTION & ALIGNMENT
BEDROOM	Pale Blue, White	Calm, peaceful	Perfectly aligned (no change needed)
HOME OFFICE	Beige, Dark Brown	Tired, uninspired	Needs brighter, energizing colors
KITCHEN	Soft Gray, White	Indifferent, sterile	Needs warm, inviting tones

This simple audit helps you identify rooms needing emotional color adjustments.

FINAL THOUGHTS ON THE PSYCHOLOGY OF COLOR

Understanding color psychology transforms interior design into a deeply personal and emotional art form. Your spaces are no longer merely aesthetically pleasing—they become intentional sanctuaries designed specifically to nurture, support, and enhance your emotional well-being and everyday experiences.

Remember, the emotional connection to color is uniquely individual. Use general psychological insights as guidelines but remain sensitive to personal and cultural nuances. With intentionality and empathy, you become more than an interior designer—you become a thoughtful curator of emotional experiences, shaping spaces that profoundly impact lives.

BOLD VS. NEUTRAL PALETTES:
Finding Your Balance

One of the most pivotal decisions you'll make when designing your home's interior is choosing between a bold, vibrant color palette or a calming, neutral scheme. This decision profoundly influences the emotional experience, visual impact, and overall style of your spaces. Bold palettes evoke energy, personality, and drama, while neutral palettes offer timeless elegance, serenity, and versatility. But who says you must choose strictly one over the other? Finding your perfect balance between bold and neutral elements is key to crafting interiors that feel authentic, expressive, and harmonious.

In this chapter, you'll learn the strategic benefits, practical guidelines, and essential techniques for skillfully blending bold and neutral palettes. You'll be empowered to create interiors that perfectly reflect your personality, ensuring your home remains both exciting and comfortable.

BOLD PALETTES: EMBRACING VIBRANCE AND EXPRESSION

A bold palette captures attention instantly, making interiors unforgettable and deeply personal. By using saturated, vivid colors, bold interiors offer vibrancy, excitement, and creative expression.

BENEFITS OF A BOLD PALETTE

- **Energy & Excitement**: Stimulates mood, inspires creativity.
- **Personal Expression**: Bold palettes distinctly reflect personality.
- **Visual Interest**: Captivating focal points and striking contrasts.

BEST USES FOR BOLD PALETTES

- **Accent Walls**: Vibrant statement walls draw attention.
- **Social Spaces**: Living rooms, dining areas, creative studios.
- **Furniture & Accessories**: Vivid upholstery, dramatic artwork, playful decor.

NEUTRAL PALETTES: CELEBRATING CALM AND TIMELESSNESS

Neutral color schemes—featuring shades of white, beige, gray, taupe, and muted earth tones—create timeless, serene, and versatile interiors. Their inherent elegance offers a restful backdrop for daily life.

BENEFITS OF A NEUTRAL PALETTE

- **Timeless Appeal**: Remains stylish despite evolving trends.
- **Relaxing Atmosphere**: Promotes tranquility, comfort, and restfulness.
- **Design Flexibility**: Easy integration with various styles and decorative changes.

BEST USES FOR NEUTRAL PALETTES

- **Bedrooms & Bathrooms**: Quiet, restful, serene atmospheres.
- **Open Spaces**: Cohesive, continuous flow throughout the home.
- **Foundation Elements**: Walls, flooring, large furniture for versatility.

COMBINING BOLD AND NEUTRAL COLORS EFFECTIVELY

Why limit yourself when you can truly combine the best of both worlds? Integrating bold, vibrant accents into a serene, neutral background offers an exciting dynamic. This approach creates immediate visual interest without overwhelming the senses. Conversely, grounding a bold, saturated space with thoughtful neutral elements provides essential balance and prevents it from feeling too intense. This strategic combination not only adds significant visual intrigue but also injects emotional depth into any design. It allows for impactful statements while maintaining a sense of harmony and sophistication.

TECHNIQUES FOR EFFECTIVE INTEGRATION

1. Bold Accents in Neutral Spaces

Incorporate strategic bold colors into predominantly neutral interiors, creating dynamic visual focal points:

- **Accent Furniture**: A bold-colored sofa or armchair becomes an immediate focal point.
- **Art & Accessories**: Vibrant artwork or decorative accessories energize neutral backdrops.
- **Textiles & Rugs**: Rich-colored pillows, throws, or rugs introduce personality and warmth.

2. Neutral Anchors in Bold Spaces

Anchor vibrant, colorful spaces with neutral elements for visual relief and balanced design:

- **Neutral Furniture**: White sofas or gray armchairs balance boldly painted walls.
- **Natural Materials**: Wooden floors, natural fibers, neutral rugs, and organic materials tone down vibrant palettes.
- **White or Neutral Ceilings**: Provide visual breathing space, preventing overwhelming sensations.

STEP-BY-STEP GUIDE TO BALANCING BOLD AND NEUTRAL COLORS

Follow these strategic steps to achieve perfect color harmony:

01 STEP — DETERMINE YOUR BASE PALETTE

The foundational decision for your color scheme involves determining your base palette: will your dominant background be neutral or bold? This crucial choice sets the entire emotional and aesthetic direction of your room. A neutral base, utilizing shades like off-white, gray, or beige, creates a calm, versatile canvas, allowing other colors to pop. Conversely, opting for a bold dominant background, such as a deep teal or vibrant yellow, establishes an immediate sense of drama and personality, requiring more considered complementary choices.

02 STEP — CHOOSE ACCENT COLORS THOUGHTFULLY

Select complementary accent colors strategically to enhance your base palette:

DOMINANT PALETTE	IDEAL ACCENT CHOICES	INTERIOR EXAMPLE
NEUTRAL	Jewel tones, vibrant primary colors, deep pastels	Gray room with emerald green accents
BOLD	Muted earth tones, whites, soft grays	Deep blue room with beige furniture

03
STEP

BALANCE VISUAL WEIGHT

Distribute colors evenly throughout your space, balancing visual intensity:

Bold Palette: Keep large furniture neutral; use bold hues on walls and accessories.

Neutral Palette: Use bold colors selectively in smaller items and focal points.

PRACTICAL COLOR COMBINATIONS FOR PERFECT HARMONY

To inspire your creative process, consider these successful color combinations:

PALETTE STYLE	BASE COLORS	ACCENT COLORS	IDEAL ROOMS
NEUTRAL DOMINANT	Soft gray, beige	Sapphire blue, burnt orange	Living room, bedroom
BOLD DOMINANT	Rich navy, emerald	Creamy white, soft blush	Dining room, entryway
BALANCED MIX	Warm taupe, ivory	Deep teal, vibrant coral	Home office, creative space

MISTAKES TO AVOID & SOLUTIONS FOR BALANCE

MISTAKE: OVERWHELMING A ROOM WITH TOO MANY BOLD COLORS.

- **Solution**: Stick to a limited, carefully curated palette (one or two bold accents balanced with neutrals).

MISTAKE: CREATING MONOTONY WITH TOO MANY NEUTRALS.

- **Solution**: Introduce dynamic, contrasting textures or subtle tonal variations for visual interest.

MISTAKE: IGNORING ROOM SIZE AND NATURAL LIGHTING.

- **Solution**: Use bolder colors sparingly in small or poorly lit rooms; neutrals or lighter shades visually expand space.

EXPERT TIPS FOR ACHIEVING BOLD-NEUTRAL BALANCE

LAYERED TEXTURES: Enhance neutral interiors with diverse textures (linen, velvet, wool) for subtle visual richness.

SEASONAL ADAPTATION: Rotate bold-colored accessories seasonally, allowing easy, fresh updates without major renovations.

TEST SWATCHES: Evaluate color combinations in your space under multiple lighting conditions, ensuring visual harmony and emotional resonance.

PRACTICAL EXERCISE: CREATING YOUR PERSONAL BOLD-NEUTRAL PALETTE

Step 1: Gather inspiring images from magazines, social media, and nature.

Step 2: Identify recurring themes: neutral backgrounds with bold accents, or vice versa.

Step 3: Create mood boards combining paint swatches, fabric samples, and decor photos.

Step 4: Refine your palette, adjusting proportions until achieving perfect visual and emotional balance.

FINAL THOUGHTS ON BALANCING BOLD AND NEUTRAL PALETTES

Colour harmony is seldom achieved through rigid formulas; it arises from an attentive dialogue between saturation and understatement, luminosity and hush. When audacious pigments stand beside restrained neutrals, each hue gains definition, depth, and narrative weight, much as a well-curated art exhibition relies on negative space to amplify masterpieces. Deep ultramarine, for instance, gathers velvety dimension when surrounded by chalk-washed plaster, while a restrained ash-beige converses fluently with cinnabar upholstery, lending warmth without surrendering composure. Design is therefore not a battle between vibrant and muted, but an orchestration of intervals, pauses, and crescendos—an interior symphony that lets the eye rest before it roams again. Approach every room as an editor hones prose: remove excess, preserve accent, and allow silence to underline the most resonant statements. In this way, balance ceases to be static equilibrium and becomes a dynamic rhythm that animates daily rituals.

Begin your composition by mapping functional zones and the emotional cadence they deserve. A reading nook may crave tepid neutrality—a pale mushroom linen, a walnut armchair—to steady concentration, yet benefit from a singular burst of marigold in the lamp base, signalling intellectual curiosity. Conversely, an entry vestibule can withstand theatrical gestures: lacquered indigo millwork underlines arrival, while fog-soft tiles beneath temper glare and welcome. Allow light to arbitrate these maneuvers; observe how dawn cools a sage wall or dusk deepens ochre cabinetry, and adjust pigment proportions accordingly. When

doubt surfaces, borrow from nature's hierarchies: forest floors are predominantly quiet, punctuated by petals, berries, and the sudden hush of silver bark. Translate that ratio indoors by majoring in neutrals—wood grain, limestone, flax—and minoring in bravura accents measured to personal tolerance. The objective is not visual obedience but emotional calibration tailored to the room's purpose.

Resist the impulse to freeze your palette in perpetuity. Interiors, like their inhabitants, evolve; the crimson you adored last winter may feel oppressive after a luminous trip abroad, just as a once-comforting ecru can appear insipid when you crave momentum. Establish adaptable layers—textiles, artwork, movable furnishings—that let you dial chromatic intensity up or down without structural upheaval. Neutral foundations provide this elasticity, acting as a quiet gallery against which fresh statements may alight seasonally. Equally critical is restraint: limit your bold notes to a concise family of undertones so the narrative remains coherent even as accessories migrate. Edit ruthlessly, then introduce contrast where the eye lands first—mantel, headboard, banquet banquette—guiding perception with curatorial intent. Step back, squint, and sense how your heartbeat responds; physiological feedback is an unerring critic. If calm lingers yet curiosity stirs, balance is working. The elegance of adept colour choreography lies not in perfect symmetry but in the confident oscillation between serenity and exhilaration that keeps rooms alive, memorable, and unequivocally yours. Trust your intuition, edit with patience, and remember that colour, like architecture itself, is ultimately successful when it frames human experience rather than dominating it or shouting for attention.

HOW TO MIX
PATTERNS AND TEXTURES
CONFIDENTLY

Stepping into a beautifully designed room that masterfully blends patterns and textures evokes instant intrigue and warmth. It sparks curiosity and draws you into its carefully curated layers. Yet, many homeowners and even designers feel intimidated by mixing patterns and textures, fearful of creating visual chaos. Let me assure you—mastering this art is entirely achievable with a strategic, thoughtful approach. When executed confidently, blending diverse patterns and textures elevates any interior, adding personality, depth, and visual interest that transforms a room from ordinary to extraordinary.

In this chapter, you'll discover the proven guidelines, practical examples, and insider techniques for mixing patterns and textures effectively. You'll gain the confidence and knowledge to design spaces that feel harmonious yet visually exciting, nuanced yet unified.

UNDERSTANDING PATTERNS AND TEXTURES

Before diving into practical applications, let's clarify the key elements:

PATTERNS
Patterns are repeated designs, shapes, or motifs found on textiles, wallpapers, rugs, and decor.

- **Geometric**: Stripes, chevron, grids, hexagons.
- **Organic**: Florals, botanicals, animal prints.
- **Classic**: Damask, paisley, toile, checks.
- **Abstract**: Artistic, irregular, contemporary designs.

TEXTURES
Textures refer to surface qualities and tactile sensations—smooth, rough, shiny, matte, soft, or coarse—that add depth and visual richness to interiors.

- **Soft Textures**: Velvet, linen, cotton, silk, wool.
- **Rough Textures**: Jute, burlap, raw wood, stone, brick.
- **Reflective Textures**: Glass, metals, polished surfaces.
- **Matte Textures**: Ceramics, matte paint finishes, untreated fabrics.

THE ART OF MIXING PATTERNS

Mixing patterns effectively isn't random—it involves careful selection and thoughtful pairing. Here are fundamental guidelines to master this skill confidently:

1. SCALE & PROPORTION
Mix patterns of varying scales (large, medium, small) to create visual interest and avoid overwhelming the space:

- **Large-Scale Patterns**: Dominant elements such as wallpaper or area rugs.
- **Medium-Scale Patterns**: Upholstery, curtains, bedding.
- **Small-Scale Patterns**: Pillows, accessories, decorative details.

PATTERN SCALE	EXAMPLE USAGE
LARGE-SCALE	Bold floral wallpaper
MEDIUM-SCALE	Geometric patterned armchairs
SMALL-SCALE	Subtle striped throw pillows

2. COHESIVE COLOR PALETTE

Maintain visual harmony by keeping patterns within a cohesive color family:

- **Unified Palette**: Select patterns featuring similar hues for cohesion.
- **Complementary Colors**: Mix patterns in complementary tones for balanced contrast.

Practical Example:
Dominant Color: Navy blue floral curtains.
Secondary Pattern: Navy and cream striped rug.
Accent Pattern: Soft navy paisley throw pillows.

3. BALANCE AND DISTRIBUTION

Evenly distribute patterns throughout the room to create balanced visual interest without overwhelming the eye:

- Avoid concentrating patterns in a single area; disperse them evenly.
- Balance bold patterns with areas of visual relief— solid colors or subtle textures.

4. PATTERN REPETITION

Repeating similar or related patterns across different elements creates a cohesive narrative:

- Match curtain patterns subtly in throw pillows.
- Echo geometric rug shapes in furniture upholstery.

MASTERING TEXTURE COMBINATIONS

Mixing textures is essential for creating interiors that feel layered, sophisticated, and inviting:

1. CONTRAST & COMPLEMENT

Combine contrasting textures (rough/smooth, matte/shiny) to enhance depth and sensory appeal:

- **Smooth vs. Rough**: Velvet sofa with a rustic jute rug.
- **Matte vs. Reflective**: Matte painted walls contrasted with metallic accents or mirrors.

2. TEXTURE LAYERING

Strategically layer textures to build depth and visual comfort:

- **Living Room Example**: Linen curtains, velvet cushions, knitted throws, wooden coffee tables, metallic lamps.
- **Bedroom Example**: Cotton bedding, woolen blankets, silk pillows, leather headboard, textured wallpaper.

PRACTICAL STEP-BY-STEP GUIDE TO MIXING PATTERNS AND TEXTURES

Follow these structured steps to confidently combine patterns and textures:

01
STEP

CHOOSE YOUR ANCHOR ELEMENT

Begin by selecting a dominant pattern or texture that will serve as your foundational starting point. This anchor piece is typically the largest or most visually impactful item in the room, such as a boldly patterned area rug, a uniquely textured sofa, or even a statement wall covering. This initial choice will guide your subsequent selections, establishing the overall mood and scale for your pattern and texture combinations.

02
STEP

BUILD COMPLEMENTARY LAYERS

Add complementary patterns or textures in varying scales and styles around your anchor element.

ANCHOR ELEMENT	COMPLEMENTARY LAYERS	ROOM EXAMPLE
GEOMETRIC RUG	Solid-color sofa, floral cushions, textured throw	Living room
VELVET SOFA	Patterned pillows, textured wallpaper, wool rug	Formal sitting area

04
STEP

ADD VISUAL RELIEF

To prevent your space from feeling too busy or overwhelming, it's crucial to incorporate solid colors or very subtle patterns. These elements act as visual resting spots, balancing the more prominent patterns and textures. Think of a plain throw blanket on a patterned chair, or simple drapes next to a textured wall.

05
STEP

REFINE AND EDIT

Finally, take a step back and objectively evaluate the room's visual balance. Look at the space as a whole; does it feel harmonious, or is one area too dominant? Don't hesitate to remove, rearrange, or adjust elements until you achieve that perfect sense of cohesive comfort and effortless style.

COMMON MISTAKES & HOW TO AVOID THEM

MISTAKE: OVERLOADING SPACES WITH TOO MANY BOLD PATTERNS.

- **Solution**: Limit to 2–3 primary patterns per room, balanced with solids or subtle textures.

MISTAKE: IGNORING PATTERN SCALES.

- **Solution**: Always pair large patterns with smaller ones to achieve harmonious visual balance.

MISTAKE: NEGLECTING TACTILE TEXTURES.

- **Solution**: Intentionally introduce diverse textures—soft, rough, reflective—to enhance depth and sensory appeal.

EXPERT TIPS FOR CONFIDENT PATTERN AND TEXTURE MIXING

VISUAL MOOD BOARD: Collect pattern swatches and textures, arranging them visually before finalizing choices.

NEUTRAL BASE ELEMENTS: Start with neutral foundational furniture or wall colors, layering patterns and textures afterward.

PATTERN CONFIDENCE LEVELS: If hesitant, introduce bold patterns gradually through accessories first, gaining comfort over time.

PRACTICAL EXERCISE: PATTERN AND TEXTURE AUDIT

Evaluate an existing room, identifying current patterns and textures:

ITEM	CURRENT PATTERN/TEXTURE	BALANCE & ADJUSTMENT NEEDED
AREA RUG	Large geometric pattern	Good anchor, needs medium contrast
SOFA & CHAIRS	Solid neutral texture	Ideal base, add small patterns
DECORATIVE ITEMS	Mostly smooth textures	Needs rough textures & visual relief

This audit helps you strategically refine your patterns and textures, identifying precisely where adjustments are needed.

FINAL THOUGHTS ON MIXING PATTERNS AND TEXTURES CONFIDENTLY

Mastering patterns and textures is among the most rewarding interior design skills—transforming spaces from flat and uninspiring into rich, dynamic environments filled with personality and warmth. Rather than fearing complexity, embrace the endless creative possibilities and expressive freedom that thoughtful pattern and texture mixing provides.

Remember, successful design isn't about rigid rules but confident experimentation and thoughtful choices. Allow your personality to shine through, trust your instincts, and follow these strategic guidelines to ensure your home resonates deeply and beautifully.With practice, mixing patterns and textures becomes intuitive, empowering you to create interiors that not only look visually spectacular but feel inviting, expressive, and uniquely your own.

SPACE PLANNING AND
Layout Essentials

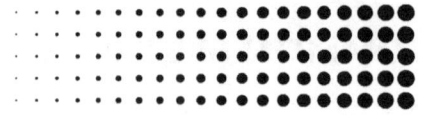

CHAPTER 4

UNDERSTANDING SCALE AND
Proportion in Your Space

Step into a thoughtfully designed space, and you'll sense it immediately—an atmosphere of ease, balance, and visual clarity. This effect doesn't emerge by chance. At its core lies an understanding of scale and proportion: two fundamental principles that distinguish merely furnished interiors from those that feel intentional, cohesive, and quietly sophisticated.

Scale relates to the size of objects within a room in relation to one another and to the space itself. A well-scaled interior ensures that furnishings neither dominate nor disappear but strike a poised dialogue with their surroundings. Proportion, on the other hand, is the relationship between parts of an object or composition. Whether it's the dimensions of a window frame or the curve of a chair back, proportion influences how the eye moves through a space—and how the mind interprets its harmony.

Mastering these principles transforms the way a room feels. A tall ceiling demands more than just taller furniture—it invites airier compositions and broader spatial rhythms. A smaller room benefits from refined balance, where even a slender lamp carries visual weight. When scale and proportion are calibrated with care, every element—from a statement chandelier to the spacing of wall art—contributes to a sense of visual equilibrium.

In the chapters that follow, we explore how these timeless concepts can guide your decisions and elevate your interior compositions. The result: rooms that are not only aesthetically pleasing, but also intuitively comfortable, quietly confident, and entirely your own.

WHAT IS SCALE AND PROPORTION?

Before mastering their practical use, it's crucial to clearly understand these concepts:

Scale: Refers to the size of an object relative to the overall space or the human body. It ensures your furnishings, decor, and architectural features feel appropriately sized within their surroundings.

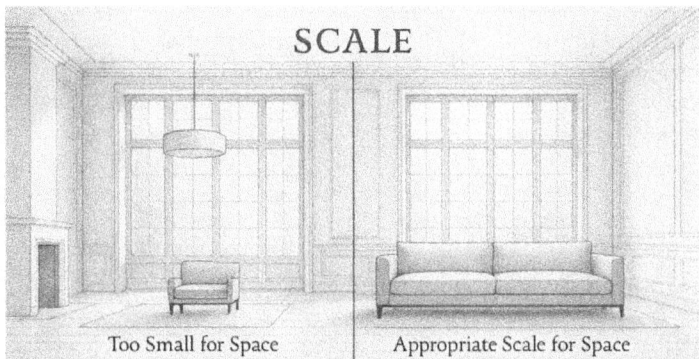

SCALE

Too Small for Space | Appropriate Scale for Space

Proportion: Refers to the relationship of individual elements to each other—how they visually balance and harmonize together within a space. Good proportion creates visual harmony and prevents any single element from overpowering the room.

PROPORTION

Poor Proportion Between Furniture | Balanced proportion Between furniture

WHY SCALE AND PROPORTION MATTER IN INTERIOR DESIGN

Scale and proportion significantly impact a room's overall aesthetic and emotional atmosphere:

Visual Balance: Proper scale and proportion prevent awkward or uncomfortable feelings caused by oversized furniture in small spaces or tiny decor pieces in spacious rooms.

Harmony and Comfort: When elements align proportionally, interiors feel more comfortable and inviting, fostering a sense of ease and well-being.

Functional Efficiency: Correct scaling ensures spaces function optimally, promoting practical and ergonomic room layouts.

THE GOLDEN RATIO AND PROPORTIONAL GUIDELINES

One powerful tool designers universally employ is the Golden Ratio—a mathematical ratio of approximately 1:1.618, renowned for its natural harmony and visual appeal. This ratio guides proportional relationships, from furniture selection to artwork placement.

USING THE GOLDEN RATIO:

- **Furniture Sizing**: For example, a coffee table should typically be about two-thirds (approximately 1:1.618) the length of the sofa for balanced proportions.
- **Artwork Placement**: Wall art ideally occupies approximately two-thirds of the wall width above furniture pieces, maintaining pleasing proportional harmony.

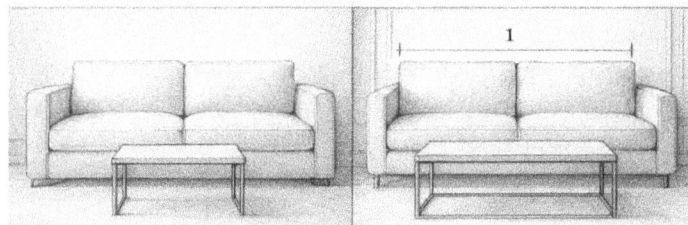

FURNITURE SIZING (GOLDEN RATIO 1:1,618)

Poor Furniture Proportion | Ideal Golden Ratio (1:1,618)

ARTWORK PLACEMENT (GOLDEN RATIO 1:1,618)

Incorrect Artwork Proportion | Golden Ratio Applied (1:1,618)

PRACTICAL RULES OF SCALE AND PROPORTION

Apply these essential practical guidelines to confidently create harmonious interiors:

1. FURNITURE TO ROOM PROPORTION

Ensure furniture feels appropriately sized for your space:

ROOM SIZE	IDEAL FURNITURE PROPORTION	EXAMPLE
SMALL SPACE	Slim, compact furniture (small sectional, streamlined chairs)	Studio apartments
MEDIUM SPACE	Moderately scaled furniture (standard sofa, accent chairs)	Average living rooms
LARGE SPACE	Oversized pieces (large sectional, substantial armchairs)	Open-concept living rooms

Small Space — Compact Furniture   Medium Space — Moderately Scaled Furniture   Large Space — Oversized Furniture

2. CEILING HEIGHT AND SCALE

The height of a room's ceiling significantly influences the appropriate scale choices for your furnishings and fixtures, impacting the overall feel.

Low Ceilings (Below 8ft)
For rooms with lower ceilings, it's best to use vertically compact furniture. Opt for low-profile lighting, such as flush mounts or recessed, to maintain an open and airy feel.

Standard Ceilings (8–10ft)
Rooms with standard ceiling heights offer more flexibility. Here, regular-sized furniture and standard lighting fixtures will typically look proportionate and well-suited.

High Ceilings (Above 10ft)
In spaces with impressive high ceilings, you can confidently select taller furniture pieces, like bookcases or large art. Statement chandeliers or grand pendant lighting are excellent choices to visually occupy this vertical space.

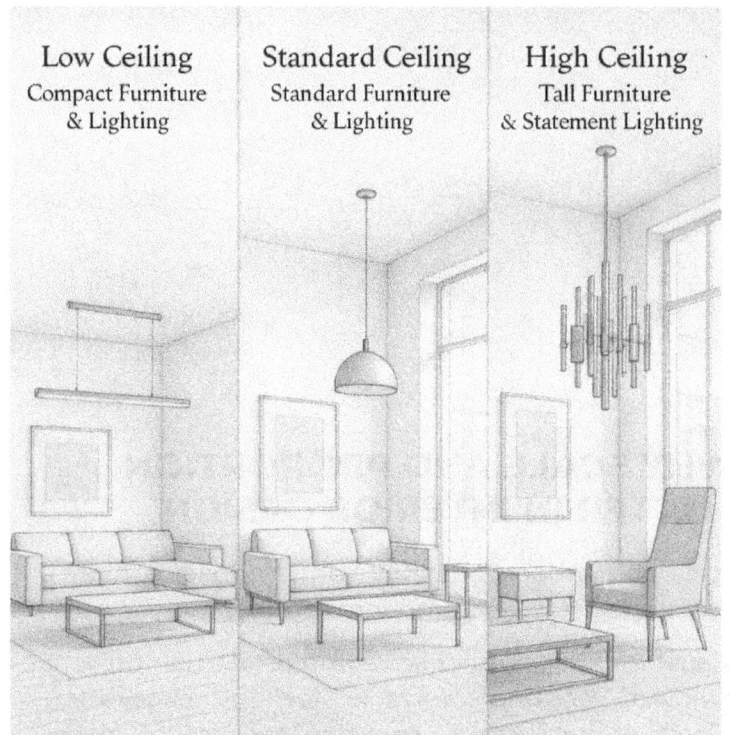

Low Ceiling
Compact Furniture
& Lighting

Standard Ceiling
Standard Furniture
& Lighting

High Ceiling
Tall Furniture
& Statement Lighting

HOW TO IDENTIFY AND CORRECT COMMON SCALE MISTAKES

Awareness of frequent scale errors empowers you to confidently correct or avoid them:

MISTAKE 1: OVERSIZED FURNITURE IN SMALL SPACES

- **Issue**: Makes room cramped and cluttered.
- **Correction**: Choose slimline, multifunctional pieces to visually expand the room.

MISTAKE 2: UNDERSIZED RUGS

- **Issue**: Disrupts proportional harmony, making furniture feel disconnected.
- **Correction**: Select rugs large enough to anchor seating areas, ideally with all furniture legs comfortably placed upon them.

Mistake	Correction
Oversized Furniture Crowded Space	Corrected with Slimline, Munfunctional Furniture

Mistake	Correction
Undersized Rug Furniture Feels Disconnected	Corrected with Appropriately Sized Rug

STEP-BY-STEP GUIDE TO ACHIEVING IDEAL SCALE AND PROPORTION

Follow this structured, practical approach to masterfully apply scale and proportion:

01 STEP — MEASURE YOUR SPACE CAREFULLY

Start by accurately measuring your room's dimensions. This includes not just the length and width, but also the height of the walls, as well as the dimensions of doorways, windows, and any prominent architectural features like fireplaces or columns.

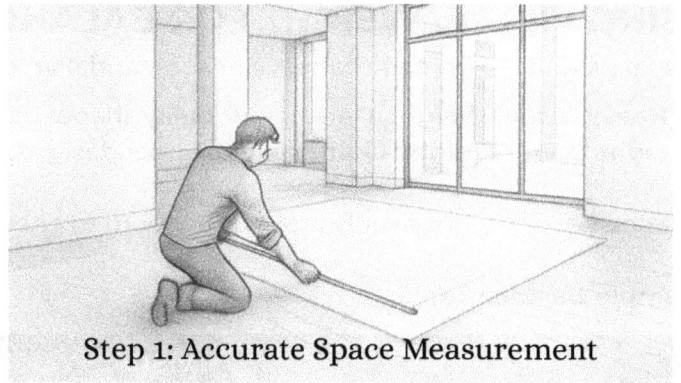

Step 1: Accurate Space Measurement

02 STEP — CREATE A BASIC FLOOR PLAN

Draw a scaled floor plan of your room. You can do this by hand on graph paper or use a digital tool. Make sure to clearly indicate the placement and dimensions of all fixed elements like windows, doors, built-ins, and outlets.

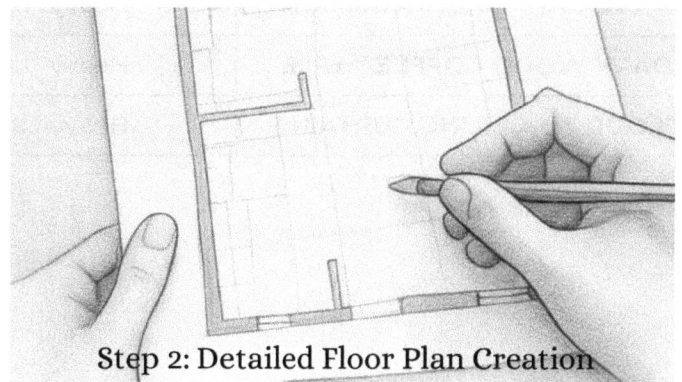

Step 2: Detailed Floor Plan Creation

03 STEP
IDENTIFY APPROPRIATE FURNITURE SIZES

Using your completed floor plan, identify suitable furniture sizes and proportions that will fit comfortably within the space. Think about how pieces relate to each other and to the room's overall dimensions. Always consider crucial factors like traffic flow and the functional needs of the space.

Step 3: Selecting Proportionate Furniture

04 STEP
ARRANGE AND ADJUST FURNITURE LAYOUTS

Finally, test various furniture arrangements on your floor plan or using painter's tape on the actual floor. This helps you find the optimal balance, harmony, and functionality. Don't hesitate to adjust furniture scale or placement until you achieve a layout that feels both comfortable and visually pleasing.

Step 4: Furniture Arrangement & Proportion Adjustment

USING VISUAL WEIGHT FOR BALANCE

"Visual weight" refers to how heavy or substantial an object appears, influenced by color, material, and design:

- **Heavy Visual Weight**: Dark colors, bulky shapes, large scale.
- **Light Visual Weight**: Light colors, slender designs, transparent materials.

Balance visual weight evenly around the room to ensure visual comfort and harmony.

Example Balance Table:

ELEMENT	VISUAL WEIGHT	BALANCE ADJUSTMENT
LARGE DARK SECTIONAL SOFA	Heavy	Balance with lighter-colored accent chairs
DARK WOOD COFFEE TABLE	Heavy	Pair with lighter-hued rug and decorative accents
FLOOR-TO-CEILING CURTAINS	Heavy	Offset with lighter furniture or neutral walls

Unbalanced (Heavy Visual Weight Clustered)

Balanced (Visual Weight Evenly Distributed)

EXPERT TIPS FOR MASTERING SCALE AND PROPORTION

VISUAL MOCK-UPS: Tape out furniture dimensions on the floor to visualize actual scale before purchase.

USE VISUAL REFERENCES: Photograph spaces, observing them objectively to identify proportion and scale imbalances.

CONSULT GUIDELINES, NOT RIGID RULES: Allow personal intuition and functional needs to guide proportional adjustments confidently.

VISUAL MOCK-UPS
(Furniture Dimensions
Taped on Floor)

USE VISUAL REFERENCES
(Photographing Space for
Objective Assessment)

PRACTICAL EXERCISE: SCALE & PROPORTION ASSESSMENT

Evaluate one of your current rooms objectively:

ROOM ELEMENT	CURRENT SCALE/PROPORTION ISSUE	ADJUSTMENT NEEDED
SOFA	Too large for small living room	Replace with smaller, streamlined sofa
COFFEE TABLE	Too small, disproportionate to seating	Upgrade to larger, proportional size
RUG	Incorrect size, feels disconnected	Choose larger rug anchoring seating area

This practical assessment identifies specific adjustments required, helping you confidently create a balanced, harmonious interior.

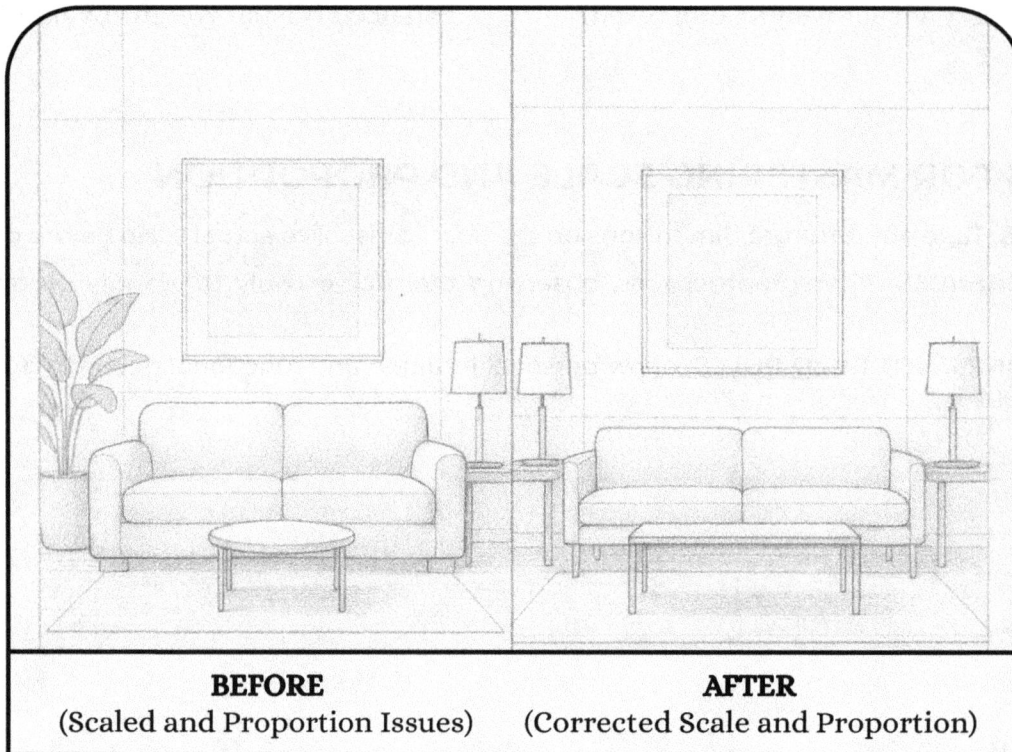

BEFORE
(Scaled and Proportion Issues)

AFTER
(Corrected Scale and Proportion)

FINAL THOUGHTS ON UNDERSTANDING SCALE AND PROPORTION

Mastering scale and proportion transforms ordinary spaces into thoughtfully designed environments—harmonious, comfortable, and visually appealing. While these principles might initially seem technical, their impact is deeply emotional, directly influencing how rooms feel and function daily.

Embrace these guidelines as powerful tools rather than rigid rules, combining your newfound knowledge with personal intuition. By thoughtfully considering scale and proportion, you'll effortlessly create interiors that feel naturally balanced, profoundly comfortable, and beautifully tailored to your individual lifestyle and personality.

CREATING
Functional Room Layouts
(WITH DIAGRAMS)

Great interior design isn't just about aesthetics; it's equally about creating functional, comfortable spaces tailored precisely to your daily life. Designing room layouts that support effortless movement, purposeful interactions, and harmonious living is at the heart of excellent home design. Imagine walking through your home without awkward obstructions, comfortably engaging in conversation, and smoothly transitioning between daily tasks—this is the art of functional space planning.

In this detailed, practical chapter, you'll learn how to create highly effective room layouts that perfectly blend form with function. With illustrated diagrams, practical examples, and expert guidelines, you'll be empowered to confidently plan and optimize every space in your home.

ESSENTIAL PRINCIPLES OF FUNCTIONAL ROOM LAYOUTS

Functional design goes beyond visual aesthetics; it prioritizes practicality, accessibility, and comfort. Follow these core principles to craft spaces that seamlessly support your lifestyle:

1. Clear Purpose
Every room must serve a clearly defined function. Identify and prioritize the primary purpose for each space (socializing, relaxing, dining, working), shaping your layout decisions accordingly.

2. Comfort & Accessibility
Furniture arrangements should promote effortless conversation, comfort, and ease of movement. Ensure adequate spacing and strategic placements for optimal accessibility.

3. Effective Zoning
Especially in open-plan spaces, clearly defined zones ensure visual coherence and practical use. Use rugs, furniture groupings, and focal points to define distinct areas.

4. Balanced Visual Flow
Arrange furniture thoughtfully to guide eyes and movement naturally around the room. Avoid overcrowding or leaving empty areas that disrupt visual balance.

PRACTICAL GUIDE TO CREATING FUNCTIONAL ROOM LAYOUTS

Use this detailed, step-by-step process to confidently plan optimal room layouts:

01
STEP

MEASURE YOUR SPACE

Precisely measure your room, noting dimensions of doors, windows, built-ins, electrical outlets, and architectural features. Accurate measurements ensure realistic and effective planning.

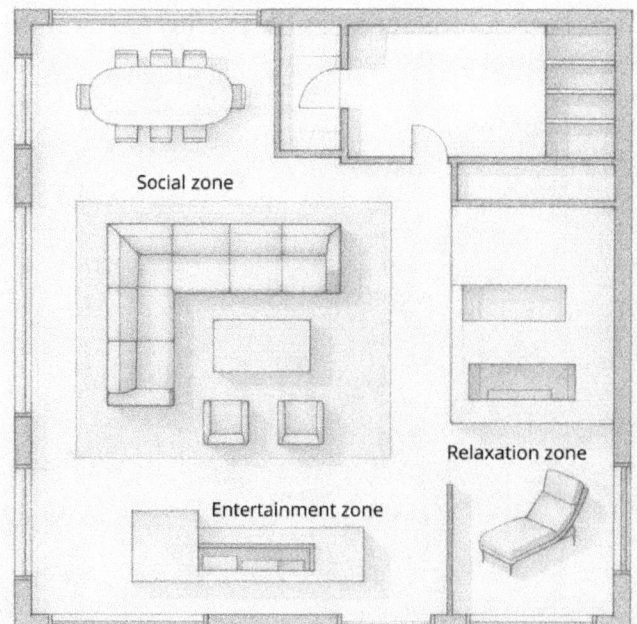

Social zone

Relaxation zone

Entertainment zone

02 STEP
IDENTIFY ROOM FUNCTION AND PRIORITIES

Clearly define your room's primary functions, prioritizing activities and furniture accordingly.

ROOM TYPE	PRIMARY FUNCTION	FURNITURE PRIORITIES
LIVING ROOM	Social interaction, relaxation	Seating, coffee table, entertainment console
DINING ROOM	Dining, entertaining	Table and chairs, serving furniture
BEDROOM	Rest, relaxation	Bed, nightstands, dressers, seating
HOME OFFICE	Productivity, focus	Desk, ergonomic seating, storage

03 STEP
CREATE A SCALED FLOOR PLAN

Draw a scaled layout (by hand or digitally), clearly marking windows, doors, and permanent features. This visual guide is crucial for precise, realistic planning.

KEY LAYOUT TYPES WITH ILLUSTRATED EXAMPLES

Explore these proven, practical layout options tailored for common room types.

1. LIVING ROOM LAYOUTS
Aim for conversation-friendly arrangements with comfortable spacing.

- **Conversational Layout**
  - Ideal for fostering interaction.
  - Furniture placed facing each other around a central coffee table.

- **Balanced Symmetrical Layout**
  - Formal, balanced, visually appealing.
  - Pairs of furniture evenly placed around a central focal point (fireplace, artwork).

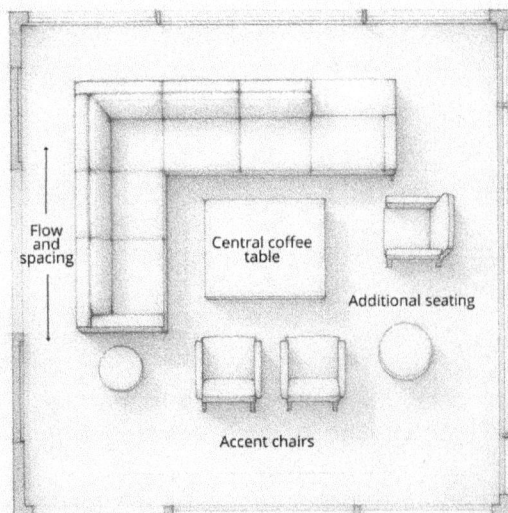

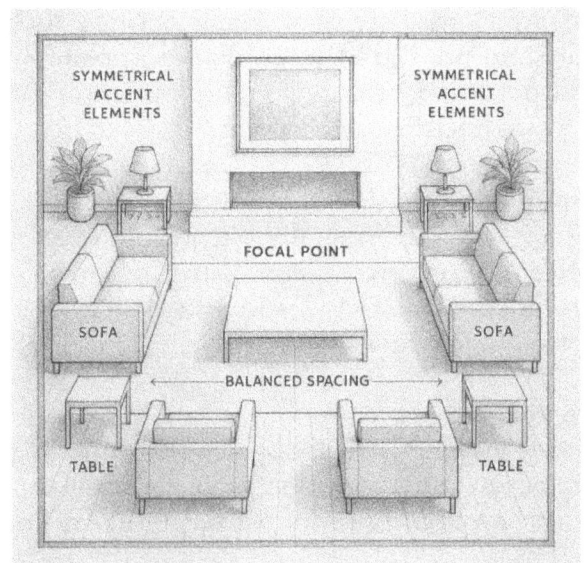

2. DINING ROOM LAYOUTS

Prioritize comfortable seating arrangements for seamless dining experiences.

- **Rectangular Dining Layout**
  - Common, practical for rectangular rooms.
  - Ensure at least 36 inches clearance behind chairs for ease of movement.

- **Round Dining Layout**
  - Encourages conversation, ideal for square or compact spaces.
  - Offers flexibility in seating arrangements.

RECTANGULAR DINING ROOM LAYOUT
WITH OPTIMAL 36-INCH CLEARANCE

OPTIMAL ROUND DINING ROOM LAYOUT
ENCOURAGING COMFORTABLE CONVERSATION

3. BEDROOM LAYOUTS

Prioritize comfort, relaxation, and functionality in your personal sanctuary.

- **Standard Bedroom Layout**
  - Bed placed opposite entry door, bedside tables on both sides.
  - Allow minimum 24 inches clearance on each side for easy movement.

- **Compact Bedroom Layout**
  - Ideal for smaller spaces, utilizing multifunctional furniture.
  - Space-saving solutions such as storage beds and floating shelves.

STANDARD BEDROOM LAYOUT
FOR OPTIMAL COMFORT AND FUNCTIONALITY

EFFECTIVE COMPACT BEDROOM LAYOUT
WITH MULTIFUNCTIONAL FURNITURE

4. HOME OFFICE LAYOUTS

Design for productivity, ergonomics, and focused work.

- **Ergonomic Office Layout**
  - Desk positioned to maximize natural light without screen glare.
  - Include ample storage and ergonomic seating.

- **Multipurpose Office Layout**
  - Encourages conversation, ideal for square or compact spaces.
  - Offers flexibility in seating arrangements.

ERGONOMIC HOME OFFICE LAYOUT
FOR MAXIMUM PRODUCTIVITY

MULTIPURPOSE HOME OFFICE LAYOUT FOR
VERSATILE WORK AND HOME USE

COMMON LAYOUT MISTAKES & HOW TO AVOID THEM

MISTAKE: BLOCKING NATURAL PATHWAYS AND DOORWAYS WITH FURNITURE.

- **Solution**: Maintain clear walkways of at least 36 inches for smooth traffic flow.

MISTAKE: FURNITURE PUSHED AGAINST WALLS UNNECESSARILY.

- **Solution**: Float furniture toward the center to encourage intimacy and visual harmony.

MISTAKE: INSUFFICIENT SPACING BETWEEN FURNITURE ITEMS.

- **Solution**: Ensure comfortable spacing (coffee table approx. 18 inches from sofa, dining chairs 36 inches clearance from walls).

EXPERT TIPS FOR PERFECTING YOUR ROOM LAYOUTS

ROOM MOCK-UPS: Use painter's tape to outline furniture placement directly on the floor for accurate visualization.

FLEXIBLE SEATING OPTIONS: Include movable seating (ottomans, lightweight chairs) for adaptable layouts.

CENTRAL FOCAL POINTS: Anchor room layouts around focal elements (fireplace, artwork, windows) for visual coherence.

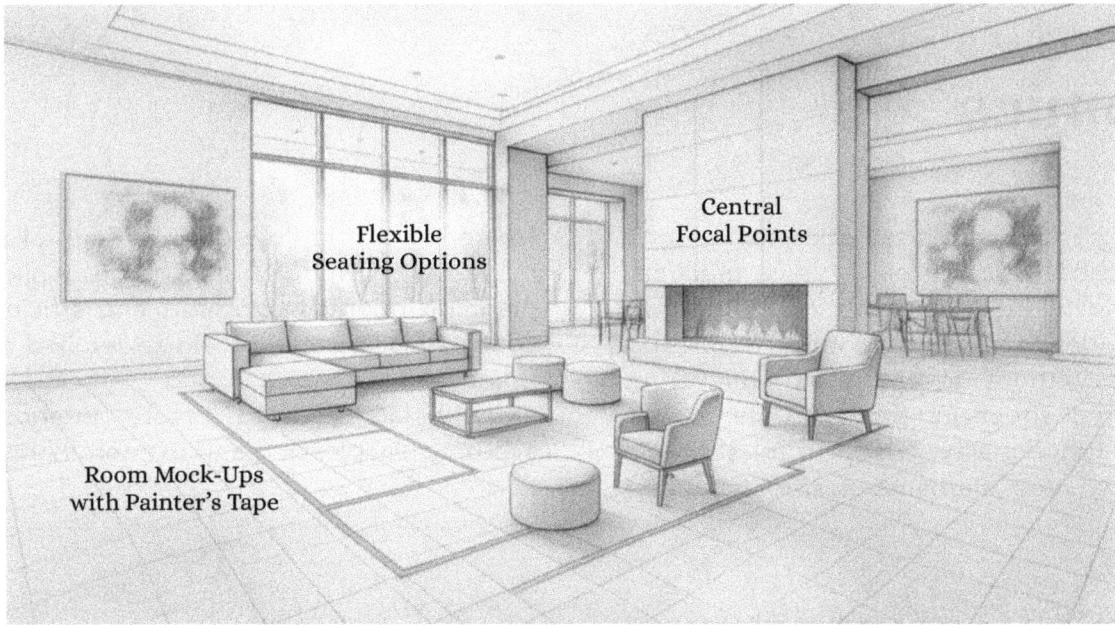

Flexible Seating Options

Central Focal Points

Room Mock-Ups with Painter's Tape

PRACTICAL EXERCISE: FUNCTIONAL ROOM LAYOUT CHECKLIST

Evaluate your current room layouts using this practical checklist:

ROOM ASPECT	IDEAL LAYOUT CRITERIA	MEETS CRITERIA?	ADJUSTMENT NEEDED
CLEAR PATHWAYS	Min. 36-inch clearance	Yes / No	Move furniture slightly
FURNITURE ARRANGEMENT	Encourages easy conversation	Yes / No	Reposition seating
ZONING & DEFINITION	Clearly defined zones	Yes / No	Add area rugs or focal points

This exercise identifies precisely what needs refining, guiding you confidently toward optimal functionality.

FINAL THOUGHTS ON UNDERSTANDING SCALE AND PROPORTION

A truly functional room layout does more than please the eye—it supports daily living with intention and ease. Exceptional design is never accidental. It emerges from a clear understanding of how a space will be used, how people move through it, and what activities it must comfortably accommodate. When form and function are given equal weight, interiors begin to serve, not just impress.

Thoughtful layouts consider circulation patterns, scale of furnishings, visual balance, and the subtle relationships between zones of activity. Whether crafting a serene reading nook, arranging a communal seating area, or integrating storage seamlessly into the background, every design choice should feel deliberate and considered.

By applying these principles, your spaces become more than decorated rooms—they become livable environments that respond to your habits, rhythms, and preferences. The result is a home that feels tailored, intuitive, and effortlessly aligned with the way you truly live.

TRAFFIC FLOW &
Ergonomics

When designing your home, aesthetics alone aren't enough. Your space must also feel intuitive, practical, and comfortable in daily life. Imagine effortlessly moving from room to room, smoothly completing everyday tasks without awkwardly maneuvering around furniture or squeezing through tight spaces. This seamless functionality arises from strategic attention to two key elements—traffic flow and ergonomics.

Mastering traffic flow ensures natural and intuitive movement through your home, while ergonomic planning prioritizes comfort and efficiency in every space. This chapter provides detailed explanations, practical examples, and precise schematics, empowering you to create interiors that are aesthetically pleasing and extraordinarily livable.

UNDERSTANDING TRAFFIC FLOW

Traffic flow refers to the natural pathways people take when moving through a home. Excellent traffic flow ensures easy, unobstructed navigation, creating comfortable, functional spaces.

KEY PRINCIPLES OF EFFECTIVE TRAFFIC FLOW

- **Clear Circulation Paths**: Establish logical routes that guide movement effortlessly between spaces.
- **Sufficient Clearance**: Maintain optimal spacing to avoid congestion or awkward movements.
- **Direct Routes**: Minimize unnecessary twists, turns, or detours between frequently used areas.

ESSENTIAL SPACE CLEARANCES
Follow these minimum clearances to ensure optimal traffic flow:

PATHWAY TYPE	RECOMMENDED CLEARANCE
Primary Circulation Paths	Minimum 36–48 inches
Secondary Paths (around furniture)	Minimum 24–36 inches
Dining Table Clearance	Minimum 36 inches behind chairs

STRATEGIC TRAFFIC FLOW IN KEY ROOMS

LIVING ROOM TRAFFIC FLOW
Prioritize direct, comfortable access to seating areas and entertainment spaces. Paths should never intersect in ways causing frustration or interruption.

Optimal Living Room Flow:
- Establish primary circulation paths around seating arrangements.
- Provide clear routes from entry to seating and between seating and entertainment zones.

KITCHEN TRAFFIC FLOW
Efficiency and practicality define kitchen flow. The "work triangle" between sink, stove, and refrigerator is crucial for smooth task performance.

Key Guidelines:
- Maintain clear pathways of 42–48 inches around islands and between counters.
- Avoid intersecting main traffic paths with cooking zones to ensure safety and ease of movement.

BEDROOM TRAFFIC FLOW

Bedrooms require direct, comfortable pathways from entrances to beds, storage, and bathroom access.

Practical Recommendations:
- Allow at least 24–36 inches clearance around beds.
- Provide unobstructed routes from entry doors to key furniture pieces.

COMMON TRAFFIC FLOW MISTAKES & SOLUTIONS

Recognizing frequent errors helps you confidently optimize traffic flow:

COMMON MISTAKE	SOLUTION & BEST PRACTICES
Furniture obstructing main paths	Reposition furniture, ensure clear passage
Crowded entryways	Simplify layout, ensure spacious entry paths
Ignoring secondary pathways	Maintain clearances around all furniture

UNDERSTANDING ERGONOMICS

Ergonomics focuses on creating environments that optimize comfort, safety, and efficiency. Proper ergonomic design ensures spaces accommodate human proportions, promoting health, wellbeing, and productivity.

Essential Ergonomic Considerations

- **Furniture Comfort**: Prioritize supportive seating, proper desk heights, and reachable storage solutions.
- **Optimal Heights and Distances**: Adjust furniture and fixtures to suitable ergonomic dimensions, reducing strain and discomfort.
- **Ease of Use**: Furniture, fixtures, and appliances should be intuitively positioned for ease of everyday use.

DETAILED ERGONOMIC GUIDELINES BY ROOM

LIVING ROOM ERGONOMICS

FURNITURE ITEM	ERGONOMIC RECOMMENDATION
Sofa & Seating	Seat height 16–18 inches, depth 20–24 inches
Coffee Table	Height 1–2 inches lower than sofa seat
Side Tables	Height level with sofa arms

DINING ROOM ERGONOMICS

FURNITURE ITEM	ERGONOMIC RECOMMENDATION
Dining Chair	Seat height approximately 18 inches
Dining Table	Height approximately 28–30 inches
Clearance Behind Chairs	Minimum 36 inches

KITCHEN ERGONOMICS

KITCHEN ELEMENT	ERGONOMIC RECOMMENDATION
Countertops	Standard height 36 inches
Upper Cabinets	Bottom shelf approximately 54 inches above floor
Work Triangle Distances	4–9 feet between appliances

HOME OFFICE ERGONOMICS

FURNITURE ELEMENT	ERGONOMIC RECOMMENDATION
Desk Height	Approximately 28–30 inches
Chair Height	Adjustable, seat height 16–20 inches
Monitor Positioning	Eye-level top of screen

STEP-BY-STEP GUIDE: OPTIMIZING TRAFFIC FLOW AND ERGONOMICS

Implement these clear steps to achieve excellent functionality and comfort:

Step 1: Identify Traffic Patterns
Analyze natural movement patterns through your home—consider how you move between key areas daily.

Step 2: Map Optimal Pathways
On a scaled floor plan, map clear, comfortable traffic paths, ensuring minimum clearances for smooth movement.

Step 3: Apply Ergonomic Measurements
Adjust furniture placements according to ergonomic guidelines ensuring comfort and efficiency.

Step 4: Test and Refine Layouts
Physically walk through your space, adjust placements based on comfort, ease, and practical experience.

EXPERT TIPS FOR SUPERIOR TRAFFIC FLOW & ERGONOMICS

REAL-LIFE SIMULATIONS: Tape furniture outlines on floors, physically testing pathways and furniture positions.

PRIORITIZE FREQUENT ROUTES: Ensure high-traffic areas are clear, accessible, and easy to navigate daily.

ADJUST FOR INDIVIDUAL COMFORTS: Ergonomic standards are general—customize specific dimensions based on personal comfort and physical needs.

PRACTICAL EXERCISE: FUNCTIONAL ROOM LAYOUT CHECKLIST

Evaluate a room in your home objectively:

ASPECT EVALUATED	CURRENT ISSUE	ADJUSTMENT NEEDED	ASPECT EVALUATED
ENTRY PATHWAYS	Narrow due to furniture	Relocate furniture for clear paths	Entry Pathways
SEATING COMFORT	Incorrect furniture heights	Adjust/replace furniture ergonomically	Seating Comfort
WORKSPACE SETUP	Inefficient placement	Rearrange for productivity & comfort	Workspace Setup

Conducting this assessment identifies specific, actionable improvements.

HOW TO DRAW AND
Plan A Room Layout
(STEP-BY-STEP GUIDE)

Every successful interior design project begins with a clear, accurate room layout. Consider it your essential road map, guiding decisions from furniture selection to décor details, ensuring the end result aligns perfectly with your vision. Imagine confidently visualizing your space, effortlessly testing different arrangements, and precisely predicting how everything will fit together. This chapter will empower you to accomplish just that—equipping you with the skills to accurately draw and plan your room layouts like a seasoned professional.

Whether you're redesigning your living room or starting fresh with a new home, this detailed, step-by-step guide, complete with clear illustrations, will help you create practical, beautiful spaces tailored precisely to your daily needs and aesthetic goals.

01 STEP — GATHER ESSENTIAL TOOLS AND MATERIALS

Begin with the right tools to ensure accuracy and ease during your planning phase:

- **Graph Paper**: Helps keep your drawing to scale (¼ inch = 1 foot recommended).
- **Measuring Tape**: For accurate measurements of room dimensions and furniture.
- **Ruler**: Ensures precise straight lines and neat, professional drawings.
- **Pencil and Eraser**: Use pencils for easy adjustments; keep erasers handy to refine layouts.
- **Colored Pencils or Markers** (Optional): Useful for distinguishing furniture and elements clearly.

GRAPH PAPER
(1/4 INCH = 1 FOOT)

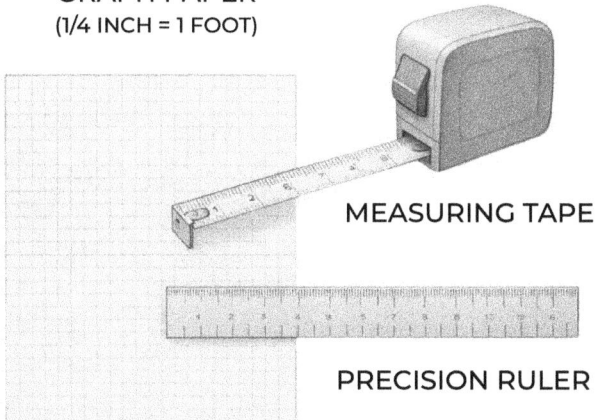

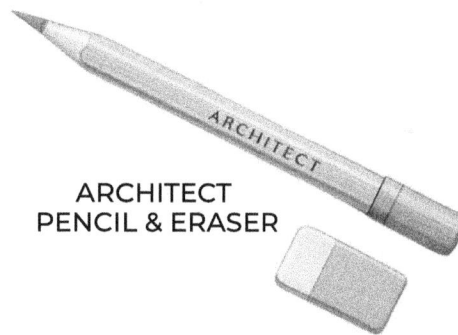

MEASURING TAPE

ARCHITECT
PENCIL & ERASER

COLORED PENCILS

PRECISION RULER

02 STEP — MEASURE YOUR SPACE ACCURATELY

Precise measurements lay the foundation for effective room planning:

- **Overall Room Dimensions**: Measure length, width, and ceiling height accurately.
- **Door and Window Locations**: Note dimensions and exact positions relative to corners and walls.
- **Architectural Elements**: Measure built-ins, radiators, fireplaces, electrical outlets, and switches—include dimensions and placement details.

Evaluate a room in your home objectively:

ELEMENT	MEASUREMENT NEEDED
Room Length & Width	Wall to wall measurements
Ceiling Height	Floor to ceiling
Windows	Width, height, distance from floor and corners
Doors	Width, height, and swing direction
Architectural Features	Dimensions and precise locations

When designing your home, aesthetics alone aren't enough. Your space must also feel intuitive, practical, and comfortable in daily life. Imagine effortlessly moving from room to room, smoothly completing everyday tasks without awkwardly maneuvering around furniture or squeezing through tight spaces. This seamless functionality arises from strategic attention to two key elements—traffic flow and ergonomics.

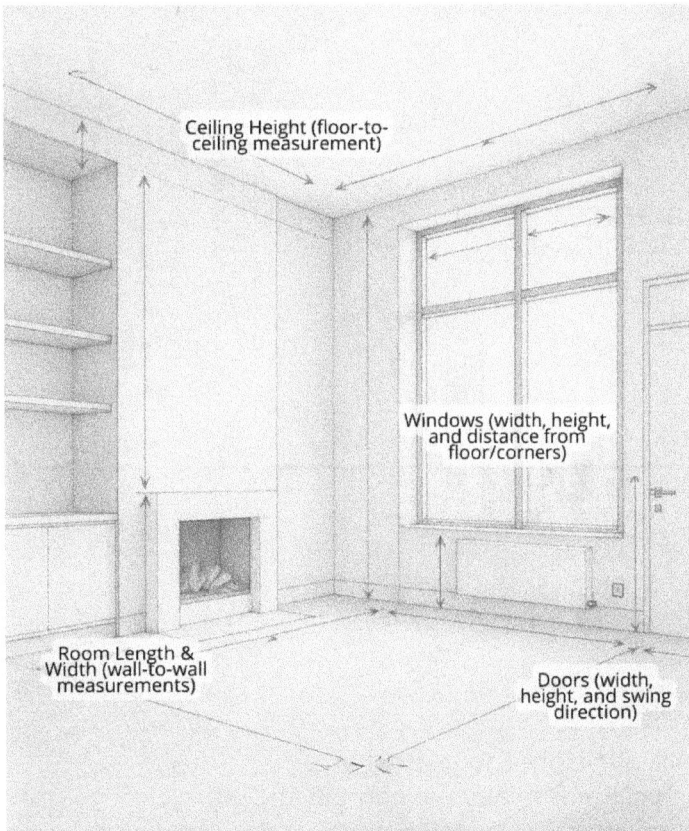

03 STEP DRAW YOUR SCALED ROOM OUTLINE

Convert your measurements into a scaled drawing using graph paper (recommended scale: ¼ inch = 1 foot):

- **Draw Room Perimeter**: Outline room dimensions clearly.
- **Mark Windows & Doors:** Indicate openings accurately; use arcs to represent door swings.
- **Identify Architectural Features**: Clearly draw built-ins, fireplaces, heating elements, and other fixed features.

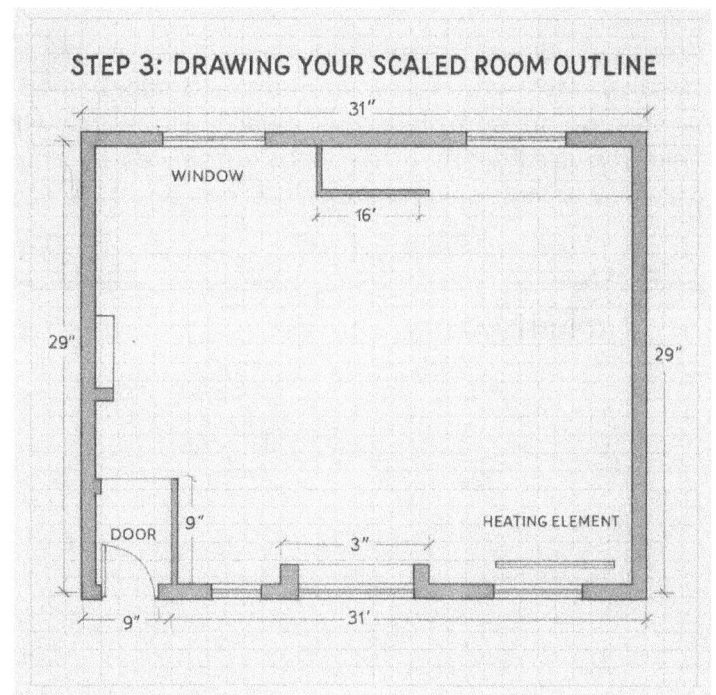

STEP 3: DRAWING YOUR SCALED ROOM OUTLINE

04 STEP CREATE FURNITURE TEMPLATES

Making scaled furniture templates enables flexible, easy experimentation with different layouts:

- Using graph paper, draw your furniture pieces accurately to scale (same as room scale).
- Cut out each furniture template, clearly labeling each piece.

Common Furniture Dimensions (for reference):

FURNITURE PIECE	STANDARD DIMENSIONS (APPROX.)
Sofa	84 inches x 36 inches
Armchair	35 inches x 35 inches
Coffee Table	48 inches x 24 inches
Dining Table	72 inches x 36 inches
Queen Bed	60 inches x 80 inches
Desk	60 inches x 30 inches

STEP 4: CREATING FURNITURE TEMPLATES

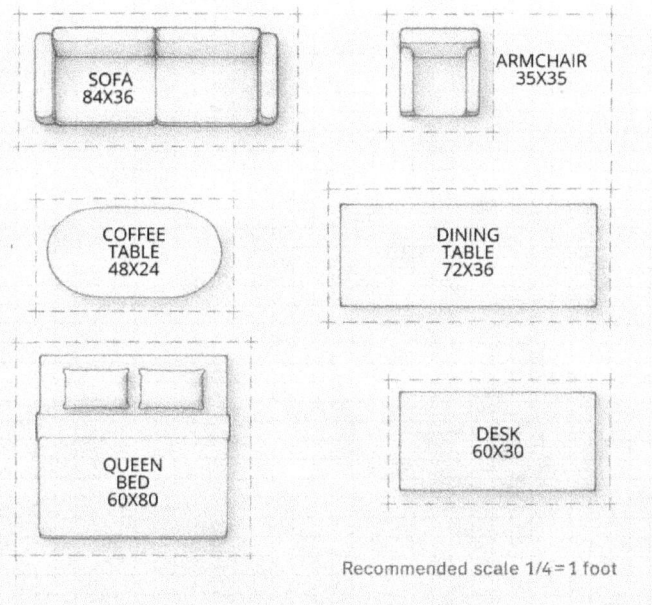

SOFA 84X36

ARMCHAIR 35X35

COFFEE TABLE 48X24

DINING TABLE 72X36

QUEEN BED 60X80

DESK 60X30

Recommended scale 1/4 = 1 foot

05 STEP
EXPERIMENT WITH FURNITURE ARRANGEMENTS

With your scaled room outline and furniture templates prepared, begin experimenting freely:

- **Prioritize Functional Requirements**: Arrange furniture based on room function and traffic flow.

- **Evaluate Spacing**: Ensure adequate clearances for comfortable movement (typically 36 inches for main pathways).

- **Visualize Realistically**: Consider how each arrangement feels visually and practically.

Arrangement Tips:

- Maintain clear focal points (fireplace, windows, artwork).

- Group seating for easy conversation.

- Ensure functional zones are clearly defined and logically placed.

STEP 5: EXPERIMENTING WITH FURNITURE ARRANGEMENTS

06 STEP
FINALIZE YOUR LAYOUT

After experimenting, choose the layout that best combines functionality, comfort, and aesthetics:

- Permanently affix your furniture templates to the room layout, clearly marking their exact locations.

- Make note of specific dimensions (distance between furniture pieces, pathway widths, etc.) directly on your plan for reference.

Final Checks:

- Confirm clear pathways and ergonomic comfort.

- Verify alignment with room functions and intended usage.

- Double-check measurements and clearances.

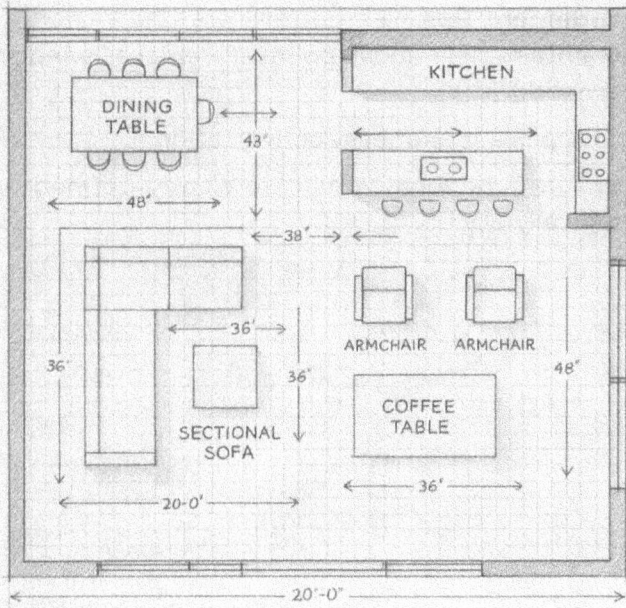

COMMON ROOM PLANNING MISTAKES & SOLUTIONS

Recognizing and addressing common errors ensures a smooth, effective planning process:

MISTAKE	RECOMMENDED CORRECTION
Incorrect Scale	Always double-check measurements
Overcrowding Furniture	Allow clear traffic paths & spacing
Neglecting Architectural Features	Integrate built-ins & features effectively

07
STEP

ADD VISUAL AND DECORATIVE ELEMENTS

Once your functional layout is finalized, enhance your plan by incorporating decorative features and visual interest:

- **Lighting Placement**: Indicate fixture locations (ceiling, wall, floor lamps) clearly.
- **Area Rugs**: Define seating and dining areas using scaled rug templates.
- **Art and Accessories**: Mark ideal placements for wall art, mirrors, and decorative shelves.

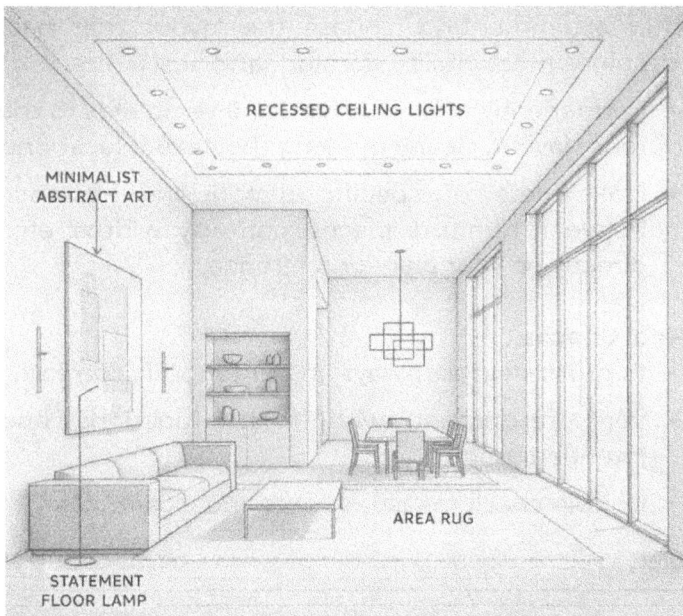

EXPERT TIPS FOR PROFESSIONAL ROOM LAYOUT PLANNING

TEST LAYOUTS PHYSICALLY: Use painter's tape or cardboard cut-outs on the actual floor for tangible visualization.

PHOTOGRAPH AND ASSESS: Take photos of taped layouts to view objectively.

FLEXIBILITY IS KEY: Remain open to adjustments based on real-life practicality and comfort.

PRACTICAL EXERCISE: CREATE YOUR OWN ROOM LAYOUT

Apply your new skills practically by planning your own room layout:

TASK	COMPLETED (Y/N)	NOTES & ADJUSTMENTS
Measure and document room accurately		
Create scaled outline on graph paper		
Draw and cut out furniture templates		
Experiment with furniture placements		
Finalize your preferred layout		
Verify clearances and functionality		

This practical exercise solidifies your layout planning skills, leaving you confident and ready for real-world application.

FINAL THOUGHTS ON ROOM LAYOUT PLANNING

An expertly drafted room layout is the architect's equivalent of a finely tuned blueprint—an elegant intersection where inspiration meets measurable reality. By translating intuition into scale drawings and precise annotations, you move beyond abstract musings and step into a realm where proportion, axis, and circulation are coherently choreographed. In this calibrated space, every sofa aligns with sightlines, every console negotiates traffic flow, and every pendant light falls exactly where shadow once collected, elevating mere rooms into deliberately orchestrated interiors.

Achieving such precision begins with an uncompromising survey. Measure wall lengths, window heights, and niche depths as a surveyor records a city block; small discrepancies multiply once furnishings arrive. Next, transpose these dimensions into a scaled plan, then audition each piece of furniture with tracing paper or digital layers. Rotate, shift, and subtract until the arrangement breathes. The dialogue between negative space and mass should feel effortless, like a pause between notes in a sonata, allowing movement to glide through the composition without collision or visual clutter. Trust your eye but verify with dimension lines; elegance is born from disciplined exactitude.

Lighting, color, and texture complete the orchestration. Arrange sources of illumination in layers—ambient, task, accent—so that each surface receives a considered glow, revealing depth rather than flattening the tableau. Select hues that support the room's orientation and the natural light it gathers, remembering that cooler tones retreat while warm pigments advance. When layering textiles and finishes, contrast matte with gloss, boucle with metal, to compose visual tempo. These nuances ensure that the plan transcends two-dimensional geometry and blossoms into a sensory narrative, inviting occupants to experience comfort as an aesthetic event throughout the day.

The discipline of layout planning rewards patience. What begins as a measured sketch evolves into a living environment that anticipates the rituals of its inhabitants. Stand back, survey the composition, and make final refinements until silence settles; then, the room will speak fluently on your behalf with effortless grace.

PART II
ROOM-BY-ROOM
GUIDE TO DESIGN

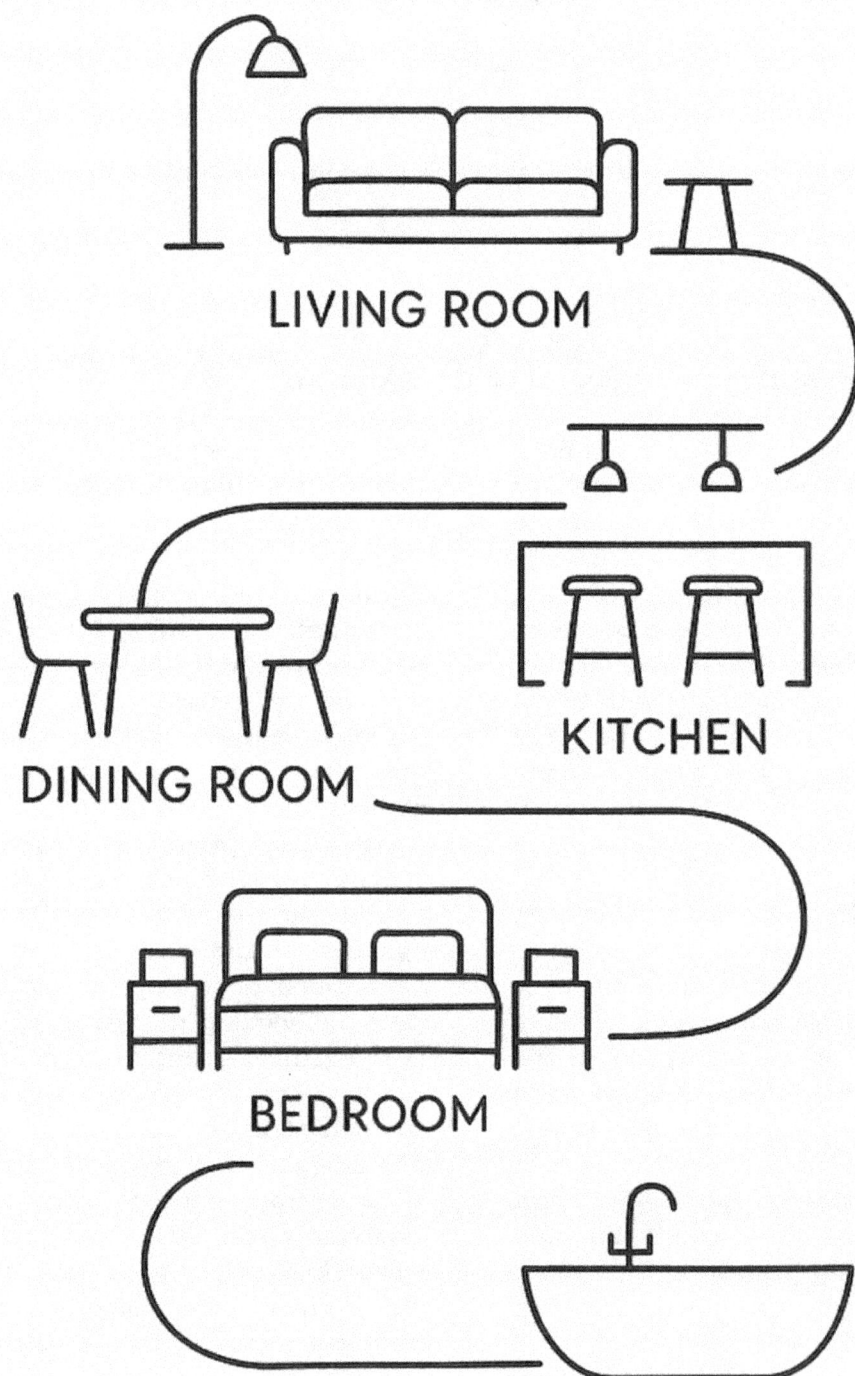

LIVING ROOM

DINING ROOM

KITCHEN

BEDROOM

ENTRYS AND
Hallways

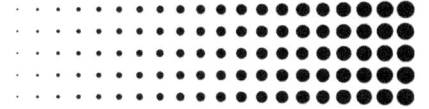

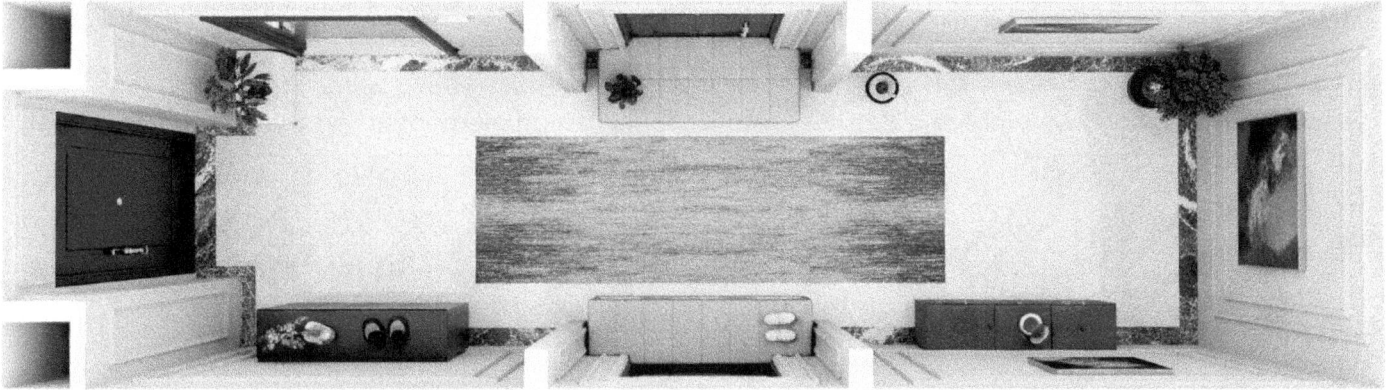

CHAPTER 5

FIRST IMPRESSIONS:
Creating Inviting Entryways

The threshold of a home transcends its literal function as a mere point of entry; it is, in essence, the opening statement of your dwelling's narrative. This initial encounter, akin to a meticulously orchestrated overture, sets the entire tone for the architectural symphony within. An entryway, whether grand in its proportions or intimate in its scale, possesses the singular capacity to extend a warm embrace, foreshadow the home's distinctive character, and seamlessly integrate practical utility into its design. It is here that the art of arrival truly manifests, transforming a simple transition into a profound experience for both resident and guest.

Consider the entryway as the home's most eloquent handshake—a gesture that is at once firm yet welcoming, offering a subtle prelude to the refined aesthetics and personal ethos that lie beyond. This pivotal space demands a design approach that marries visual splendor with intuitive functionality.

Every element, from the deliberate choice of materials to the strategic placement of light, contributes to a cohesive impression that resonates long after one has stepped inside. This section will delve into the foundational principles and refined techniques that allow for the transformation of any entryway into an exquisitely designed introduction, ensuring it not only captures attention but also invites further exploration of the sanctuary it precedes. From the subtle interplay of textures underfoot to the carefully curated vista that unfolds upon entry, each detail is an opportunity to articulate a sense of belonging and anticipation. We will explore how thoughtful spatial planning, combined with a discerning selection of furnishings and decor, can elevate the entryway from a mere passageway to a captivating prelude, reflecting the unique personality and sophisticated taste of its inhabitants.

THE IMPORTANCE OF THE ENTRYWAY

Your entryway is your home's "welcome mat," immediately communicating your personal style and the ambiance within. A well-designed entryway achieves three essential objectives:

- **Creates Visual Impact**: Instantly expresses your design style, setting expectations for the rest of your interior.
- **Enhances Functionality**: Provides convenient space for coats, shoes, keys, and other daily essentials.
- **Establishes Warmth and Welcome**: Makes guests feel comfortable and welcomed, offering a glimpse into the home's overall character.

CORE ELEMENTS OF AN INVITING ENTRYWAY

To create an inviting entryway, incorporate these foundational design elements thoughtfully and cohesively:

01 FOCAL POINT

Every entryway should have a clear visual focal point to immediately draw attention. Ideal focal points might include:

- A statement mirror or artwork
- A uniquely designed console table
- A striking pendant light fixture
- Bold wallpaper or wall treatment

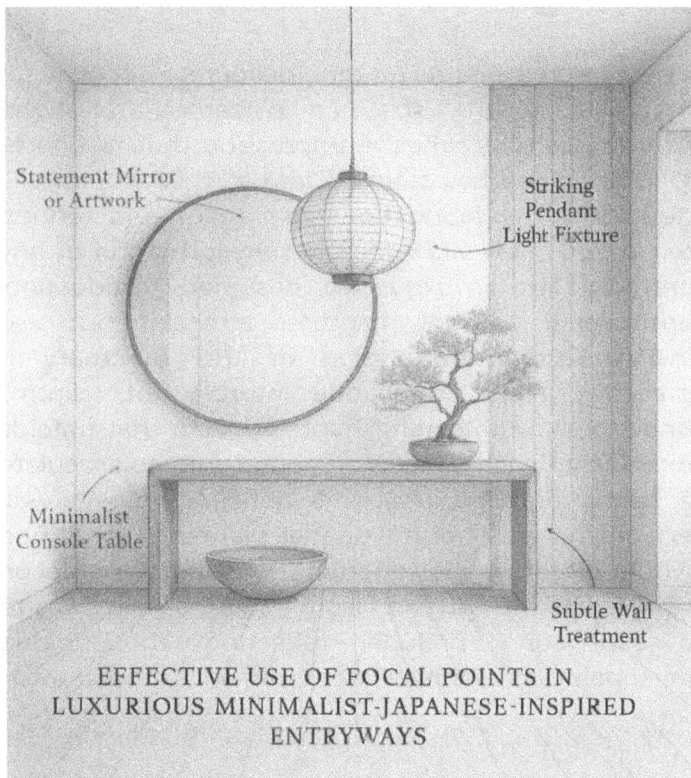

EFFECTIVE USE OF FOCAL POINTS IN LUXURIOUS MINIMALIST-JAPANESE-INSPIRED ENTRYWAYS

02 FUNCTIONAL STORAGE SOLUTIONS

Entryways are practical spaces—storage is key. Consider the following solutions:

- **Console Tables with Drawers**: Perfect for keys, mail, and daily essentials.
- **Shoe Storage Benches**: Combining seating and discreet storage.
- **Wall Hooks & Coat Racks**: Convenient for outerwear and bags.
- **Built-in Storage**: Ideal for larger entryways, offering a streamlined look.

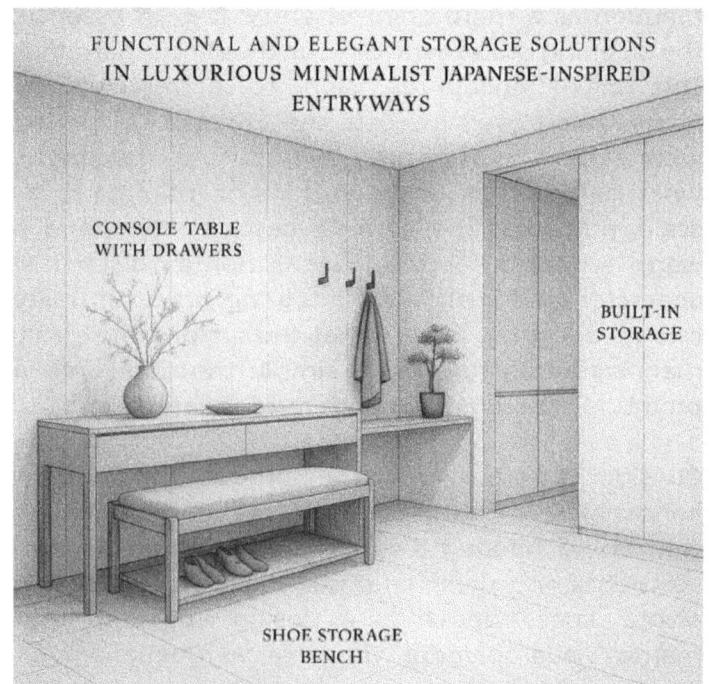

FUNCTIONAL AND ELEGANT STORAGE SOLUTIONS IN LUXURIOUS MINIMALIST JAPANESE-INSPIRED ENTRYWAYS

03 APPROPRIATE SEATING

Providing a seating area significantly enhances an entryway's comfort and usability:

- **Benches**: Functional and decorative, ideal for putting on or removing shoes.
- **Small Accent Chairs**: Perfect for compact entryways, adding charm and personality.
- **Ottomans**: Compact, portable options ideal for limited spaces.

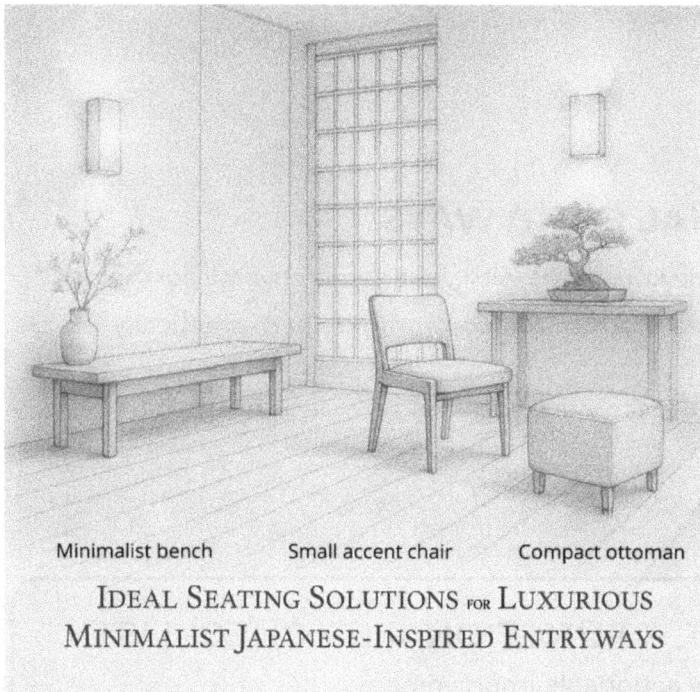

Minimalist bench   Small accent chair   Compact ottoman

IDEAL SEATING SOLUTIONS FOR LUXURIOUS MINIMALIST JAPANESE-INSPIRED ENTRYWAYS

04 ADEQUATE LIGHTING

Proper lighting enhances your entryway's functionality and mood:

- **Ambient Lighting**: Ceiling-mounted or recessed lights create inviting general illumination.
- **Accent Lighting**: Wall sconces or picture lights highlight artwork or decorative features.
- **Task Lighting**: Lamps or wall lights help with practical activities like finding keys or sorting mail.

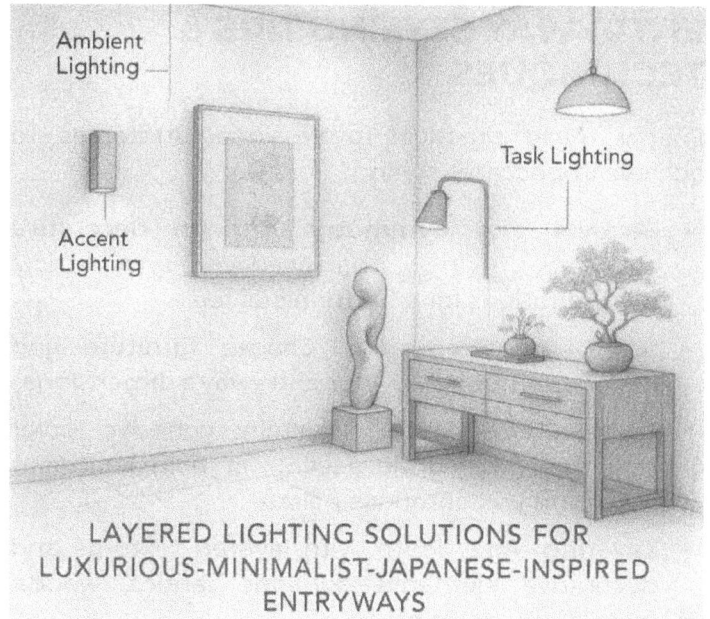

LAYERED LIGHTING SOLUTIONS FOR LUXURIOUS-MINIMALIST-JAPANESE-INSPIRED ENTRYWAYS

05 PERSONALIZED DECORATIVE ELEMENTS

Reflect your personality through carefully chosen décor:

- **Artwork & Photography**: Showcase personal style and create visual interest.
- **Mirrors**: Make small entryways feel larger and brighter.
- **Plants & Natural Elements**: Add life, freshness, and warmth.
- **Area Rugs**: Define the space clearly and add comfort.

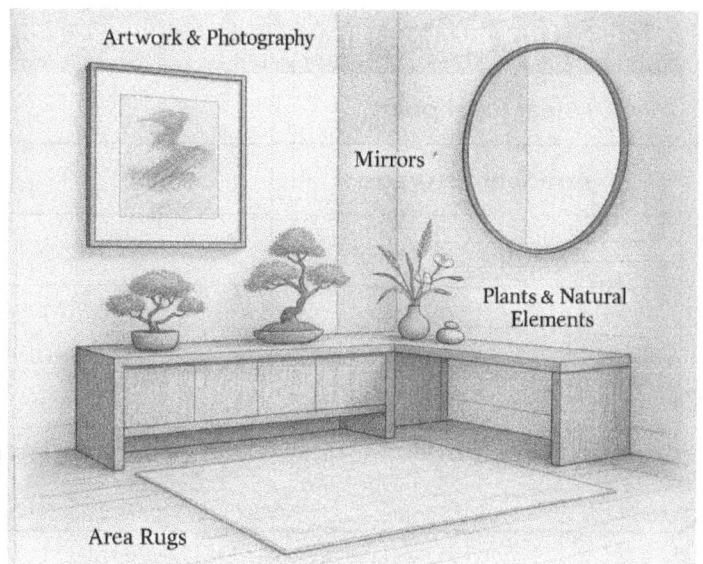

ENTRYWAY STYLING TIPS & TECHNIQUES

Follow these practical, professional strategies to achieve impeccable styling:

- **Balance and Symmetry**: Arrange decorative elements in balanced, symmetrical configurations for a harmonious feel.
- **Scale and Proportion**: Choose furniture and décor appropriate to your entryway's dimensions.
- **Color Coordination**: Maintain cohesive color schemes with subtle accents or bold contrasts, reflecting your interior's palette.
- **Layering**: Add depth with layered textures and decorative elements—combine fabrics, woods, metals, and greenery.

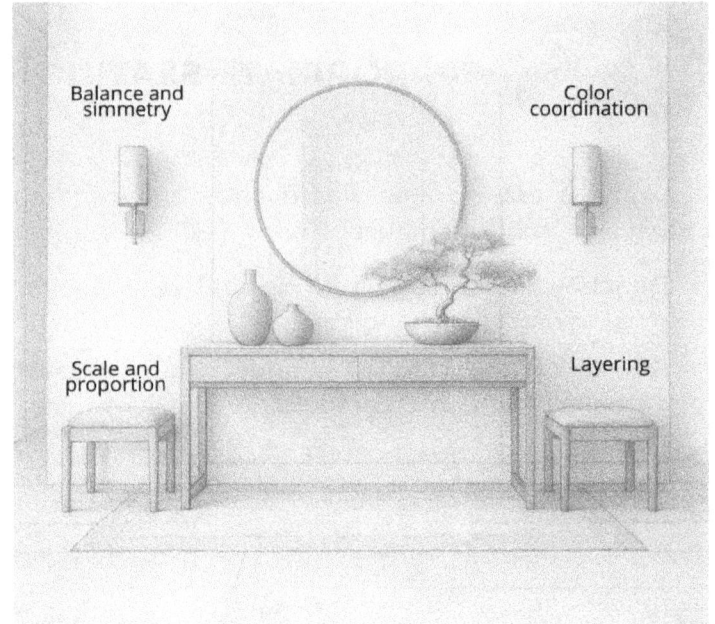

EXPERT TIPS FOR CREATING EXCEPTIONAL ENTRYWAYS

REFLEF YOUR HOME'S INTERIOR STYLE: Keep entryway style consistent with your home's overall aesthetic.

PRIORITIZE COMFORT & USABILITY: Ensure entryways are welcoming, comfortable, and practically usable every day.

PERSONALIZE THOUGHTFULLY: Add meaningful, personal decorative touches to make the space uniquely yours.

PRACTICAL EXERCISE: ENTRYWAY STYLE & FUNCTIONALITY CHECKLIST

Evaluate your entryway's current effectiveness and identify actionable improvements:

FEATURE EVALUATED	MEETS CRITERIA? (Y/N)	ADJUSTMENTS NEEDED
Clear focal point		
Adequate storage		
Seating availability		
Lighting adequacy		
Decorative elements		

Conducting this evaluation gives you clear direction for achieving a perfectly designed entryway.

Solutions for
SMALL AND NARROW SPACES

Designing small or narrow entryways can be challenging, but think of these spaces as unique design puzzles waiting to be solved creatively. With the right strategies, your compact entryway can feel spacious, functional, and visually stunning—defying its limited dimensions to leave a memorable first impression.

In this detailed guide, you'll discover professional solutions that cleverly optimize small and narrow entryways. We'll explore spatial design principles, practical furniture selections, creative storage solutions, and visual techniques to transform tight spaces into attractive, comfortable, and efficient entry points.

SPATIAL DESIGN PRINCIPLES FOR COMPACT ENTRYWAYS

Applying these core design principles helps visually expand tight spaces and maximize practical use:

01 USE VERTICAL SPACE WISELY

When floor space is limited, direct your attention upwards:

- **Floating Shelves**: Provide storage without occupying floor space.
- **Wall-Mounted Hooks**: Free up floor area while offering essential hanging storage.
- **Vertical Storage Units**: Tall, slim cabinets store shoes, bags, and umbrellas effectively.

Effective Vertical Space Solutions for Compact Entryways – Scandinavian & Hygge inspired style

02 CREATE VISUAL DEPTH

Enhance visual perception, making narrow spaces appear deeper and more spacious:

- **Mirrors**: Strategically placed mirrors reflect light and visually double space depth.
- **Artwork Placement**: Hang artwork or mirrors at eye-level to draw the gaze upwards, enhancing perceived height.
- **Lighting Direction**: Utilize directional wall sconces to highlight vertical elements and elongate visual lines.

CREATING VISUAL DEPTH IN COMPACT ENTRYWAYS –
SCANDINAVIAN & HYGGE INSPIRED STYLE

03 MAINTAIN OPEN PATHWAYS

Preserve clear traffic flow, vital in tight spaces:

- **Slim Profile Furniture**: Choose narrow consoles or wall-mounted furniture that doesn't obstruct walking paths. These space-saving choices help maximize floor area while keeping everything accessible, visually open, and easy to move around. Pieces like floating shelves, leggy sideboards, or slender benches can deliver both function and form without becoming obtrusive.

- **Avoid Overcrowding**: Select fewer, more functional items to prevent cramped, cluttered spaces. Prioritize multi-use furnishings that enhance utility without consuming too much square footage or interfering with movement, especially near doorways, corners, or passage zones. Leave room to breathe—negative space isn't empty; it's useful.

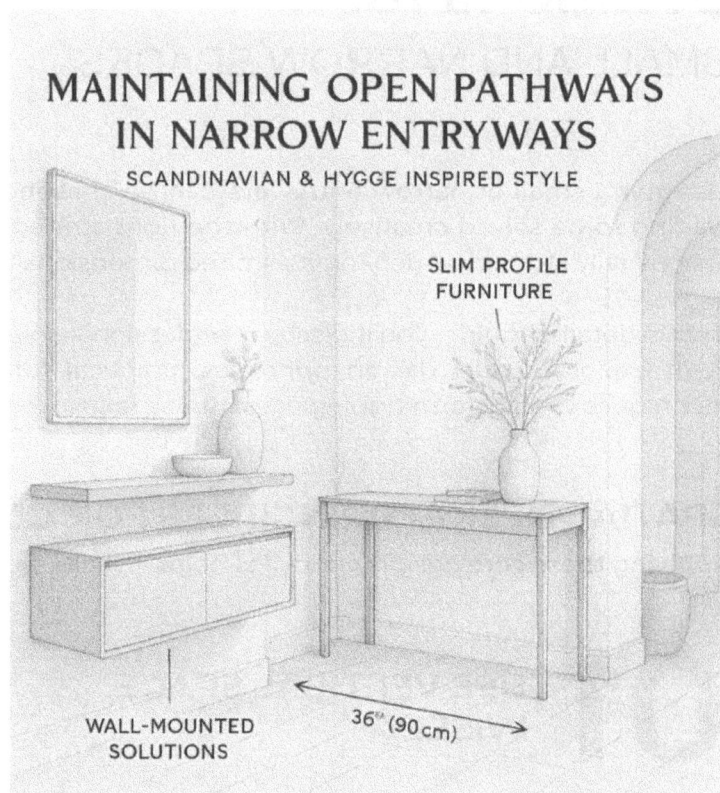

MAINTAINING OPEN PATHWAYS IN NARROW ENTRYWAYS

SCANDINAVIAN & HYGGE INSPIRED STYLE

SLIM PROFILE FURNITURE

WALL-MOUNTED SOLUTIONS

36" (90 cm)

- **Clearance Guidelines**: Maintain at least 36 inches clearance for main entry pathways when possible. This buffer improves accessibility, reduces hazards, supports both daily comfort and emergency navigation, and ensures that everyone—regardless of mobility—can pass through easily. In dining areas or around seating, aim for at least 24–30 inches to allow chairs to pull out comfortably and people to pass by without squeezing.

IDEAL FURNITURE FOR NARROW ENTRYWAYS

Selecting appropriate furniture tailored specifically to limited spaces is crucial:

- **Wall-Mounted Consoles**: Space-saving design for keys and small items, with open floor space underneath.
- **Compact Benches**: Narrow benches with built-in shoe storage combine functionality with minimal footprint.
- **Multipurpose Pieces**: Ottomans or stools that serve as seating, storage, and decorative accents simultaneously.

Furniture Dimensions for Reference:

FURNITURE TYPE	IDEAL DIMENSIONS FOR NARROW ENTRYWAYS
Wall-Mounted Console	Depth: 8–12 inches, Width: 24–36 inches
Narrow Bench	Depth: 12–15 inches, Length: 24–36 inches
Compact Ottoman	Diameter/Depth: 12–15 inches

CREATIVE STORAGE SOLUTIONS

Maximizing storage without overwhelming the space:

- **Built-In Niches**: Ideal for shoes, keys, or mail—seamlessly integrated into walls.
- **Hidden Storage**: Choose furniture with hidden compartments (e.g., benches with lift-up seats or drawers).
- **Under-Bench Storage**: Use baskets under benches for easy, attractive storage.

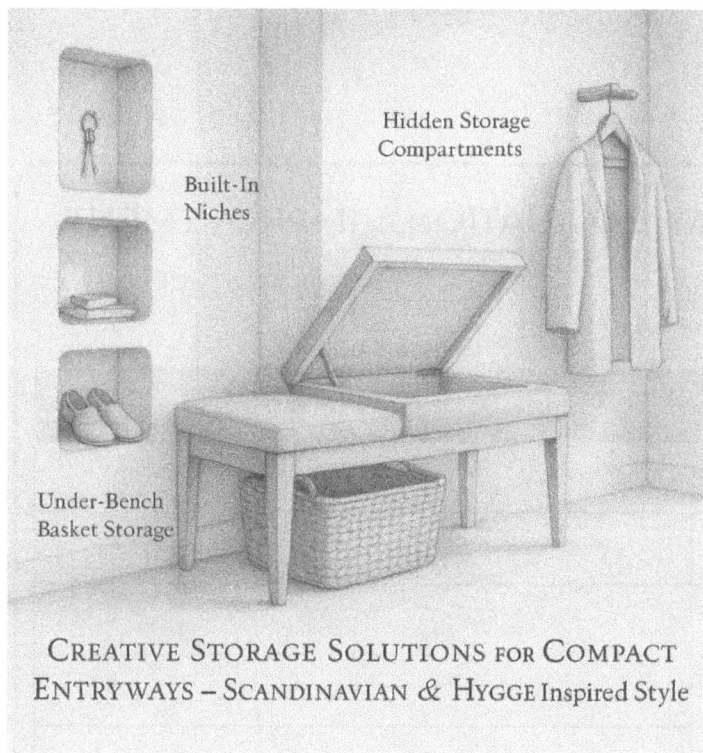

CREATIVE STORAGE SOLUTIONS FOR COMPACT ENTRYWAYS – SCANDINAVIAN & HYGGE Inspired Style

LIGHTING TECHNIQUES TO ENLARGE NARROW SPACES

The right lighting dramatically improves a small entryway's atmosphere and perception of space:

- **Layered Lighting**: Combine overhead fixtures, wall sconces, and table lamps for balanced illumination.
- **Wall Washers & Spotlights**: Visually expand narrow walls and highlight design features.
- **Natural Light Enhancement**: Keep windows unobstructed and use sheer window treatments to maximize natural brightness.

EFFECTIVE USE OF COLOR AND PATTERN

Strategic color choices and patterns significantly influence spatial perception:

- **Light & Neutral Colors**: Bright whites, creams, and soft grays expand space visually.
- **Vertical Stripes**: Subtle vertical wallpaper patterns or paint effects make walls appear taller.
- **Contrasting Accents**: Sparing use of bold colors directs focus to specific elements, avoiding visual clutter.

COMMON MISTAKES TO AVOID IN NARROW ENTRYWAYS

Recognizing typical pitfalls ensures successful design outcomes:

MISTAKE	RECOMMENDED CORRECTION
Oversized Furniture	Opt for slim and wall-mounted solutions
Poorly Planned Lighting	Implement layered and directional lighting
Overuse of Dark Colors	Prefer light palettes to expand perception

STEP-BY-STEP GUIDE: OPTIMIZING SMALL & NARROW ENTRYWAYS

Follow this systematic approach to achieve maximum functionality and style:

Step 1: Evaluate and Measure Space
- Document precise entryway dimensions.
- Identify primary storage and functional requirements.

Step 2: Choose Compact, Functional Furniture
- Select slim-profile or multipurpose furniture based on space constraints.

Step 3: Maximize Vertical Storage
- Plan wall-mounted and vertical storage solutions to optimize available space.

Step 4: Enhance Lighting & Color Schemes
- Implement layered lighting; choose light colors and subtle vertical patterns.

Step 5: Strategically Incorporate Decorative Elements
- Use mirrors, artwork, and carefully selected décor to enhance visual depth and interest.

EXPERT TIPS FOR SMALL ENTRYWAY DESIGN

MINIMALIST MINDSET: Keep décor and furniture simple and purposeful.

VERTICAL EMPHASIS: Always utilize vertical space to its fullest potential.

VISUAL TRICKERY: Leverage mirrors, lighting, and colors to create optical illusions of greater space.

PRACTICAL EXERCISE: SMALL ENTRYWAY EVALUATION & IMPROVEMENT CHECKLIST

Use this exercise to critically evaluate and enhance your entryway:

FEATURE EVALUATED	MEETS CRITERIA? (Y/N)	SPECIFIC IMPROVEMENTS NEEDED
Vertical space utilized		
Adequate clear pathways		
Optimal furniture selection		
Effective storage solutions		
Appropriate lighting & color		

Performing this evaluation provides actionable insights and clear direction for optimizing your entryway design.

FINAL THOUGHTS ON SMALL & NARROW ENTRYWAY DESIGN

Designing small entryways may initially seem restrictive, but these spaces present unique opportunities for creativity and innovative design solutions. By implementing these strategies—embracing verticality, optimizing storage, selecting slim-profile furniture, and employing visual techniques—you'll craft an entryway that's not only functional but also inviting and aesthetically pleasing.

With thoughtful design choices, even the most compact entryway becomes a remarkable introduction, reflecting your personal style and providing comfort and efficiency daily.

MUST HAVE
Entryway Elements
(CHECKLIST)

Your entryway is the introduction to your home's personality and style. However, beyond aesthetics, it serves a critical daily function—providing organization, practicality, and comfort. To create the ideal entryway, certain elements are indispensable. In this section, you'll discover the key entryway components every home should include. Organized into a clear and comprehensive checklist format, you'll find it simple to apply these guidelines to your space, ensuring a perfect balance of form and function.

ENTRYWAY ESSENTIALS CHECKLIST
Consider this checklist as your ultimate guide to designing a functional, welcoming, and beautiful entryway.

01 FUNCTIONAL STORAGE SOLUTIONS

Storage is the foundation of any well-designed entryway, effectively eliminating clutter and enhancing usability:

- **Console Table or Credenza**: Ideal for keys, mail, and essentials.
- **Shoe Storage** (Bench or Cabinet): Streamlines daily shoe management.
- **Coat Rack or Hooks**: Provides instant access to jackets, scarves, and bags.
- **Baskets or Trays**: Keeps small items organized and easy to find.

02 COMFORTABLE SEATING

Entryway seating offers practicality and comfort, significantly enhancing usability:

- **Bench with Cushioning**: Functional and inviting for removing or putting on shoes.
- **Compact Stool or Ottoman**: Ideal for smaller spaces, providing easy, movable seating.
- **Built-in Seating**: Seamless, space-efficient solution, ideal for larger entryways.

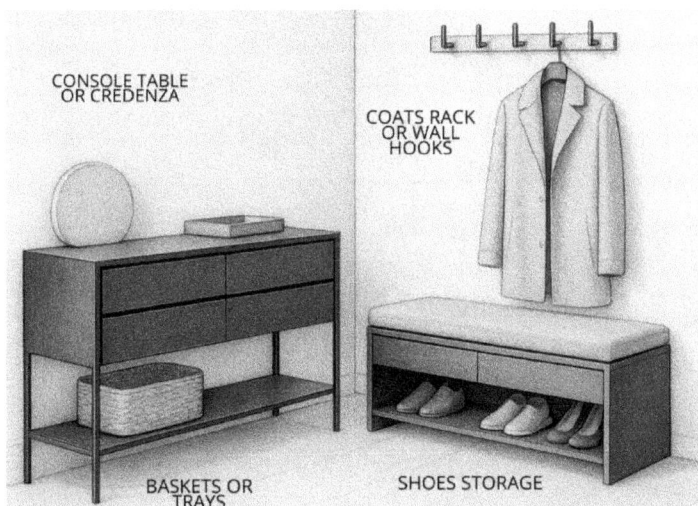

CONSOLE TABLE OR CREDENZA

COATS RACK OR WALL HOOKS

BASKETS OR TRAYS

SHOES STORAGE

FUNCTIONAL STORAGE SOLUTIONS FOR ENTRYWAYS – MODERN & MINIMALIST INSPIRED STYLE

BENCH WITH CUSHIONING

BUILT-IN SEATING

COMPACT STOOL OR OTTOMAN

Comfortable Entryway Seating Solutions – Farmhouse & Rustic Charm Inspired Style

03 ADEQUATE LIGHTING

Lighting significantly affects your entryway's mood, function, and visual appeal:

- **Ambient Overhead Lighting**: Ensures sufficient general illumination.
- **Wall Sconces or Accent Lights**: Highlights decorative elements or creates welcoming atmosphere.
- **Table Lamp**: Adds warmth, character, and a personal touch, if space permits.

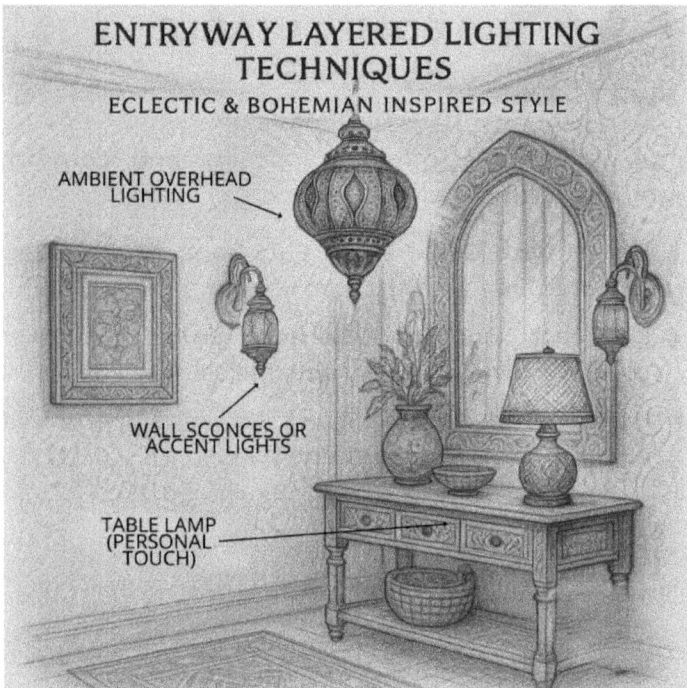

ENTRYWAY LAYERED LIGHTING TECHNIQUES
ECLECTIC & BOHEMIAN INSPIRED STYLE

AMBIENT OVERHEAD LIGHTING

WALL SCONCES OR ACCENT LIGHTS

TABLE LAMP (PERSONAL TOUCH)

04 MIRROR FOR FUNCTIONALITY AND SPACE PERCEPTION

Mirrors not only serve practical purposes but visually enlarge and brighten the space:

- **Wall Mirror**: Strategically positioned at eye level for convenience and aesthetic appeal.
- **Full-Length Mirror**: Ideal if space allows, enhancing functionality for checking outfits.
- **Decorative Mirror**: Adds character and reflects your unique style.

Full-Length Mirror

Wall Mirror

Decorative Mirror

EFFECTIVE MIRROR PLACEMENT & TYPES in ENTRYWAYS
– Traditional & Classic Inspired Style

05 DURABLE, WELCOMING RUG

An appropriate rug defines your entryway space and protects your floors:

- **Size**: Choose proportional to your entryway; large enough to stand comfortably but leaving some flooring visible.
- **Material**: Select easy-to-clean, durable materials suited to high-traffic areas (jute, polypropylene, or indoor/outdoor materials).
- **Design**: Opt for a design complementary to your entryway's overall style and color scheme.

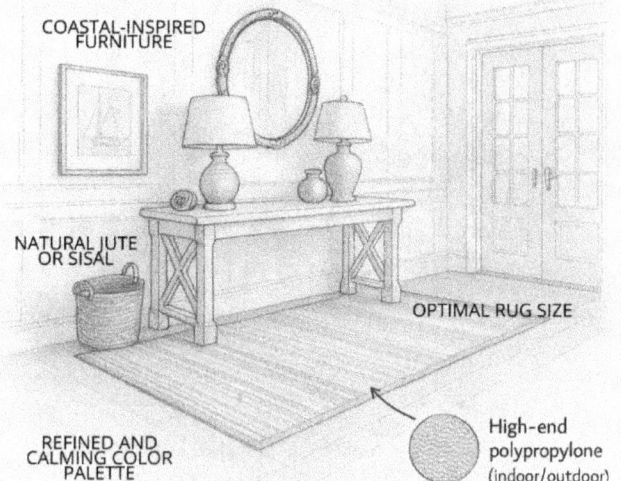

Ideal Entryway Rug Sizes, Placements & Materials – Coastal & Nautical Inspired Style

COASTAL-INSPIRED FURNITURE

NATURAL JUTE OR SISAL

OPTIMAL RUG SIZE

REFINED AND CALMING COLOR PALETTE

High-end polypropylone (indoor/outdoor)

06 PERSONALIZED DÉCOR & ACCESSORIES

Adding personal elements to your entryway is what turns it from just a functional space into something that feels like home. Small details can make a big difference, giving visitors a glimpse of your personality the moment they walk in.

- **Artwork or Photography**: Hanging a favorite piece of art or a meaningful photo can instantly create a visual anchor. Whether it's a bold abstract painting or a quiet black-and-white landscape, it adds character and sets the tone for the space.

- **Plants or Floral Arrangements**: A potted plant or seasonal floral bouquet brings in a natural touch that softens the environment. It's an easy way to introduce life, color, and a bit of freshness, especially if the rest of the entry is more neutral.

- **Accent Pieces** (vases, sculptures): Decorative objects like unique vases, small sculptures, or ceramic bowls help express your taste without overwhelming the area. Choosing just one or two eye-catching pieces keeps things interesting while maintaining a clean, uncluttered feel.

07 EFFICIENT DROP ZONE

Your entryway should work for you, not against you. Setting up a designated drop zone helps prevent everyday chaos by giving your essentials a consistent home. It makes coming and going feel smoother and more intentional.

- **Tray or Bowl for Keys and Coins**: A decorative tray or ceramic bowl can do more than just look nice—it keeps your keys, loose change, and other small items in one dependable place. Instead of digging through bags or pockets, everything is ready and waiting when you need it.

- **Mail Organizer or Slot**: Whether it's a freestanding organizer, a wall-mounted file, or a simple letter tray, having a dedicated place for mail keeps paper clutter in check. It allows you to sort quickly—urgent items stay visible while junk mail can be set aside.

- **Charging Station** (Optional): A small charging area near the entry can be a smart addition, especially for households with multiple devices. It offers a practical, out-of-the-way spot to top off batteries while helping keep cords neatly managed and out of sight.

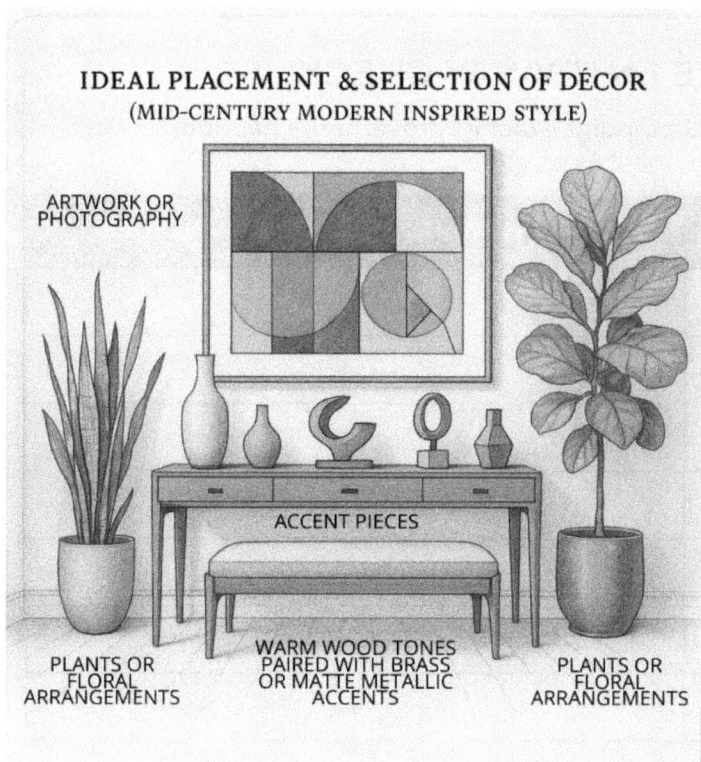

IDEAL PLACEMENT & SELECTION OF DÉCOR
(MID-CENTURY MODERN INSPIRED STYLE)

ARTWORK OR PHOTOGRAPHY

ACCENT PIECES

PLANTS OR FLORAL ARRANGEMENTS

WARM WOOD TONES PAIRED WITH BRASS OR MATTE METALLIC ACCENTS

PLANTS OR FLORAL ARRANGEMENTS

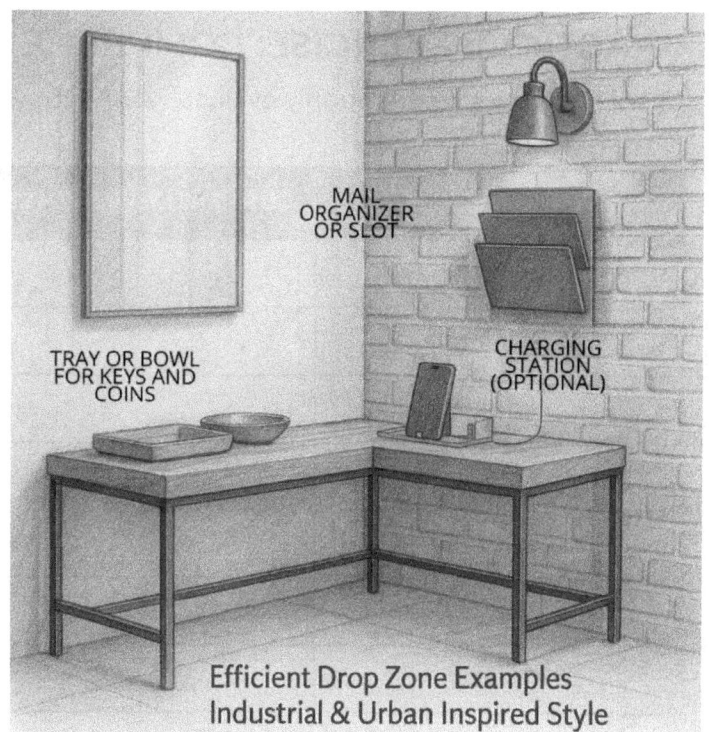

MAIL ORGANIZER OR SLOT

CHARGING STATION (OPTIONAL)

TRAY OR BOWL FOR KEYS AND COINS

Efficient Drop Zone Examples
Industrial & Urban Inspired Style

QUICK REFERENCE: ENTRYWAY ELEMENTS OVERVIEW

Use this at-a-glance reference to quickly verify essential components:

ESSENTIAL ELEMENTS	RECOMMENDED OPTIONS	NOTES / CONSIDERATIONS
Storage Solutions	Console table, shoe bench, hooks, baskets	Prioritize practical daily needs
Seating	Bench, stool, built-in seating	Match to available space
Lighting	Ceiling fixture, sconces, table lamps	Layer multiple sources
Mirror	Wall-mounted, full-length, decorative	Consider size and positioning
Rug	Durable materials, easy-clean options	Size proportionate to space
Décor & Accessories	Artwork, plants, accent items	Reflect personal style
Drop Zone	Tray, mail organizer, charging station	Organize daily essentials

EXPERT ENTRYWAY DESIGN TIPS

Apply these expert-level strategies to maximize your entryway's function and aesthetic appeal:

BALANCE PRACTICALITY & AESTHETICS: Every item should combine functional practicality with visual appeal.

MIND YOUR ENTRYWAY'S SCALE: Ensure each element is appropriately sized to avoid crowding or emptiness.

KEEP A COHESIVE STYLE: Your entryway should be a harmonious introduction to your home's overall aesthetic.

PRACTICAL EXERCISE: COMPREHENSIVE ENTRYWAY CHECKLIST

Use this exercise to thoroughly evaluate your entryway and pinpoint exact improvements needed:

ESSENTIAL ELEMENT	CURRENTLY PRESENT? (Y/N)	IMPROVEMENTS OR ADDITIONS NEEDED
Functional Storage		
Seating		
Lighting		
Mirror		
Durable Rug		
Décor & Accessories		
Drop Zone		

Living Rooms
AND LOUNGES

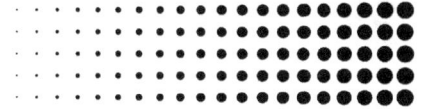

CHAPTER 6

DESIGNING FOR
Comfort & Conversation

Picture an evening glow washing over linen-clad sofas while understated brass accents catch the light like quiet jewelry. The living room is a theatre of stories, where laughter ricochets across supple cushions and silences settle into soft rugs. Every contour invites lingering; every texture hints at ease. Here, comfort is not an afterthought but the protagonist, shaping how bodies recline and voices flow freely.

Conversation, meanwhile, unfurls in subtle cues—a generous radius between lounge chairs, a low coffee table that seems to hover, a lamp casting a pool of amber that flatters both porcelain and teak. Thoughtful proportion keeps gazes level, encouraging eyes to meet. Even silence finds purpose, cushioned by fabrics that temper echoes and colors that feel familiar yet quietly captivating.

When comfort and dialogue harmonize, the room becomes a magnetic nucleus for family rituals and spontaneous gatherings alike. Children splice homework with anecdotes, friends trade confidences over citrus spritzes, and solitary afternoons bloom into restorative retreats. This choreography owes as much to measured geometry as to the mood woven through layered lighting and scented undertones.

Such a space doesn't shout design principles; it whispers them through balance, scale, and rhythm. Upholstery reads like prose—velvets and bouclés adding commas and ellipses—while curated art offers gentle exclamation. The result is a setting that feels deeply considered, an elegant backdrop where life unfolds naturally and beauty never demands attention.

CORE PRINCIPLES OF COMFORTABLE & CONVERSATIONAL DESIGN

To create spaces that feel naturally inviting, consider the following foundational principles:

01 ARRANGEMENT FOR CONVERSATION

Effective furniture placement fosters easy interaction:

- **Group Seating**: Position sofas and chairs facing each other to encourage dialogue.

- **Conversational Distances**: Seating should ideally be spaced within 4 to 8 feet to facilitate comfortable speaking and eye contact.

- **Circular or Semi-Circular Layouts**: Encourage inclusivity and visibility, enhancing group dynamics.

CIRCULAR

FACING SEATS

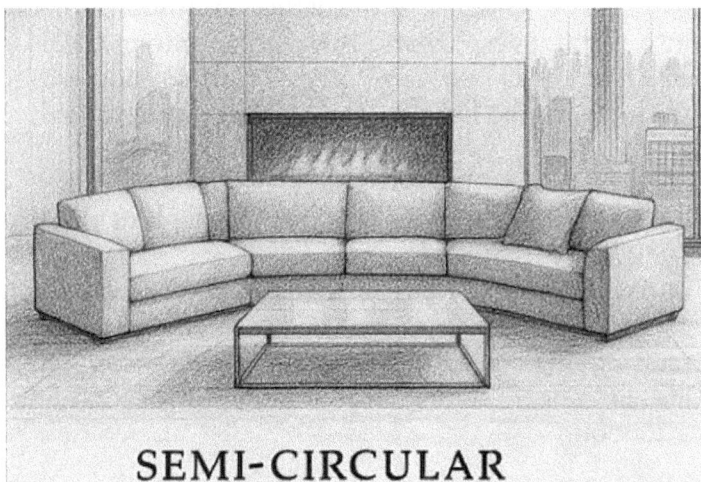

SEMI-CIRCULAR

02 PRIORITIZE COMFORT

Comfortable seating ensures guests feel welcomed and relaxed:

- **Upholstered Furniture**: Opt for plush cushions, supportive backrests, and comfortable materials.

- **Adequate Seating Depth & Height**: Ideal seat depth (20–24 inches) and height (17–19 inches) significantly influence comfort levels.

- **Accessible Side Tables**: Allow guests easy access to drinks, snacks, or personal items.

03 ACHIEVING VISUAL BALANCE

Visual balance contributes significantly to comfort:

- **Symmetrical Layouts**: Offer formal balance and stability; perfect for traditional or formal spaces.

- **Asymmetrical Layouts**: Create a relaxed, casual vibe suited for modern or eclectic interiors.

- **Balanced Furniture Sizes**: Ensure no single item dominates, maintaining visual harmony.

Symmetrical

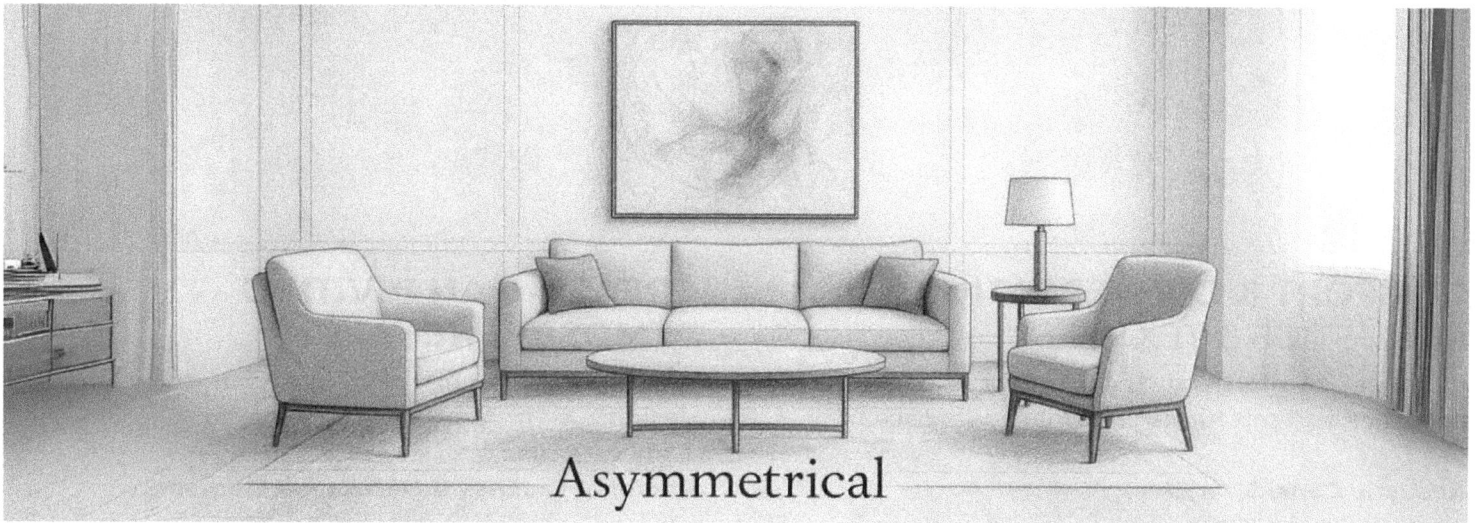

Asymmetrical

CHOOSING THE RIGHT FURNITURE FOR COMFORT & CONVERSATION

Selecting appropriate furniture is essential:

FURNITURE ITEM	RECOMMENDED FEATURES	BENEFITS
Sofa	Deep cushions, quality upholstery, armrests	Central seating piece for groups
Accent Chairs	Versatile, movable, supportive cushions	Complement main sofa; extra seating
Ottoman	Multi-use: seating, footrest, or table	Enhances versatility and comfort

IDEAL LIVING ROOM LIGHTING FOR COMFORT

Lighting significantly shapes atmosphere and comfort levels:

- **Ambient Lighting**: General illumination via ceiling fixtures or recessed lights, setting the overall brightness.

- **Task Lighting**: Targeted lighting through table lamps or floor lamps near seating for reading or focused tasks.

- **Accent Lighting**: Highlight decorative elements, enhancing visual interest and comfort through wall sconces or spotlights.

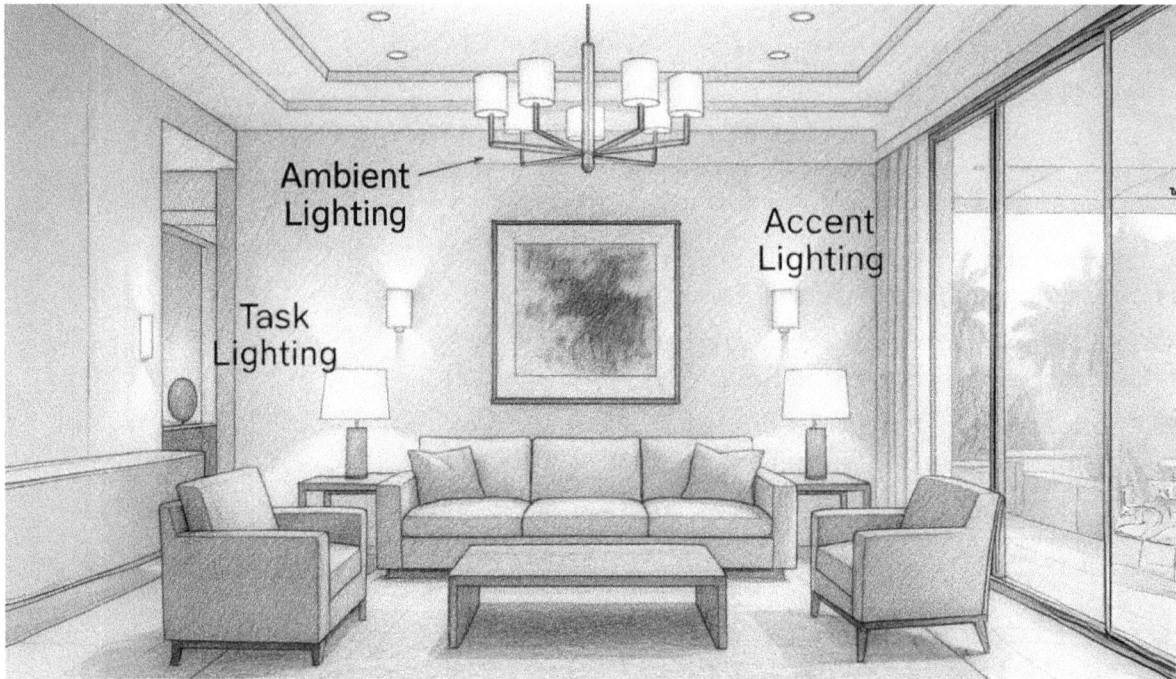

COMFORT & CONVERSATION: ACOUSTICS & TEXTILES

Enhance comfort by thoughtfully incorporating acoustics and soft furnishings into your space:

Acoustic Considerations

- **Soft Furnishings**: Rugs, drapes, and upholstered pieces help absorb sound, reduce echoes, and create a quieter, more intimate atmosphere for conversation.
- **Placement of Furniture**: Arranging seating to form enclosed zones naturally contains sound within the group, supporting clear and comfortable dialogue.

Textile Choices for Comfort

- **Area Rugs**: Define conversation areas while softening footfalls and improving acoustics with warmth and texture.
- **Throw Pillows & Blankets**: Add comfort, visual softness, and a layered aesthetic that invites relaxation.
- **Curtains & Drapes**: Frame the room with elegance, reduce noise, and enhance the room's sense of coziness and enclosure.

CREATING AN INVITING ATMOSPHERE

Atmospheric details complete your conversational design:

Personal Touches & Decorative Elements

- **Bookshelves & Displays**: Add personality and create conversation starters.
- **Plants & Natural Elements**: Introduce tranquility, improve air quality, and provide visual appeal.
- **Art & Photographs**: Reflect personality, interests, and create meaningful focal points.

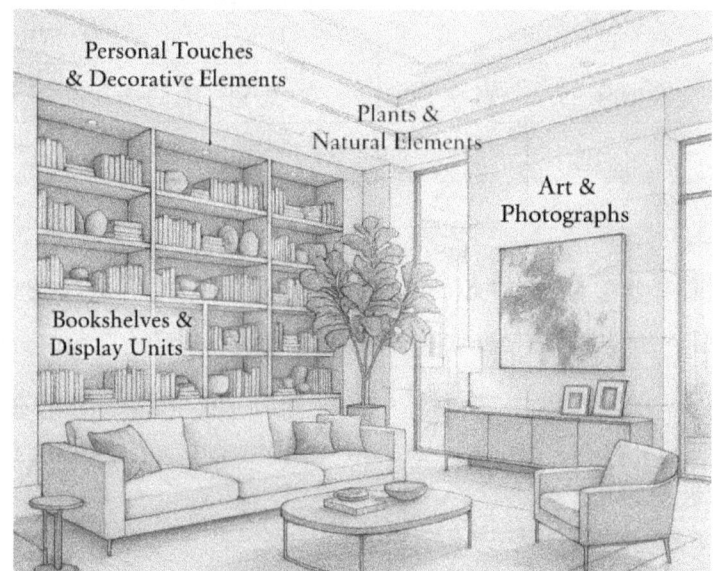

COMMON MISTAKES IN CONVERSATIONAL DESIGN (AND HOW TO AVOID THEM)

Awareness of pitfalls ensures your design remains inviting and functional:

COMMON MISTAKE	SOLUTION & RECOMMENDATIONS
Furniture Too Far Apart	Group seating closer for comfortable conversations
Overly Formal or Uncomfortable Seating	Prioritize comfort and versatility in furniture choices
Poor Lighting & Acoustics	Implement layered lighting; use soft furnishings to manage acoustics

STEP-BY-STEP GUIDE TO DESIGNING A COMFORTABLE & CONVERSATIONAL LIVING ROOM

Use this comprehensive approach to ensure successful results:

Step 1: Assess Space & Needs
- Identify primary uses: entertaining, relaxation, family activities.
- Measure and evaluate spatial constraints and opportunities.

Step 2: Choose Conversational Furniture Layout
- Opt for arrangements facilitating interaction (circular, semi-circular, or facing).

Step 3: Select Comfortable Furniture
- Prioritize upholstered, supportive seating and multi-use furniture items.

Step 4: Implement Layered Lighting & Textiles
- Use ambient, task, and accent lighting combined with textiles to enhance atmosphere and acoustics.

Step 5: Personalize & Accessorize Thoughtfully
- Add artwork, plants, bookshelves, and accessories that reflect your personality and enhance conversational comfort.

EXPERT TIPS FOR COMFORTABLE, CONVERSATIONAL DESIGN

MIX & MATCH FURNITURE STYLES: Combine formal and relaxed pieces to cultivate a space that feels collected, welcoming, and visually rich. The contrast between tailored and casual elements adds warmth and individuality, supporting a range of seating preferences.

CREATE MULTIPLE SEATING ZONES: Particularly effective in open-concept or generously sized rooms, defining a few smaller seating areas encourages intimate conversation, accommodates groups of varying sizes, and brings purpose and scale to the overall layout.

ALWAYS CONSIDER FLOW: Prioritize open pathways and natural circulation between pieces to ensure the room feels spacious, accessible, and harmonious. Clear movement lines not only improve comfort but also support spontaneous gathering and relaxed interaction.

Mix & Match Furniture Styles
Elegantly blend formal furniture pieces

Multiple Seating Zones
Secondary conversational zone

Consider Flow and Circulation
Clear, generously spaced pathways (minimum 56--48 inches)

PRACTICAL EXERCISE: COMFORT & CONVERSATION LAYOUT ASSESSMENT

Evaluate your living room's conversational effectiveness with this structured exercise:

FEATURE EVALUATED	MEETS CRITERIA? (Y/N)	IMPROVEMENT NEEDED
Furniture arrangement for conversation		
Comfortable seating choices		
Layered & effective lighting		
Acoustic & textile comfort		
Personal & inviting atmosphere		

This practical assessment provides clarity on precisely how to refine your living room for optimal comfort and conversational flow.

FINAL THOUGHTS ON DESIGNING FOR COMFORT & CONVERSATION

A living room attuned to comfort and conversation is less a collection of furniture than a gentle choreography of sensations—light gliding across velvet, laughter cushioned by wool, the faint whisper of a candle as dusk settles. Walls recede when chairs invite a natural lean, and tables poised at just-so height anticipate a resting glass or an open novel. Every element collaborates, quiet yet assured, to tell guests that their presence is anticipated and their ease already measured.

Texture anchors that promise. Underfoot, an area rug edited to the exact proportions of the seating ensemble hushes footsteps and centers conversation, while brushed-brass accents catch lamplight like discreet jewelry. Hues remain subdued, yet a single flash of persimmon or indigo reminds the eye that joy lives alongside tranquility. Sound carries differently here; upholstery serves as a gentle gatekeeper, filtering background murmur so even the softest confession can float unhurried, protected by fabric and intent, echoing the gentle cadence of well-loved conversation.

Movement enjoys equal consideration. Pathways unfold like gentle currents, allowing bodies to glide without the stutter of obstacles, ensuring hosts never interrupt a story by squeezing past a corner. Seating clusters linger within arm's reach yet resist crowding, encouraging shifting constellations of people as evenings mature. One can withdraw to the edge for quiet reflection, then drift back toward the hum of dialogue with effortless grace; the room holds space for both impulses without judgment and grace.

Ultimately, such thoughtful composition becomes a silent ambassador for the household's values. Friends recall not the thread count but the way time seemed to stretch kindly, children remember the freedom to sprawl, and solitary afternoons acquire a companionable hush rather than emptiness. What endures is a feeling—an assurance that here, story and comfort share equal billing and neither is hurried. Daylight may shift and décor may evolve, yet the room continues to breathe hospitality like a living art form.

Furniture Arrangement
GUIDELINES

Furniture arrangement is both art and science. It can transform a simple room into a space that's inviting, functional, and visually appealing. Thoughtful furniture placement affects traffic flow, conversation ease, and overall comfort, shaping your living environment in subtle yet profound ways. In this section, we'll uncover the secrets of furniture arrangement, offering precise guidelines to maximize your living space.

FUNDAMENTAL RULES FOR FURNITURE ARRANGEMENT

When planning your furniture layout, adhere to these foundational guidelines to achieve balanced and harmonious spaces.

01 IDENTIFY THE ROOM'S PRIMARY PURPOSE

Before arranging furniture, define the main activities of your room clearly. Typical purposes include:

- **Socializing**: Open arrangements promoting conversation.
- **Watching TV or Movies**: Seating facing entertainment areas.
- **Reading and Relaxation**: Quiet corners with cozy armchairs.

02 PRIORITIZE THE LARGEST PIECE

Begin by positioning your largest furniture piece, such as the sofa or sectional, as this anchors your room.

- **Optimal Placement**: Usually opposite the main focal point (fireplace, TV, large window).
- **Clearance**: Allow 3 feet of space for comfortable movement around it.

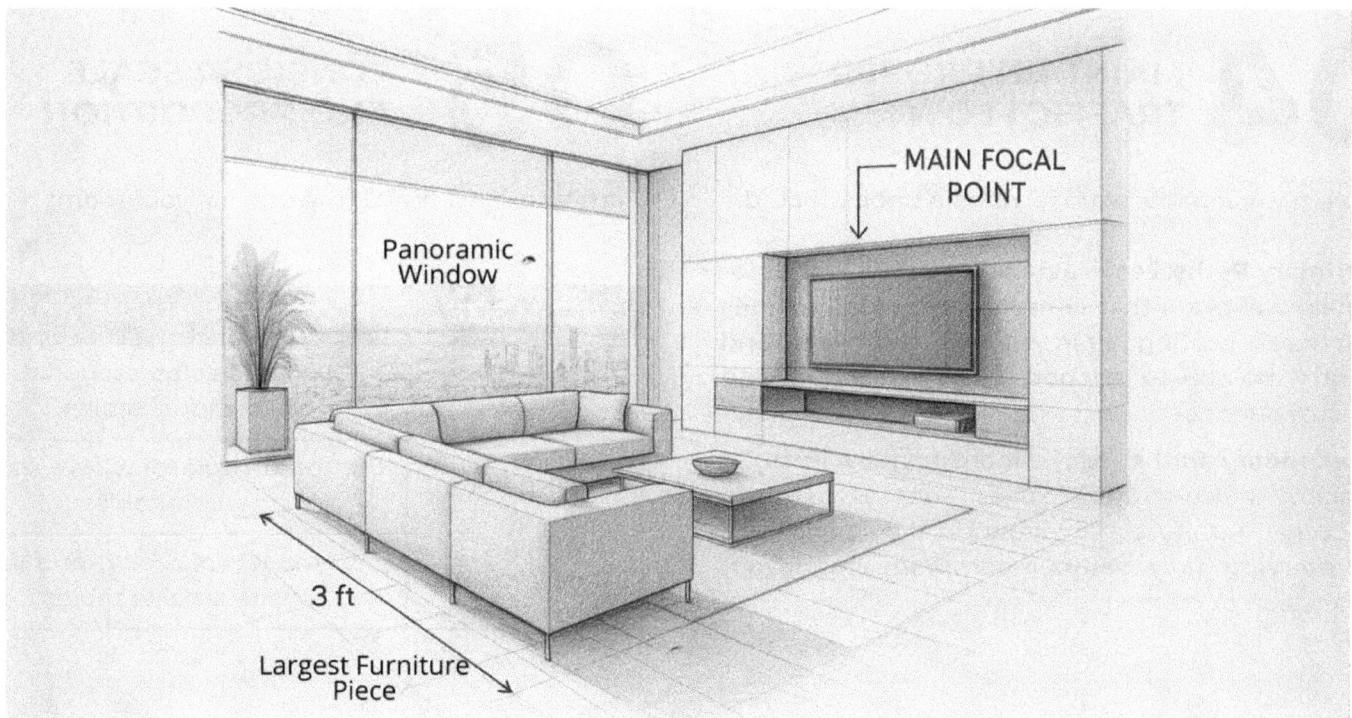

MAIN FOCAL POINT

Panoramic Window

3 ft

Largest Furniture Piece

03 FACILITATE NATURAL CONVERSATION

Aim to create groupings that facilitate easy conversation:

- **Face-to-Face**: Chairs and sofas placed directly opposite or angled toward each other.
- **Comfortable Distance**: Ideally, seating should be spaced between 4–8 feet apart.
- **Circular Arrangements**: Preferred for larger groups to ensure inclusivity.

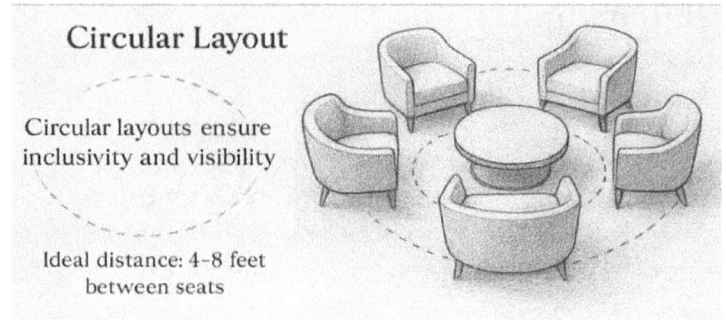

Circular Layout

Circular layouts ensure inclusivity and visibility

Ideal distance: 4–8 feet between seats

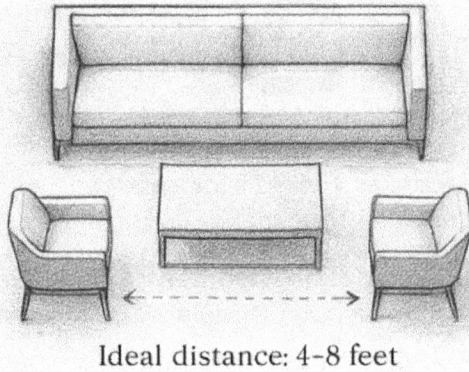

Face-to-Face Layout

Ideal distance: 4–8 feet

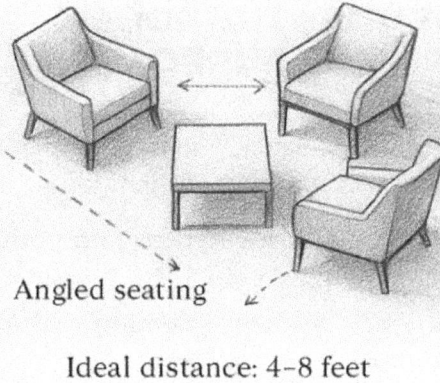

Angled Layout

Angled seating

Ideal distance: 4–8 feet

04 MAINTAIN PROPER TRAFFIC FLOW

Ensure natural paths of travel remain unobstructed:

- **Primary Paths**: Leave a minimum of 36 inches for main walkways that connect key areas—such as between seating arrangements, doorways, and entry points—to support easy circulation and visual openness.
- **Secondary Paths**: Allow approximately 18 to 24 inches in lower-traffic zones, such as between accent furniture or around the perimeter, preserving flow without compromising layout cohesion or intimacy.

05 CONSIDER SCALE AND PROPORTION

Furniture must match the scale of your room:

ROOM SIZE	RECOMMENDED FURNITURE
Large Rooms	Oversized sofas, sectionals, substantial tables
Medium Rooms	Standard-sized sofas, loveseats, medium tables
Small Rooms	Compact sofas, slim-profile chairs, smaller tables

SPECIFIC ARRANGEMENT TECHNIQUES

Let's examine popular arrangement techniques suitable for various spaces.

SYMMETRICAL ARRANGEMENT

Perfect for formal, balanced aesthetics, creating calm and order.

- **Ideal For**: Traditional and formal living rooms.
- **Technique**: Mirror furniture placements around a central focal point (e.g., fireplace, artwork).

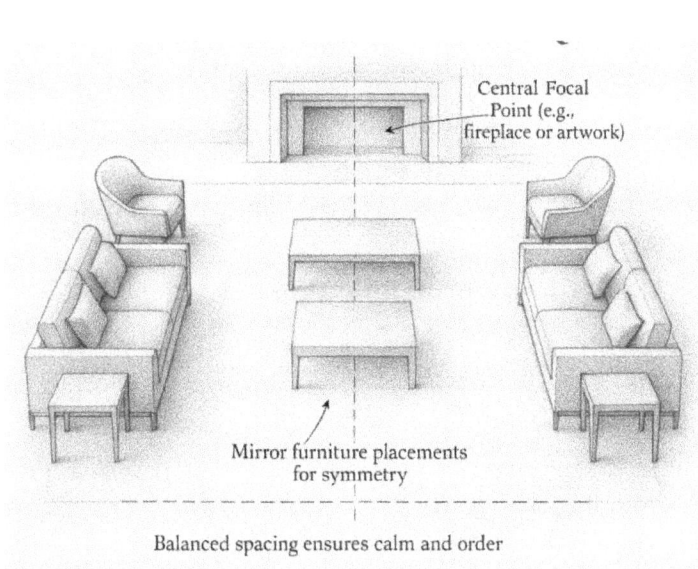

Central Focal Point (e.g., fireplace or artwork)

Mirror furniture placements for symmetry

Balanced spacing ensures calm and order

ASYMMETRICAL ARRANGEMENT

Offers a relaxed, contemporary look and feel.

- **Ideal For**: Modern, eclectic, casual interiors.
- **Technique**: Balance visual weight creatively by offsetting furniture items in size and number.

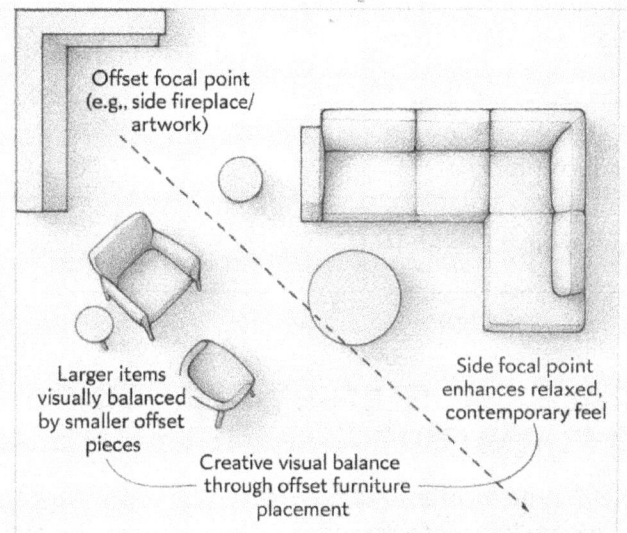

Offset focal point (e.g., side fireplace/ artwork)

Larger items visually balanced by smaller offset pieces

Side focal point enhances relaxed, contemporary feel

Creative visual balance through offset furniture placement

ZONING ARRANGEMENT

Creates visually and functionally distinct areas within open-plan layouts to bring structure, clarity, and purposeful flow to the space.

- **Ideal For**: Multifunctional living areas, open-concept homes, lofts, and studio apartments where a single room must accommodate varied activities without the use of permanent walls. Zoning helps define how each area is meant to be used while maintaining an open, cohesive feel.
- **Technique**: Use large area rugs to anchor each zone, arrange furniture into thoughtful groupings based on function, and incorporate layered lighting—such as chandeliers above dining tables, floor lamps by seating areas, or task lighting near desks—to visually differentiate zones for dining, relaxing, reading, or working, all while maintaining an elegant sense of unity.

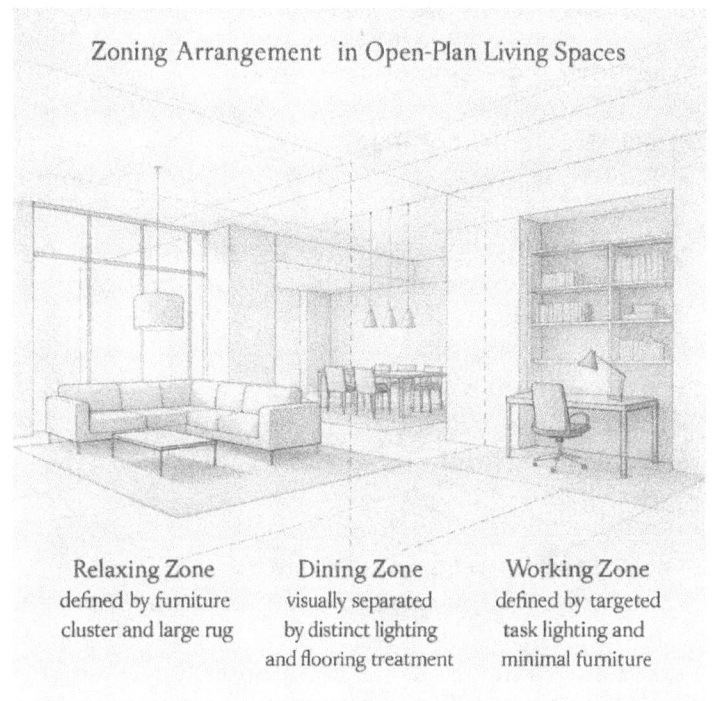

Zoning Arrangement in Open-Plan Living Spaces

Relaxing Zone
defined by furniture cluster and large rug

Dining Zone
visually separated by distinct lighting and flooring treatment

Working Zone
defined by targeted task lighting and minimal furniture

ESSENTIAL FURNITURE SPACING GUIDELINES (CHEAT SHEET)

Use this handy cheat sheet for quick reference while arranging your furniture.

FURNITURE ELEMENT	RECOMMENDED SPACING
Sofa to Coffee Table	14–18 inches
Seating Arrangement (distance)	4–8 feet for comfortable conversation
Walkway Clearance (main paths)	At least 36 inches
Walkway Clearance (secondary paths)	18–24 inches
TV Viewing Distance	1.5 to 2.5 times the diagonal TV measurement

PRACTICAL STEP-BY-STEP GUIDE TO FURNITURE ARRANGEMENT

Follow these practical steps to arrange furniture effectively in any space:

Step 1: Measure Your Space
- Take precise measurements of the room.
- Note doorways, windows, fireplaces, electrical outlets, and architectural elements.

Step 2: Create a Floor Plan
- Sketch a basic floor plan or use an online planning tool.
- Experiment digitally or physically (use cut-out paper shapes) to explore arrangement possibilities.

Step 3: Define the Room's Purpose
- Clearly list out all intended uses of the room.
- Determine furniture essentials based on these activities.

Step 4: Start with Largest Furniture
- Position your largest piece first to anchor the room.
- Arrange smaller pieces subsequently around this anchor.

Step 5: Arrange Remaining Pieces
- Ensure conversational layouts, proper spacing, clear pathways.
- Adjust for comfort, aesthetics, and functionality.

Step 6: Test and Refine
- Physically test the arrangement by moving through and interacting in the space.
- Adjust furniture based on comfort, ease of use, and aesthetics.

FURNITURE ARRANGEMENT FOR SMALL SPACES

Small rooms require specialized techniques:

- **Use multifunctional furniture**: Storage ottomans, sleeper sofas.
- **Prioritize vertical space**: Shelving, mounted storage.
- **Float furniture slightly**: Creates an illusion of spaciousness.

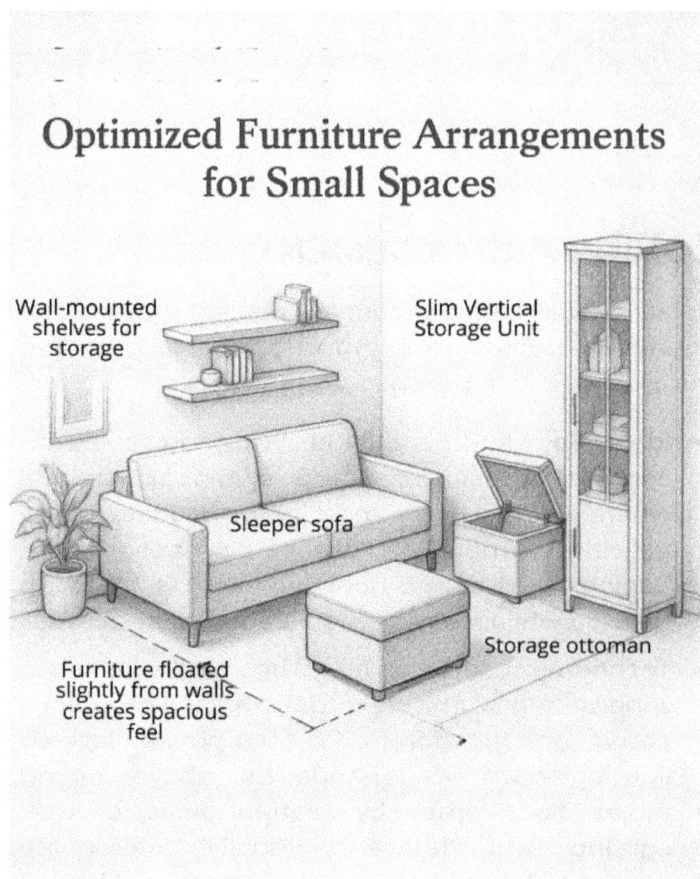

Optimized Furniture Arrangements for Small Spaces

Wall-mounted shelves for storage

Slim Vertical Storage Unit

Sleeper sofa

Furniture floated slightly from walls creates spacious feel

Storage ottoman

FURNITURE ARRANGEMENT TIPS FOR LARGE SPACES

Expansive rooms benefit from intentional zoning and careful attention to scale and proportion:

- Create multiple seating areas: Establish distinct conversation groupings within the room to encourage intimacy and variety in social interaction.

- Use substantial furniture: Choose pieces with presence to fill the space comfortably, helping the room feel balanced rather than sparse or underfurnished.

- Include anchor elements: Incorporate large area rugs, generously sized coffee tables, or sectional sofas to ground each zone and visually organize the layout.

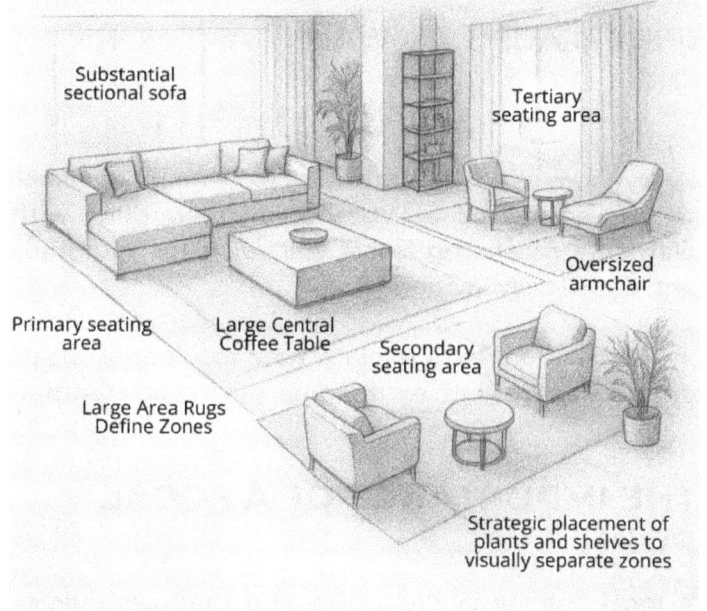

EXPERT TIPS FOR PERFECT FURNITURE ARRANGEMENT

BALANCE FORM AND FUNCTION: Furniture should serve practical needs without sacrificing style.

EXPERIMENT: Don't be afraid to try unconventional arrangements; you might discover unexpected, wonderful solutions.

CONSIDER SIGHTLINES: Maintain clear, attractive sightlines, especially towards focal points or views.

EXERCISE: EVALUATE YOUR CURRENT FURNITURE LAYOUT

Use this quick evaluation to see how your current furniture arrangement measures up:

EVALUATION CRITERIA	MEETS CRITERIA? (Y/N)	IMPROVEMENTS NEEDED
Clear focal point established		
Furniture spacing optimal		
Traffic flow unobstructed		
Comfortable conversation areas		
Visual balance and proportion		

Conduct this evaluation and make adjustments to perfect your furniture layout.

Creating Focal Points
(FIREPLACES, TV WALLS, ARTWORK)

Every room needs a captivating focal point—a visual anchor that immediately draws attention and sets the tone for the entire space. Whether you're working with a fireplace, a TV wall, stunning artwork, or architectural elements, mastering focal points elevates your interior design, ensuring your room feels cohesive, harmonious, and effortlessly inviting.

In this section, we'll explore how to identify, emphasize, and even create striking focal points, transforming ordinary spaces into extraordinary living environments.

THE IMPORTANCE OF A FOCAL POINT

A focal point provides clarity and purpose, guiding visual flow and shaping furniture arrangements. Its impact extends beyond mere aesthetics, enhancing usability and emotional comfort.

Benefits of Effective Focal Points:
- **Visual Clarity**: Clearly defines the room's purpose.
- **Design Cohesion**: Ties different elements together.
- **Enhanced Ambiance**: Creates mood and evokes emotion.
- **Structured Layouts**: Organizes furniture arrangement logically.

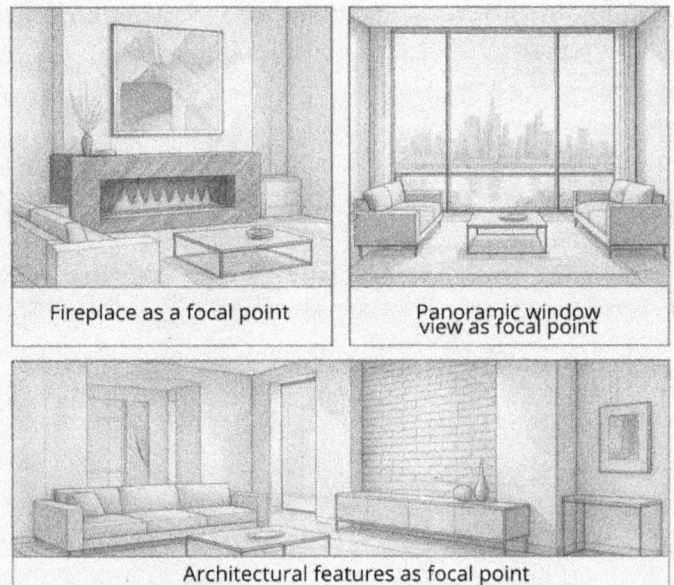

Natural Focal Points for Modern Interiors

Fireplace as a focal point

Panoramic window view as focal point

Architectural features as focal point

IDENTIFYING YOUR ROOM'S NATURAL FOCAL POINT

Before creating a new focal point, check if your room already has a natural anchor, such as:

- Fireplace
- Large Windows with Beautiful Views
- Built-in Shelves or Bookcases
- Architectural Details (exposed brick walls, columns, arches)

If one of these elements exists, consider enhancing it rather than competing against it.

CREATING A FOCAL POINT: FIREPLACES

Fireplaces naturally command attention, symbolizing warmth, comfort, and home.

Enhancing Fireplace Focal Points:
- **Mantel Styling**: Balance decorative items such as mirrors, artwork, or sculptural accents.
- **Symmetrical or Asymmetrical Layouts**: Achieve formal symmetry with matching items, or informal asymmetry for relaxed charm.
- **Framing Elements**: Built-ins, bookshelves, or sconces enhance the visual weight of your fireplace.

Central Mirror/Art

Matching Decorative Items
Built-In Shelves
(Symmetrical)

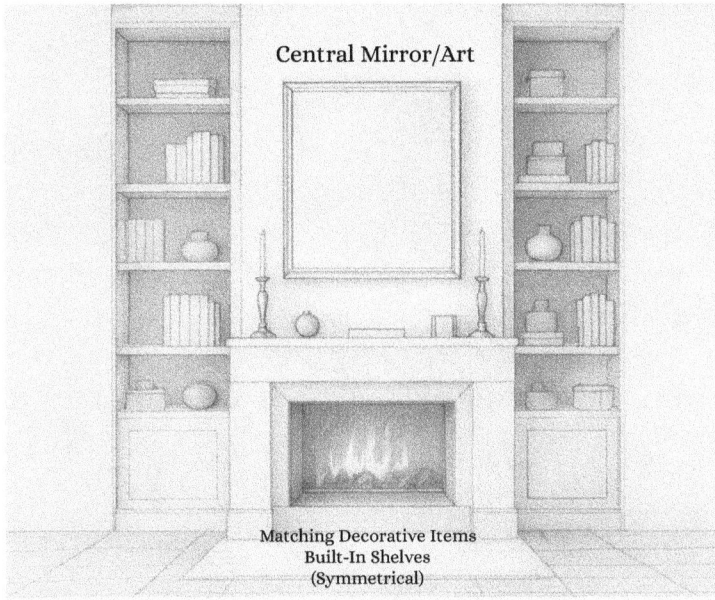

SYMMETRICAL MANTEL STYLING

Strategic
Symmetrical

ASYMMETRICAL MANTEL STYLING

CREATING A FOCAL POINT: TV WALLS

TV walls have evolved dramatically, becoming stylish focal points in modern homes rather than mere functional zones.

TV Wall Design Techniques:

- **Accent Wall**: Paint, wallpaper, or textured panels behind the TV for contrast.
- **Integrated Storage**: Built-in shelving and cabinetry surrounding the TV for aesthetic appeal and functionality.
- **Artful Mounting**: Surrounding TV with artwork or gallery arrangements to blend technology with decor seamlessly.

ACCENT WALL
EXAMPLE

- Paint, wallpaper, or textured panels behind the TV for contrast
- Minimalist shelving or console

INTEGRATED STORAGE
EXAMPLES

- Built-in storage cabinets
- Elegant decorative elements

ARTFUL MOUNTING
EXAMPLE

- Gallery style art arrangement
- Strategic accent lighting

RECOMMENDED TV MOUNTING HEIGHTS & VIEWING DISTANCES

TV Size	Ideal Viewing Height (from)	Ideal Seating Distance
42-55 inches	42-56 inches	6-10 feet
55-70 inches	48-60 inches	8-12 feet
70+ inches	54-66 inches	10-15 feet

Viewing Height

OPTIMAL VIEWING DISTANCE

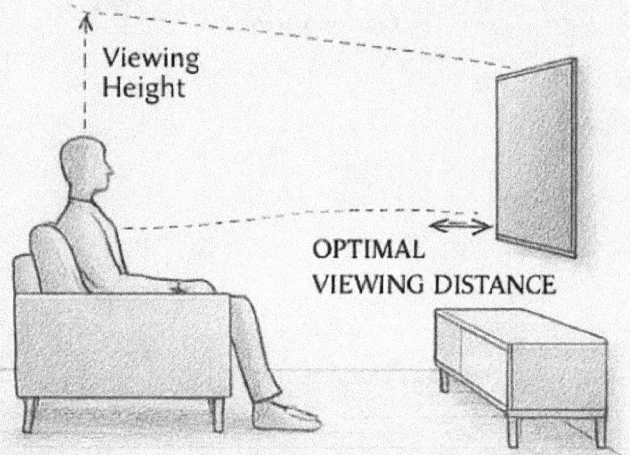

OPTIMAL VIEWING DISTANCE →

CREATING A FOCAL POINT: ARTWORK

Art pieces serve as powerful visual statements, infusing personality and culture into your space.

Artwork as Focal Point Techniques:

- **Large Statement Piece**: A single bold artwork placed strategically on the main wall.
- **Gallery Walls**: Thoughtfully arranged collection of smaller pieces forming a cohesive, visually exciting composition.
- **Balanced Lighting**: Use picture lights or spotlights to highlight artwork dramatically.

Guidelines for Optimal Artwork Placement:

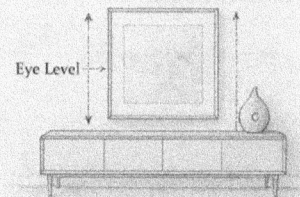

- **Eye Level**: Center artwork at approximately 57–60 inches from the floor.
- **Scale & Proportion**: Artwork should cover around two-thirds to three-quarters of the available wall space.

LUXURY ARTWORK FOCAL POINTS & PLACEMENT GUIDELINES

ARTWORK FOCAL POINT TECHNIQUES

Large Statement Piece

Gallery Wall

Single Bold Artwork as Central Focus Creates Visual Impact

Eclectic, Informal Gallery Wall Salon Style Arrangement

Ledge Display

ARTWORK PLACEMENT

Eye Level

Floating Shelves Art Display Flexible & Casual Approach

Gallery Wall Layout Ideas:

STYLE	DESCRIPTION
Grid Arrangement	Symmetrical, organized rows for formal spaces.
Salon Style	Asymmetrical, eclectic groupings for casual areas.
Ledge Display	Floating shelves displaying framed art informally.

LAYERING MULTIPLE FOCAL POINTS

In larger or open-plan spaces, layering multiple focal points can effectively zone your room into functional, harmonious sections.

Effective Techniques:

- **Primary & Secondary Points**: Establish one dominant focal point (like a fireplace) with smaller, complementary ones (artwork or windows).
- **Visual Hierarchy**: Ensure secondary points don't compete but rather support the primary focal point.
- **Furniture Groupings**: Cluster furniture around focal points to enhance distinct zones.

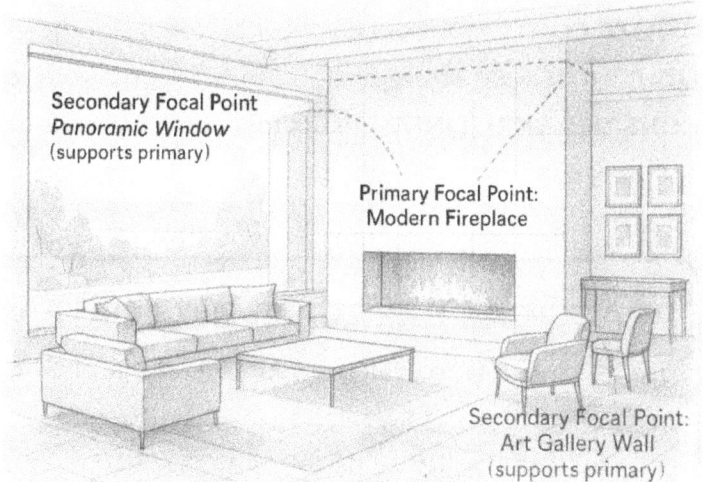

Layering Multiple Focal Points for Open-Plan Interiors

Secondary Focal Point
Panoramic Window
(supports primary)

Primary Focal Point:
Modern Fireplace

Secondary Focal Point:
Art Gallery Wall
(supports primary)

COMMON MISTAKES WHEN CREATING FOCAL POINTS

Avoid these typical pitfalls for maximum visual appeal and effectiveness:

MISTAKE	SOLUTION
Too Many Competing Focal Points	Clearly identify and prioritize one dominant focal point
Poor Scale and Proportion	Match focal point size with room scale
Neglecting Balance & Symmetry	Ensure visual balance around focal points

STEP-BY-STEP GUIDE TO CREATING A SUCCESSFUL FOCAL POINT

Follow this detailed guide to establish a striking and cohesive focal point in any room:

Step 1: Choose Your Focal Element
- Select or identify the most naturally commanding feature—such as a fireplace, statement art piece, TV wall, or architectural element—that draws attention and suits the room's purpose.

Step 2: Determine Positioning
- Place your focal point on a central or prominently visible wall to ensure it naturally anchors the room and immediately captures the eye upon entry.

Step 3: Scale Appropriately
- Ensure the focal element is scaled in proportion to both the room and surrounding furniture—neither overpowering nor underwhelming—so it feels balanced within the space.

Step 4: Enhance & Style
- Layer with intentional accessories such as artwork, lighting, shelving, or decor accents that frame and emphasize the focal point without cluttering it.

Step 5: Furniture Alignment
- Position key pieces like sofas or chairs to face or subtly angle toward the focal point, reinforcing its importance and supporting comfort and function.

Step 6: Test and Refine
- Step back to evaluate both aesthetics and flow. Make thoughtful adjustments until the focal point feels visually harmonious, well-integrated, and naturally commanding.

EXPERT TIPS FOR IMPACTFUL FOCAL POINTS

UTILIZE CONTRAST: Bold colors or textures significantly enhance visibility and attractiveness.

LIGHTING IS KEY: Strategic lighting highlights your focal points dramatically.

CONSIDER SIGHTLINES: Ensure focal points are visible from primary seating and entry areas.

PRACTICAL EXERCISE: EVALUATE YOUR ROOM'S FOCAL POINT

Use this exercise to evaluate your existing or planned focal points:

EVALUATION CRITERIA	MEETS CRITERIA? (Y/N)	IMPROVEMENTS NEEDED
Clear, dominant focal point		
Appropriate scale & proportion		
Enhanced by lighting & decor		
Furniture alignment & visibility		

Complete this exercise to understand clearly how effectively your focal points function.

CONCLUSION

A well-considered focal point is never merely decorative—it is the subtle conductor of the room's rhythm, the quiet magnet that draws the eye and anchors the experience of space. Whether it's the architectural strength of a fireplace, the commanding elegance of curated art, or the sculptural silhouette of a statement light fixture, the focal point offers clarity and cohesion. It brings intention to the layout and mood, giving the room a sense of direction without rigidity.

When lighting grazes a textured wall or silhouettes a sculptural form, the space comes alive with dimensional grace. The interplay between focal elements and surrounding furnishings builds a kind of visual conversation—measured, fluid, and refined. It is in this harmony that the room begins to express something personal, something unmistakably lived in yet distinctly composed.

Scale and proportion do more than maintain balance; they elevate presence. A focal point scaled correctly doesn't shout—it resonates. It invites without dominating, guiding the gaze gently and naturally. The room feels finished, not because every surface is styled, but because there is a center—a quiet anchor around which life can move freely.

Such spaces linger in memory. They offer both visual captivation and emotional ease, reminding us that thoughtful design is never accidental. It's an orchestration of form and feeling, where every detail supports the whole with elegance and quiet confidence.

Rugs & Textile
LAYERING ILLUSTRATED

Imagine walking barefoot into a room, immediately feeling warmth, softness, and a distinct sense of style beneath your feet. This isn't accidental; it's the magic of thoughtfully chosen rugs and layered textiles. Rugs and fabrics are the unsung heroes of interior design, seamlessly merging beauty, comfort, and personality into a cohesive space.

In this comprehensive guide, we'll delve into the art and science of selecting, layering, and styling rugs and textiles to elevate your room from merely attractive to effortlessly luxurious.

WHY RUGS AND TEXTILE LAYERING MATTER

A carefully selected rug or beautifully layered textiles can dramatically transform your living area. More than mere decoration, these elements fulfill key roles:

- **Defines Spaces**: Clearly delineates areas in open-concept rooms.
- **Adds Warmth & Comfort:** Enhances the tactile and visual comfort of your space.
- **Provides Visual Interest**: Introduces patterns, textures, and colors that captivate the eye.
- **Improves Acoustics**: Absorbs sound, reducing echoes in large rooms.
- **Protects Flooring**: Shields your floors from wear and tear, especially in high-traffic zones.

Correct: Front legs of furniture placed comfortably on rug (8' x 10')

Incorrect: Furniture entirely off rug or rug too small, breaking visual harmony

UNDERSTANDING RUG SIZES & PLACEMENT

Selecting the correct rug size and placement ensures visual harmony and functional usability. Here's a detailed guide to commonly recommended rug sizes and arrangements:

Common Rug Sizes and Best Uses

RUG SIZE	BEST FOR	FURNITURE ARRANGEMENT
5' x 8'	Small living spaces or seating nooks	Furniture partially on/off rug
8' x 10'	Standard living room or dining area	Front legs of seating furniture on the rug
9' x 12'+	Large living rooms or open layouts	All furniture comfortably on the rug

OPTIMAL RUG PLACEMENT for SMALL & COZY LIVING AREAS

Correct:
Front legs of furniture partially on rug (5' x 8)

Incorrect:
Rug completely under or entirely separate from furniture

Correct:
All furniture fully placed on large rug (9' x 12'+). Creates cohesive, harmonious visual connection.

Incorrect:
Rug too small, furniture partially off rug; creates visual imbalance and disconnected seating area."

LAYERING RUGS LIKE A DESIGNER

Layering rugs adds dimension, personality, and an artful mix of textures to your interiors. Follow these expert-approved methods to layer confidently:

Layering Techniques:

- **Size Variation**: Place a smaller, decorative rug over a larger, neutral base rug.
- **Texture Contrast**: Combine smooth flat-weaves with plush or shaggy rugs.
- **Pattern Mixing**: Pair bold patterns with subtler prints or solids for visual harmony.

Effective Rug Layering Combinations:

BASE RUG	TOP LAYER RUG	RESULTING STYLE/EFFECT
Neutral Jute or Sisal	Patterned Kilim or Vintage Rug	Eclectic and warm
Solid Color Rug	Smaller textured sheepskin	Cozy, inviting, and luxurious
Large Flat-Weave	Smaller patterned Persian rug	Bohemian, globally inspired

CHOOSING RUG MATERIALS

The choice of rug material greatly influences durability, maintenance, and feel underfoot:

- **Wool**: Durable, naturally stain-resistant, luxurious feel, ideal for high-traffic areas.
- **Cotton**: Budget-friendly, washable, soft, suitable for casual spaces.
- **Silk**: Luxurious sheen, delicate, best for low-traffic, formal areas.
- **Jute & Sisal**: Eco-friendly, natural texture, durable for casual living spaces.
- **Synthetic** (Polypropylene, Nylon): Affordable, stain-resistant, great for families and pets.

QUICK REFERENCE GUIDE:

MATERIAL	DURABILITY	MAINTENANCE	COMFORT	COST (USD / SQ FT)
Wool	High	Moderate	Very High	$20 – $200
Cotton	Moderate	Easy	High	$10 – $50
Silk	Low	High	Very High	$50 – $400
Jute / Sisal	High	Moderate	Moderate	$3 – $10
Synthetic	Very High	Easy	Moderate	$5 – $30

WOOL RUG
Durable, naturally stain-resistant, very high comfort, luxurious comfort,

COTTON
Soft, washable, budget-friendly, casual apperance

SILK
Luxurious sheen, delicate, ideal for formal, low traffic-areas

JUTE & SISAL
Eco-friendly, textured, highly durable, naturally aesthetic

SYNTHETIC
Affordable, highly stain-resistant, practical, suitable for family and pets

TEXTILE LAYERING ESSENTIALS

Beyond rugs, textiles such as curtains, throws, pillows, and upholstery fabric play a vital role in creating comfort and visual depth.

Expert Tips for Layering Textiles:

- **Consistency in Palette**: Maintain a cohesive color palette while varying patterns and textures.
- **Balancing Scale**: Mix large-scale prints with small-scale patterns and solids.
- **Texture Mix**: Blend smooth materials (silk, cotton) with tactile textures (velvet, linen, wool).

Sample Textile Layering Combination:

- **Curtains**: Light linen or sheer fabric for softness.
- **Throw Pillows**: Velvet and patterned cotton for texture and visual interest.
- **Throw Blanket**: Chunky knit or faux fur for warmth and depth.
- **Upholstery**: Neutral, durable fabrics to anchor the visual composition.

CREATING BALANCE WITH RUGS & TEXTILES

Proper balance between rugs and textiles creates visual harmony and prevents overwhelming the space.

Key Balance Strategies:

- **Visual Weight**: Heavy or patterned rugs balanced by simpler textiles.
- **Color Distribution**: Dominant rug color subtly repeated in pillows or curtains.
- **Pattern Moderation**: Highly patterned rugs paired with neutral or lightly patterned textiles.

PRACTICAL STEP-BY-STEP GUIDE TO RUG SELECTION & LAYERING

Follow this comprehensive guide for successful rug placement and layering:

Step 1: Measure Your Space
Record precise room dimensions and furniture positions.

Step 2: Determine Rug Size
Use the sizing guide above to select ideal dimensions.

Step 3: Choose Primary Rug Material & Style
Base choice on room function, traffic, and desired comfort.

Step 4: Select a Layering Rug
Smaller size, complementary pattern, or contrasting texture.

Step 5: Integrate Complementary Textiles
Pillows, throws, curtains, and upholstery to enhance visual balance.

Step 6: Test and Adjust
Review and modify placements for visual harmony and practical comfort.

QUICK RUG & TEXTILE LAYERING CHECKLIST

Use this practical checklist as a final evaluation:

- Rug size proportional to space
- Rugs and textiles complement each other in color and pattern
- Adequate balance between texture, pattern, and color

- Functional material choices based on room usage
- Visual and tactile comfort achieved
- Layered textiles enhance overall aesthetic without overwhelming space

COMMON RUG & TEXTILE MISTAKES TO AVOID

MISTAKE	HOW TO CORRECT
Rug Too Small	Choose larger size based on furniture layout
Overwhelming Patterns	Pair busy rugs with simpler textiles
Ignoring Material & Function	Match rug durability to room use
Poor Textile Balance	Distribute color and texture strategically

CONCLUSION

Rugs whisper character across a room the way seasoned floors once did, grounding everything in quiet confidence. Layered thoughtfully, they soften acoustics, define proportion, and infuse a tactile rhythm that walls alone cannot provide. A hint of cashmere-soft wool alongside a nubby jute border creates dialogue between refinement and rustic ease; matte cotton runners add punctuation, guiding the gaze without ceremony. Color lives differently when filtered through pile and weave—deep indigo absorbs afternoon light, while cinnamon notes glow at dusk, coaxing warmth from every surface.

Pattern, too, becomes narrative rather than decoration: a vintage kilim hints at distant craftsmanship, a modern geometric tuft promises playful clarity, yet together they create a story uniquely tethered to the present occupant. Textiles manage climate, inviting bare feet in winter and cool respite in August. Within such layered luxury, life unspools gracefully, every footstep cushioned by intention and beauty that lingers long after dusk.

Kitchen
AND DINING AREAS

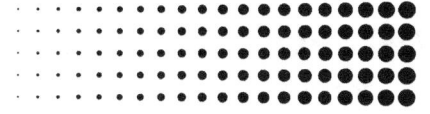

CHAPTER 7

Optimal Kitchen Layouts:
ISLAND, L-SHAPE, U-SHAPE, GALLEY

Morning light pours across polished quartz, revealing the choreography at the centre of every well-composed kitchen. Shapes may vary—an expanse anchored by a sculptural island, an L that hugs the room's perimeter, a generous U with arms that welcome, or a streamlined galley built for precision—but each arrangement succeeds when form listens to function. Paths glide without collision, work surfaces align with instinct, and appliances sit like seasoned sous-chefs, ready at the perfect reach. The island layout becomes a social stage where simmering pots share conversation with bar-height stools. An L-shape, graceful in modest footprints, grants clear sight-lines so one can sauté while admiring garden blooms. The enveloping U offers full immersion, tools circling the cook like a bespoke atelier.

Meanwhile, the galley, beloved by culinary purists, channels movement in a deliberate, almost nautical rhythm, every step calculated yet effortless. Hardware gleams, cabinetry whispers its soft-close promise, and layered lighting paints zones of focus and repose. Consider how aromas travel, how steam escapes, how the clink of glasses plays against marble or oak; these sensory notes reveal whether the chosen geometry truly serves the life unfolding within it. Crafting such synergy is less about following rigid templates than recognising the subtle dialogue between architecture and appetite, between familial bustle and solitary midnight tea. In the right configuration, the kitchen transcends utility, evolving into a habitat where nourishment, style, and memory find perfect alignment and welcomes gatherings that have yet arrived.

WHY YOUR KITCHEN LAYOUT MATTERS

An ideal kitchen layout does more than improve aesthetics—it enhances your daily routine by promoting efficiency, comfort, and ease of use. Before we explore each layout, consider these core concepts:

The Kitchen Work Triangle: The triangle formed between the stove, refrigerator, and sink. Optimal layouts reduce distances between these points, facilitating ease of movement.

Traffic Flow: Well-planned layouts minimize congestion and allow multiple people to comfortably use the space simultaneously.

Storage Accessibility: Thoughtful layouts ensure commonly used items are conveniently within reach.

01 ISLAND KITCHENS

Island kitchens are open, inviting, and incredibly functional. An island serves as a multifunctional centerpiece, ideal for cooking, dining, storage, and entertaining.

BEST FOR:

Large, open floor plans, families or those who frequently entertain

KEY FEATURES & BENEFITS:

- Additional countertop workspace
- Informal dining area with bar seating
- Convenient extra storage beneath the island
- Potential for appliance integration (sinks, cooktops, wine coolers)

IMPORTANT DIMENSIONS:

- Minimum clearance of 36-42 inches around the island for comfortable movement
- Ideal island width: 2-4 feet; Length: typically 4-10 feet, depending on kitchen size

POPULAR ISLAND CONFIGURATIONS:

- Cooking-focused island (integrated stove)
- Social-centric island (bar seating, entertaining zone)

Island size: Width (2-4 feet), Length (4-10 feet).

Minimum clearance: 36-42 inches around the island.

COOKING-FOCUSED ISLAND
Stove Integrated

Island size: Width (2-4 feet), Length (6-10 feet).

Minimum clearance: 36-42 inches around the island.

SOCIAL-CENTRIC ISLAND
Informal seating & entertainment area

FUNCITIONAL ISLAND
Sink, dishwasher, storage integration

02 L-SHAPED KITCHENS

L-shaped kitchens are highly versatile, working well in both compact and spacious homes. This layout places cabinets and appliances along two adjoining walls, forming an "L".

BEST FOR:

Small to medium-sized kitchens, open-plan spaces or studios, maximizing corner space

KEY FEATURES & BENEFITS:

- Efficient workflow with natural work triangle formation
- Easy integration of dining tables or islands
- Optimizes corner storage with rotating shelves or pull-out units

IDEAL DIMENSIONS:

Maintain a minimum distance of 4-6 feet between major appliances for optimal functionality.

COMMON L-SHAPE VARIATIONS:

- Basic L-shape with free-standing table or island
- Extended L-shape (with peninsula counter or additional seating area)

03 U-SHAPED KITCHENS

Known as the most efficient layout for cooks, a U-shaped kitchen maximizes counter and storage space by placing cabinets and appliances around three walls.

BEST FOR:

Medium to large kitchens, passionate cooks requiring expansive workspace, kitchens with dedicated zones for cooking, prepping, and cleaning

KEY FEATURES & BENEFITS:

- Excellent workflow with minimized distance between workstations
- Large countertop space ideal for multiple cooks
- Storage options for cookware and pantry items

IDEAL DIMENSIONS:

Minimum clearance of 42-48 inches between parallel countertops for comfortable movement

POPULAR U-SHAPE ENHANCEMENTS:

- Central island addition (for larger U-shaped kitchens)
- Peninsula extension creating informal dining or workspace

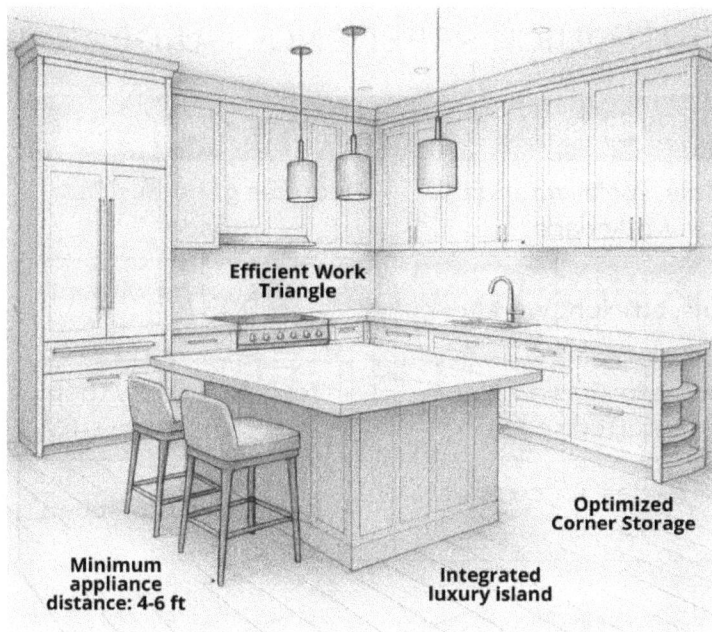

Efficient Work Triangle

Optimized Corner Storage

Minimum appliance distance: 4-6 ft

Integrated luxury island

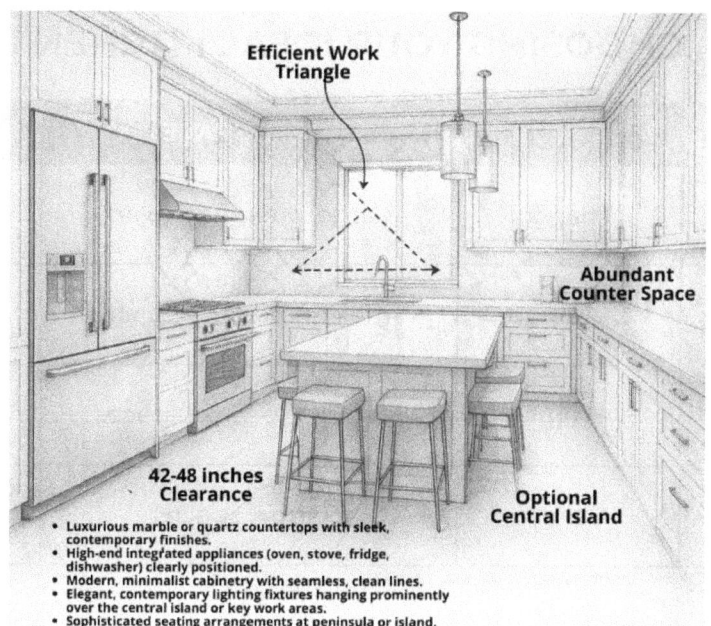

Efficient Work Triangle

Abundant Counter Space

42-48 inches Clearance

Optional Central Island

- Luxurious marble or quartz countertops with sleek, contemporary finishes.
- High-end integrated appliances (oven, stove, fridge, dishwasher) clearly positioned.
- Modern, minimalist cabinetry with seamless, clean lines.
- Elegant, contemporary lighting fixtures hanging prominently over the central island or key work areas.
- Sophisticated seating arrangements at peninsula or island.

04 GALLEY KITCHENS

Also known as corridor kitchens, Galley kitchens feature two parallel counters, providing efficient and compact workspace. This layout is renowned for efficiency and ease of use in smaller spaces.

BEST FOR:

- Narrow, elongated spaces
- Compact apartments and condos
- Efficient cooking spaces requiring minimal steps

KEY FEATURES & BENEFITS:

- Exceptional efficiency with everything within reach
- Easy and affordable layout to install
- Enhanced functionality in limited square footage

IMPORTANT DIMENSIONS:

Optimal distance of 36-48 inches between parallel counters for comfortable workflow and easy appliance access

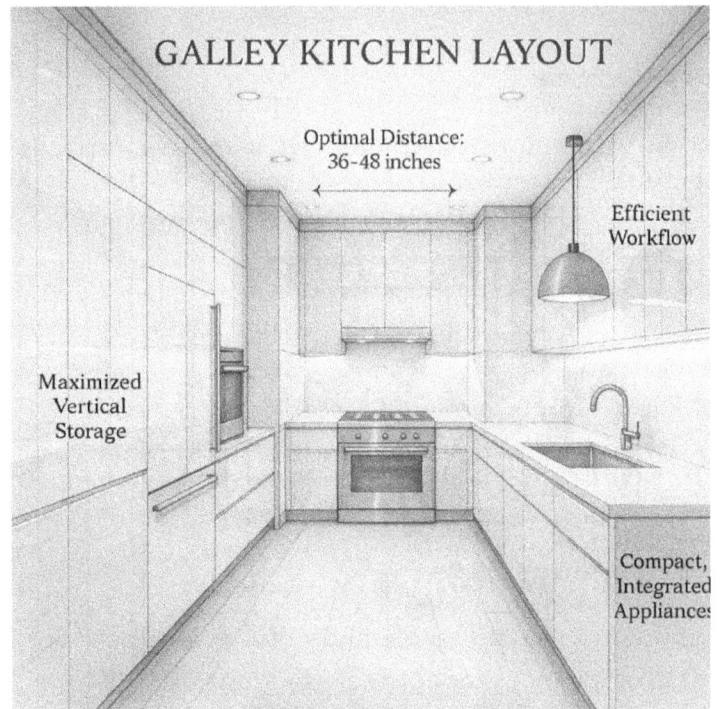

GALLEY KITCHEN LAYOUT

Optimal Distance: 36-48 inches

Efficient Workflow

Maximized Vertical Storage

Compact, Integrated Appliances

EXPERT TIPS FOR GALLEY KITCHENS:

- Bright lighting and reflective surfaces to open the space visually
- Maximized vertical storage to reduce clutter
- Compact appliances and streamlined cabinetry for seamless integration

CHOOSING YOUR IDEAL KITCHEN LAYOUT: QUICK REFERENCE GUIDE

LAYOUT	IDEAL SPACE	PROS	CONS
Island	Large, open floor plan	Versatile, social, abundant workspace	Requires generous floor space
L-shaped	Small to medium spaces	Flexible, efficient workflow	Limited storage without an island
U-shaped	Medium to large spaces	Maximum storage and countertop space	Can feel enclosed without openness
Galley	Narrow spaces	Efficient, ideal for compact spaces	Limited social interaction

FINAL CONSIDERATIONS FOR CHOOSING A LAYOUT

As you finalize your kitchen's layout, reflect on the rhythms of daily life. Consider how often you simmer sauces for gatherings or breeze through morning routines with a cup of coffee. Measure available square footage against the movement between sink, stove, and refrigerator, ensuring each triangle feels natural. Factor in the number of guests you host, from casual brunches to formal dinner parties, adapting aspirations to your space's practical parameters.

No single arrangement suits every home; each configuration reveals its virtues through your habits and room geometry. Pay attention to natural light, material textures to heighten the sense of luxury. Embrace the design principles but let your story guide the selection, creating a kitchen that harmonizes functionality with refined elegance.

COMMON KITCHEN LAYOUT MISTAKES TO AVOID

Ignoring Workflow: Always prioritize the kitchen work triangle connecting sink, stove, and refrigerator. Neglecting this essential alignment forces excessive steps, disrupts meal preparation flow, and can create congestion when multiple family members or guests share the space during busy moments.

Overlooking Storage: Ensure ample, well-placed storage solutions tailored to your routines. Failing to account for cookware sizes, pantry organization, and everyday essentials often leads to cluttered counters, wasted vertical space, and frustration when unpacking groceries or reaching for frequently used items.

Incorrect Island Dimensions: Avoid overcrowding by maintaining at least 107 cm (42 inches) of clearance around the island. An island that is too large or small can hinder appliance accessibility, obstruct traffic flow, and undermine seating comfort for breakfasts or entertaining gatherings.

Poor Lighting: Integrate layered lighting strategies, combining under-cabinet task lights, pendant fixtures, and ambient sources. Inadequate illumination casts shadows on work surfaces, strains the eyes during even detailed tasks, and diminishes the kitchen's inviting atmosphere, compromising both function and design appeal.

QUICK LAYOUT SELECTION CHECKLIST

- Kitchen size and available space assessment
- Workflow efficiency (kitchen triangle)
- Traffic flow analysis (multiple cooks, guests)
- Adequate clearance for movement
- Storage solutions integration
- Appliance accessibility and arrangement
- Social and entertainment functionality

CONCLUSION

Your kitchen's layout is far more than just a floor plan; it's the very foundation of your daily life, profoundly influencing everything from the seamlessness of your culinary endeavors to the joy of social gatherings. The thoughtful selection of a layout, be it a dynamic Island, an adaptable L-shape, a capacious U-shape, or an efficient Galley, is paramount. Informed planning ensures your kitchen beautifully merges essential functionality, effortless flow, and sophisticated style into a truly seamless living experience. This isn't merely about aesthetics; it's about crafting a space that truly works for you.

To confidently navigate these pivotal decisions, leverage the insights within this guide and the accompanying illustrations. They are your trusted companions in envisioning and actualizing a kitchen that not only meets your practical needs but also elevates your culinary space from the ordinary to the extraordinary. Embrace this opportunity to create a haven where memories are made and daily life unfolds with grace and ease.

Cabinetry, Countertops
& BACKSPLASH GUIDE

In a kitchen, the elements you choose for cabinetry, countertops, and backsplash dramatically influence both aesthetics and functionality. They set the tone, create visual harmony, and impact daily usage. In this guide, we'll delve deep into how to select, combine, and maximize these three key features, equipping you to create a kitchen that perfectly reflects your personal style and cooking habits.

01 CABINETRY: THE BACKBONE OF KITCHEN DESIGN

Cabinetry shapes your kitchen's character, organization, and efficiency. Choosing the right cabinets can trasform an ordinary kitchen into a highly functional and elegant space.

MATERIALS: PROS, CONS, AND APPLICATIONS

MATERIAL	PROS	CONS	BEST SUITED FOR
Solid Wood	Timeless appeal, durable, refinishing possible	Sensitive to humidity, expensive	Traditional, Farmhouse, Luxury
Plywood	Durable, stable, resistant to moisture	Slightly higher cost	All kitchen styles
MDF	Smooth finish, affordable, ideal for paint	Vulnerable to moisture damage	Modern, painted cabinetry
Laminate	Economical, easy maintenance, numerous finishes	Lower durability, harder repair	Contemporary, budget-friendly

SOLID WOOD
Well-defined wood grain
Luxurious Finish

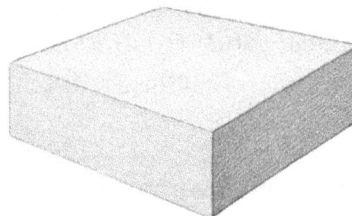

MDF
Smooth finish for painting
Uniform composition

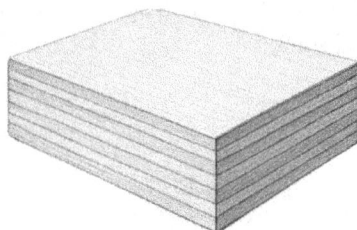

PLY WOOD
Cross-sectional ayers
Stability and durability

LAMINATE
Sleek appearance
Synthetic layered structure

DOOR STYLES: DEFINING YOUR AESTHETIC

- **Shaker Style**: Simple, clean lines suitable for modern, transitional, or traditional kitchens.
- **Raised Panel**: Elegant and traditional; ideal for classic, formal kitchens.
- **Flat-Panel** (Slab): Minimalist and sleek, perfect for modern or contemporary designs.
- **Glass-Front**: Provides visual openness, ideal for displaying dishware or collectibles.

Design Tip: Combine styles (e.g., shaker cabinets with a few glass-front doors) for visual interest and functionality.

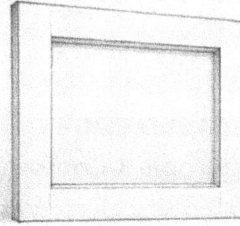

Shaker Style
Simple, Clean Lines

Raised Panel
Classic & Elegant

Flat-Panel (Slab):
Minimalist & Modern

Glass-Front
Visual Openness

02 COUNTERTOPS: A BALANCE OF BEAUTY AND DURABILITY

Countertops are work surfaces and major visual focal points. Selecting the right countertop involves balancing aesthetics, practicality, and budget.

POPULAR COUNTERTOP MATERIALS COMPARISON

MATERIAL	PROS	CONS	IDEAL USE
Quartz	Durable, non-porous, low-maintenance	Higher initial cost	High-use kitchens, modern aesthetic
Granite	Natural beauty, heat resistant, unique patterns	Requires sealing, moderate upkeep	Classic or luxurious kitchen
Marble	Elegant, cool surface ideal for baking	Susceptible to stains, regular sealing needed	Luxury, low-use areas, baking stations
Laminate	Affordable, variety of designs, easy maintenance	Less durable, sensitive to heat	Budget-friendly remodels
Butcher Block	Warm appearance, easy refinishing, practical for chopping	High maintenance, susceptible to water damage	Farmhouse, rustic, culinary enthusiasts

EDGE STYLES: FINE DETAILING

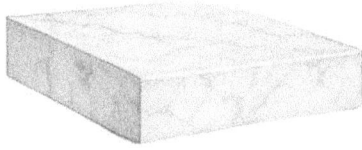

EASED EDGE
Simple & Contemporary

BULLNOSE EDGE
Safe, rounded, family-friendly

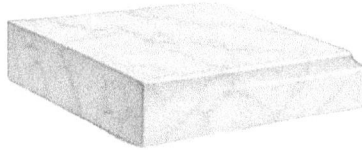

BEVELED EDGE
Adds depth, traditional appeal

OGEE EDGE
Classic, luxurious detail

03 BACKSPLASHES: THE KITCHEN'S ACCENT WALL

Backsplashes protect your walls and set visual tone. They provide an excellent opportunity to introduce color, texture, and pattern.

CHOOSING THE PERFECT MATERIAL

MATERIAL	CHARACTERISTICS & STYLE	PROS & CONS
Ceramic Tile	Classic, versatile, variety of shapes and colors	Easy maintenance; grout may stain
Glass Tile	Modern, reflective, sleek look	Easy cleaning; installation tricky
Natural Stone	Timeless, luxurious, unique variations	Requires sealing, porous surface
Stainless Steel	Industrial look, easy maintenance	Fingerprints visible; scratches possible
Subway Tile	Timeless, versatile design, suits most styles	Widely popular; requires grout upkeep

DESIGNING PATTERNS & LAYOUTS

- **Horizontal Stacked**: Clean and contemporary.
- **Herringbone**: Dynamic, visual depth, luxurious feel.
- **Chevron**: Sophisticated zigzag, energetic appearance.
- **Vertical Stacked**: Heightens ceilings visually.

Design Tip: Pair simple cabinetry with bold backsplash patterns for maximum impact.

KITCHEN BACKSPLASH: PATTERNS AND LAYOUTS

HORIZONTAL STACKED
Clean & Contemporary

HERRINGBONE
Dynamic & Luxurious

CHEVRON
Sophisticated & Energetic

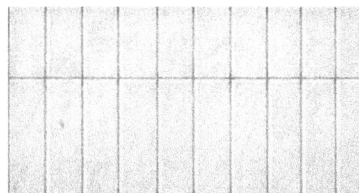

VERTICAL STACKED
Visually Heightening

CREATING VISUAL HARMONY: COMBINING CABINETS, COUNTERTOPS, AND BACKSPLASHES

Guidelines for Successful Combinations:

1. Balance Boldness with Simplicity: If cabinets are boldly colored, choose subtle countertops and backsplash, or vice versa.
2. Coordinate Color Palettes: Maintain color cohesion by using complementary or analogous colors.
3. Mix Textures Thoughtfully: Contrast smooth cabinetry with textured backsplash materials or countertops.

Practical Combination Examples:

- Modern Kitchen: Flat-panel cabinetry, quartz countertops, glass-tile backsplash.
- Farmhouse Kitchen: Shaker cabinetry, butcher-block or granite countertops, ceramic subway tile backsplash.
- Luxury Traditional: Raised-panel cabinetry, marble countertops, natural stone backsplash.

QUICK SELECTION CHECKLIST

- Choose cabinetry style/material considering function and aesthetics.
- Select countertop material based on lifestyle and maintenance preference.
- Identify backsplash that complements cabinetry and countertops.

- Determine appropriate edge profile for your countertop.
- Verify maintenance requirements align with your lifestyle.

CONCLUSION

Selecting the perfect cabinetry, countertops, and backsplashes lies at the heart of kitchen design that exudes both elegance and lasting appeal. Begin by choosing door styles and finishes that echo the room's architectural details—think subtle shaker profiles in soft, muted hues or sleek, high-gloss panels that catch natural light. Pair these with countertop materials whose textures and veining tell a story of craftsmanship, whether honed marble surfaces or the organic warmth of soapstone. Elevate the ensemble with a thoughtfully chosen backsplash: a hand-crafted mosaic tile or marble slab that subtly bridges form and function.

When each surface speaks the same refined language—complementing one another in color, scale, and pattern—you achieve a seamless tableau. This harmonious layering ensures your kitchen remains not only supremely practical but also an enduring expression of sophistication that will grace your home for years to come.

Lighting & Fixtures
ILLUSTRATED

In interior design, lighting is transformative—it shapes atmosphere, directs attention, and significantly impacts the functionality of any kitchen and dining space. Whether you're aiming for a cozy ambiance, clear task illumination, or dramatic visual statements, your lighting strategy is crucial. This guide takes you through various lighting types, fixtures, and effective strategies to illuminate your space brilliantly.

UNDERSTANDING TYPES OF LIGHTING

To expertly light your kitchen and dining area, combine three essential lighting categories:

01 AMBIENT LIGHTING

Ambient lighting offers overall illumination, ensuring even brightness throughout the space. Think of it as your foundational layer, setting the room's baseline lighting conditions.

Best Fixtures for Ambient Lighting:
- **Recessed Lights**: Discreet, functional, perfect for seamless integration.
- **Flush Mounts & Semi-Flush Mounts**: Ideal for kitchens with lower ceilings, providing diffused light.

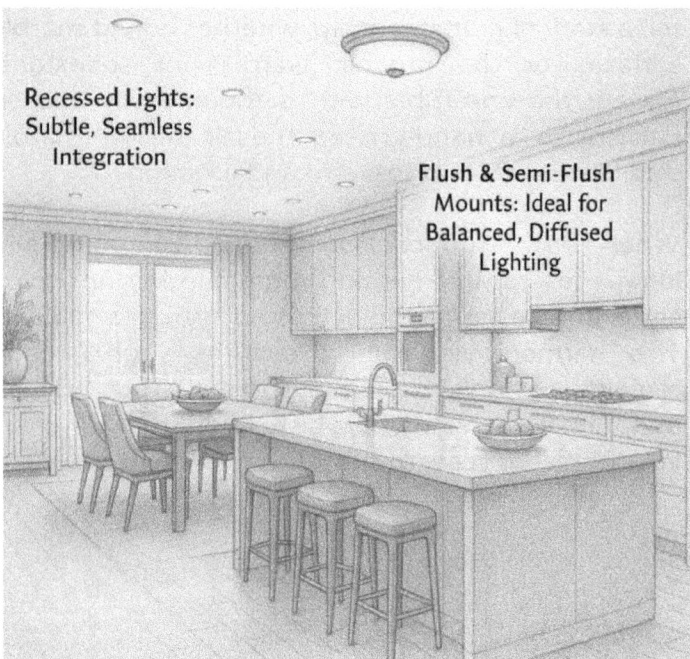

Recessed Lights: Subtle, Seamless Integration

Flush & Semi-Flush Mounts: Ideal for Balanced, Diffused Lighting

02 TASK LIGHTING

Task lighting is tailored to support specific activities such as cooking, meal preparation, or dining. It ensures safety and precision.

Effective Fixtures for Task Lighting:
- **Under-Cabinet Lighting**: Crucial for illuminating countertops, enhancing both safety and precision.
- **Pendant Lighting**: Excellent for illuminating kitchen islands and dining tables with focused beams.
- **Track Lighting**: Adjustable directionality, great for flexible task lighting needs.

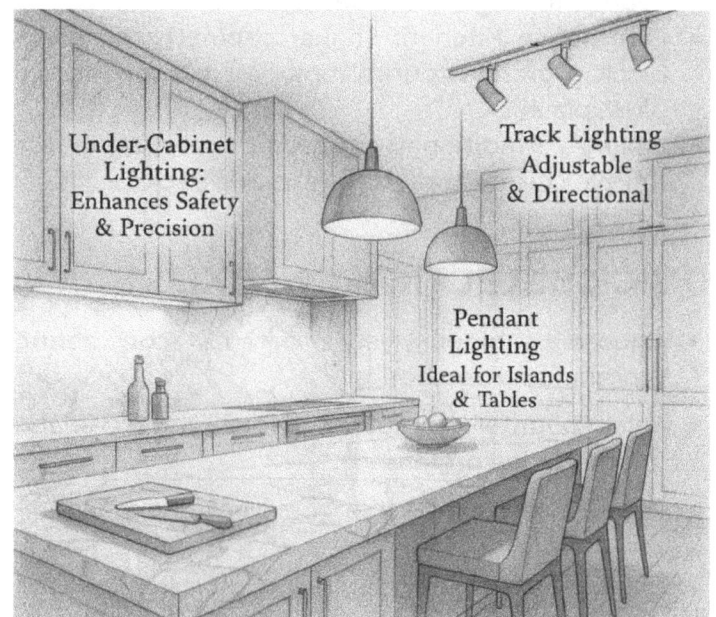

Under-Cabinet Lighting: Enhances Safety & Precision

Track Lighting Adjustable & Directional

Pendant Lighting Ideal for Islands & Tables

03 ACCENT LIGHTING

Accent lighting highlights specific features, such as artwork, architectural details, or decorative elements. It enhances visual interest and adds depth to your design.

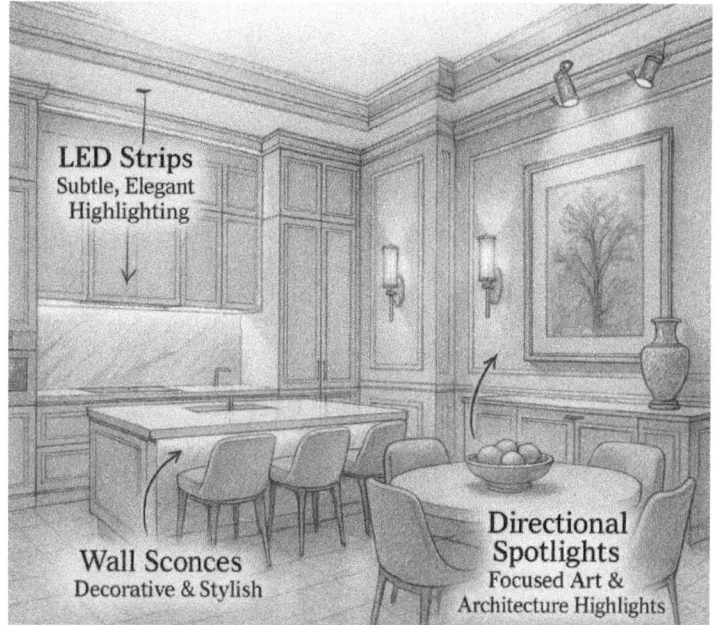

LED Strips
Subtle, Elegant Highlighting

Wall Sconces
Decorative & Stylish

Directional Spotlights
Focused Art & Architecture Highlights

Best Accent Fixtures:

- **LED Strips**: Flexible and discreet, ideal for showcasing cabinetry details, under-counter edges, or toe-kick areas. Their slim profile allows for seamless integration behind crown moulding or within shelving niches.

- **Wall Sconces**: Decorative, providing subtle yet focused highlights on framed prints, floating shelves, or textured walls. Choose dimmable options to adjust mood from bright task settings to soft evening ambiance.

- **Directional Spotlights**: Perfect for highlighting art or unique architectural features. Adjustable heads swivel to cast crisp pools of light on focal points—whether it's a sculptural vent hood or a statement backsplash.

- **In-Cabinet Puck Lights**: Compact circular fixtures mounted inside glass-front cabinets or open shelving. They deliver concentrated beams to illuminate fine china, stemware, or decorative collections with a jewel-like glow.

- **Track Lighting**: Versatile rail systems with multiple movable heads. Position each lamp precisely to accent bar seating, island décor, or accent walls—allowing you to reconfigure lighting layouts as your décor evolves.

ESSENTIAL FIXTURE TYPES ILLUSTRATED

The design of your lighting fixtures significantly influences both functionality and aesthetics. Here are critical fixture types, each offering distinct visual and practical benefits:

FIXTURE TYPE	DESCRIPTION	IDEAL PLACEMENT
Pendant	Suspended from the ceiling by a cord or chain	Over kitchen islands, dining tables
Chandelier	Ornate, multi-light fixture for dramatic impact	Dining rooms, large open-plan kitchens
Recessed	Hidden within ceilings, sleek and modern	Kitchens needing clean lines, contemporary styles
Track	Adjustable fixtures on tracks, customizable	Flexible layouts, modern or industrial kitchens
Flush Mount	Mounted flush with ceiling; minimal visual footprint	Kitchens with low ceilings, hallways
Wall Sconce	Mounted on walls, adding subtle illumination	Accent walls, dining areas, corridors

LIGHTING FIXTURE TYPES

PENDANT
Suspended Elegance

CHANDELIER
Dramatic Ornate Statement

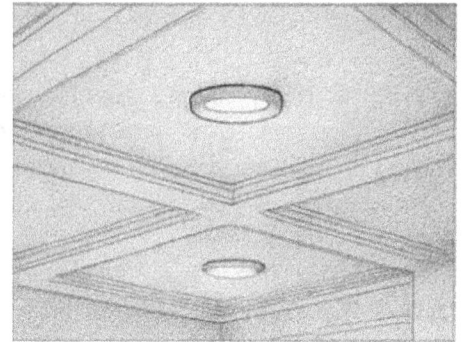

FLUSH MOUNT
Minimal Footprint

TRACK
Adjustable &
Customizable

WALL SCONCE
Subtle &
Decorative

BULB BASICS: CHOOSING THE RIGHT LIGHT

Bulb selection dramatically impacts color rendering, energy consumption, and visual comfort:

BULB TYPE	FEATURES & BENEFITS	IDEAL APPLICATION
LED	Energy-efficient, long lifespan, available in various color temperatures	Task and ambient lighting, eco-friendly
Incandescent	Warm color tone, traditional appeal	Accent and decorative fixtures
Halogen	Bright, white illumination, high-quality color rendering	Task lighting, highlighting artwork
CFL	Energy-efficient alternative, longer life than incandescent	Ambient lighting

Color Temperature Guide:

- **Warm White** (2700K-3000K): Cozy, inviting—ideal for dining spaces and ambient fixtures.
- **Neutral White** (3500K-4100K): Balanced, clear—great for task lighting areas like countertops.
- **Cool White** (5000K+): Crisp, energizing—recommended for ultra-modern kitchens and clear task lighting.

BULB TYPES

LED-BULB
Energy Efficient &
Long Lifespan

INCANDESCENT
Warm Tone &
Decorative

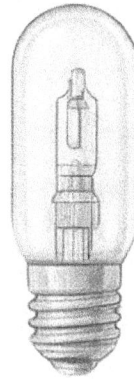

HALOGEN
Bright, White
Illumination

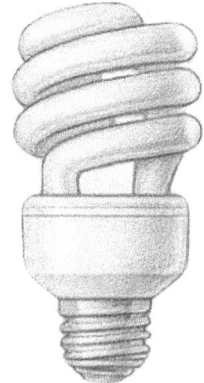

CFL
Energy-Efficient
Alternative

LIGHTING LAYOUT TIPS: KEY PLACEMENT RULES

Effectively placing your fixtures maximizes comfort, functionality, and visual harmony:

KITCHEN ISLANDS
Pendants or linear lights positioned approximately 30-36 inches above countertop height.

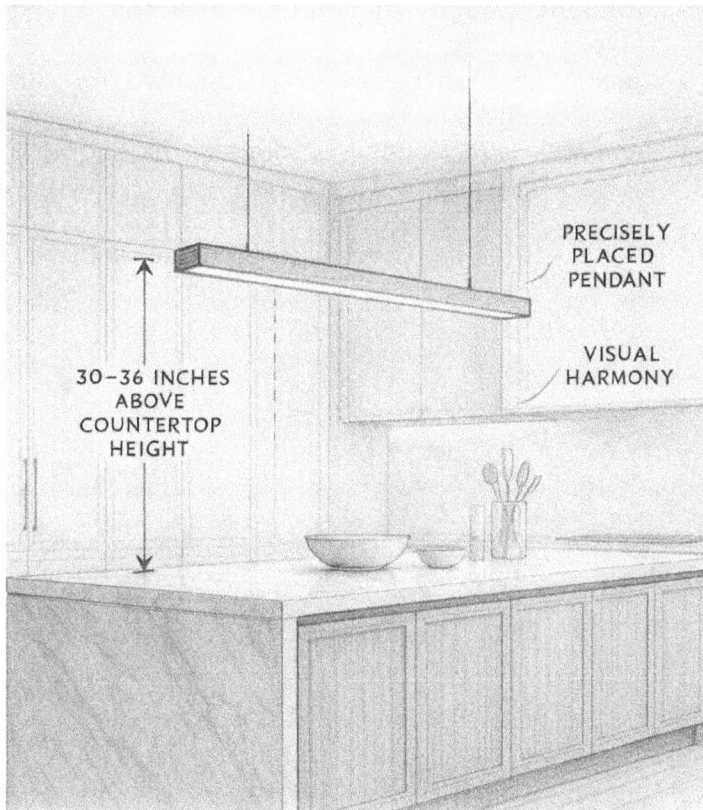

DINING TABLE
Chandeliers or pendant lights positioned 30-34 inches above tabletop, centered to ensure balanced illumination.

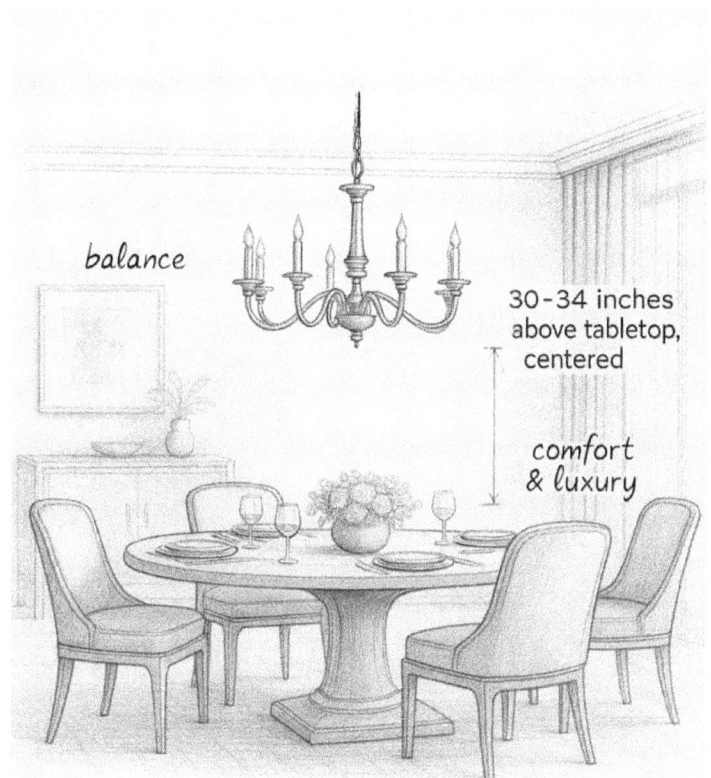

30–36 INCHES ABOVE COUNTERTOP HEIGHT

PRECISELY PLACED PENDANT

VISUAL HARMONY

balance

30-34 inches above tabletop, centered

comfort & luxury

UNDER-CABINET LIGHTING

LED strips or puck lights positioned towards the front edge of cabinetry to minimize shadows.

Lights mounted towards cabinet front edge for reduced shadows

RECESSED LIGHTING

Generally spaced 4-6 feet apart for even illumination, placed directly over key task areas.

Recessed lights 4–6 feet apart

ILLUMINATING EXAMPLES

To clarify ideal setups, here are detailed visual scenarios showcasing various lighting combinations:

1. MODERN KITCHEN EXAMPLE:

- **Ambient**: Recessed LED fixtures.
- **Task**: Under-cabinet LED strips, linear pendants above island.
- **Accent**: Directional spotlights showcasing open shelving.

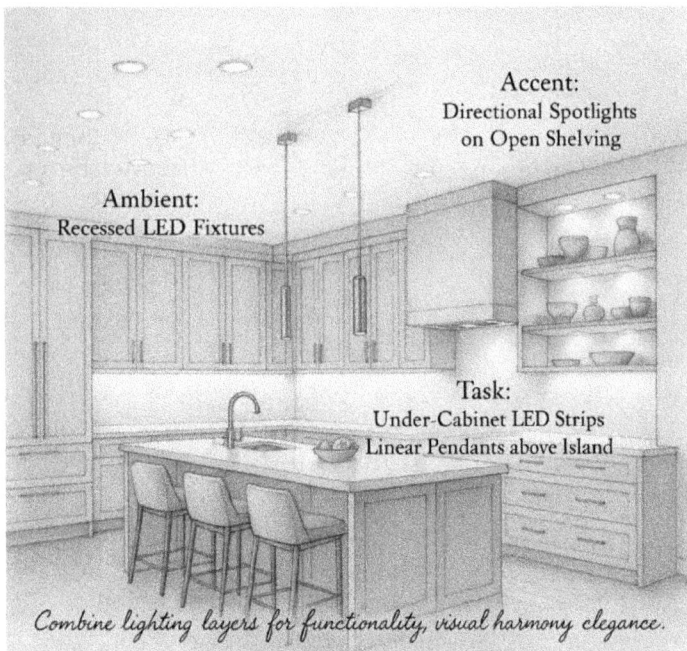

Accent: Directional Spotlights on Open Shelving

Ambient: Recessed LED Fixtures

Task: Under-Cabinet LED Strips Linear Pendants above Island

Combine lighting layers for functionality, visual harmony elegance.

2. TRADITIONAL DINING AREA EXAMPLE:

- **Ambient**: Chandelier centered over the dining table.
- **Task**: Wall sconces flanking sideboard for soft supplementary light.
- **Accent**: Directional spotlights highlighting artwork on walls.

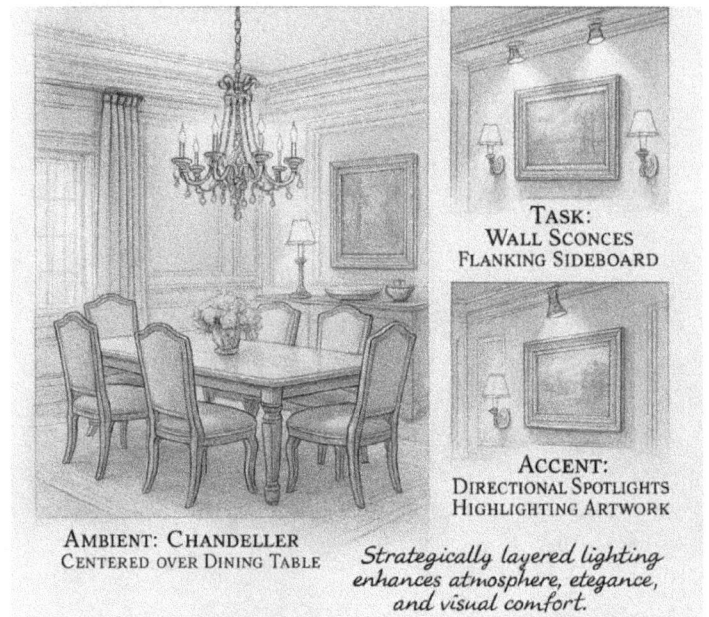

TASK: WALL SCONCES FLANKING SIDEBOARD

ACCENT: DIRECTIONAL SPOTLIGHTS HIGHLIGHTING ARTWORK

AMBIENT: CHANDELIER CENTERED OVER DINING TABLE

Strategically layered lighting enhances atmosphere, elegance, and visual comfort.

PRACTICAL LIGHTING CHECKLIST

Use this checklist to ensure comprehensive kitchen and dining area lighting:

- **Ambient Lighting**: Establish even base illumination.
- **Task Lighting**: Provide targeted illumination for cooking, prepping, and dining.
- **Accent Lighting**: Highlight key features and add visual depth.
- **Fixture Selection**: Align fixture styles with kitchen aesthetic.
- **Bulb Choices**: Select suitable bulb types and color temperatures.
- **Placement**: Ensure correct distances and heights for optimal function and comfort.

LIGHTING CONTROLS AND DIMMER SWITCHES

Lighting control is an often-overlooked element that enhances convenience and adaptability:

- **Dimmer Switches**: Essential for setting various moods, allowing you to finely tune brightness for precise cooking tasks in the morning or a softer glow during evening gatherings.
- **Motion Sensors**: Ideal for pantries, closets, or storage areas—automatically detecting movement to illuminate small spaces only when needed, reducing energy waste and hands-free convenience when your arms are full.
- **Smart Home Controls**: Offer remote and programmable operation via smartphone apps or voice assistants, enabling personalized schedules, away-mode security lighting, and the flexibility to adjust scenes from anywhere.

MAINTENANCE & SUSTAINABILITY

Keep lighting efficient and fixtures visually appealing with minimal effort:

TASK	FREQUENCY	TIPS
Cleaning fixtures	Every 1-3 months	Use microfiber cloth to avoid scratching
Checking bulbs and LEDs	Annually	Replace failing bulbs immediately
Inspecting wiring/switches	Every 1-2 years	Ensure connections remain safe

Eco-Friendly Tip: Always select LED bulbs for reduced energy consumption and greater sustainability.

CONCLUSION

Lighting is not merely functional; it's an essential part of the design language of your kitchen and dining area. With careful consideration of ambient, task, and accent lighting, combined with thoughtfully chosen fixtures and effective placement strategies, you can significantly elevate your living experience. Embrace the opportunity lighting offers to transform your kitchen and dining space into an elegant, inviting, and highly functional environment.

Styling the Dining Space
(FORMAL & INFORMAL DINING)

The dining area of a home holds a unique status. It's more than just a place to eat—it's a canvas for celebrating special occasions, sharing everyday meals, or simply gathering for meaningful conversation. Whether you prefer the timeless elegance of a formal setting or the relaxed comfort of informal dining, each style demands careful curation to perfectly align with your lifestyle. In this chapter, we explore detailed guidelines to style formal and informal dining spaces, ensuring each meal feels effortlessly special.

FORMAL DINING: CREATING ELEGANT EXPERIENCES

A formal dining room epitomizes sophistication, tradition, and structure. It's designed for entertaining guests, special occasions, and holiday dinners, where attention to detail is paramount.

FURNITURE ESSENTIALS:

- **Dining Table**: Choose substantial tables—rectangular or oval—with finishes like rich hardwood, marble, or glass tops paired with refined wooden bases.
- **Dining Chairs**: Upholstered chairs with graceful silhouettes, cushioned seats, and supportive backs elevate comfort and style.
- **Sideboard or Buffet**: Essential for storage and serving convenience, complementing your table's style and finish.

STYLING THE FORMAL TABLE: KEY ELEMENTS
Table Linens & Textiles:
- Opt for premium tablecloths or runners in subtle shades or refined patterns. Linen or silk fabrics enhance elegance.
- Cloth napkins coordinated with tablecloths complete the cohesive look.

Dinnerware & Glassware:
- Formal china sets featuring understated designs or gold/silver trims.
- Crystal stemware for water, wine, and champagne, meticulously arranged by height and usage.

Flatware & Cutlery: Polished silver or high-quality stainless steel placed meticulously in correct formal dining etiquette positions.

Centerpieces & Decorative Accents: Classic floral arrangements, elegant candelabras, or sculptural centerpieces ensure the table remains visually balanced without obstructing sightlines.

Dining Table
Luxurious finishes, substantial size for formal exteraining.

Dining Chairs
Upholstered comfort, refined silhouette.

Sideboard/Buffet
Essential storage and serving convenience.

Formal dining spaces blend sophistication, comfort, and meticulous attention to detail for memorable gatherings.

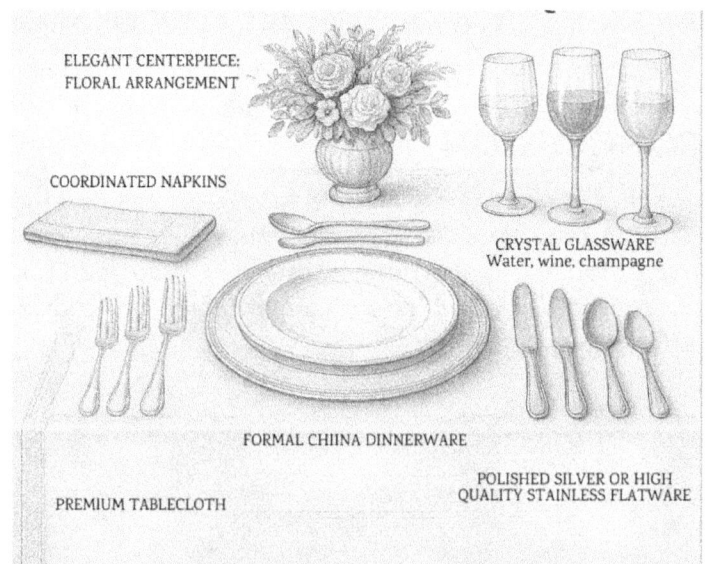

ELEGANT CENTERPIECE: FLORAL ARRANGEMENT

COORDINATED NAPKINS

CRYSTAL GLASSWARE
Water, wine, champagne

FORMAL CHIINA DINNERWARE

PREMIUM TABLECLOTH

POLISHED SILVER OR HIGH QUALITY STAINLESS FLATWARE

LIGHTING & AMBIANCE:

- Chandeliers or pendant lights positioned centrally above the table, combined with wall sconces for a layered lighting approach.
- Dimmer switches for adjustable lighting to set the mood appropriate for formal occasions.

INFORMAL DINING: INVITING COMFORT AND CASUAL ELEGANCE

An informal dining space emphasizes comfort, practicality, and versatility, often blending seamlessly with kitchen or living areas. It's designed to welcome daily meals and relaxed socializing.

FURNITURE CHOICES FOR INFORMAL SPACES:

- **Dining Table**: Round or square tables enhance conversation, while extendable tables provide flexibility.
- **Seating Options**: Benches, casual upholstered chairs, or a mix-and-match approach creates warmth and visual interest.
- **Storage & Display**: Open shelving or casual hutches display everyday dishes, glasses, or decorative accessories.

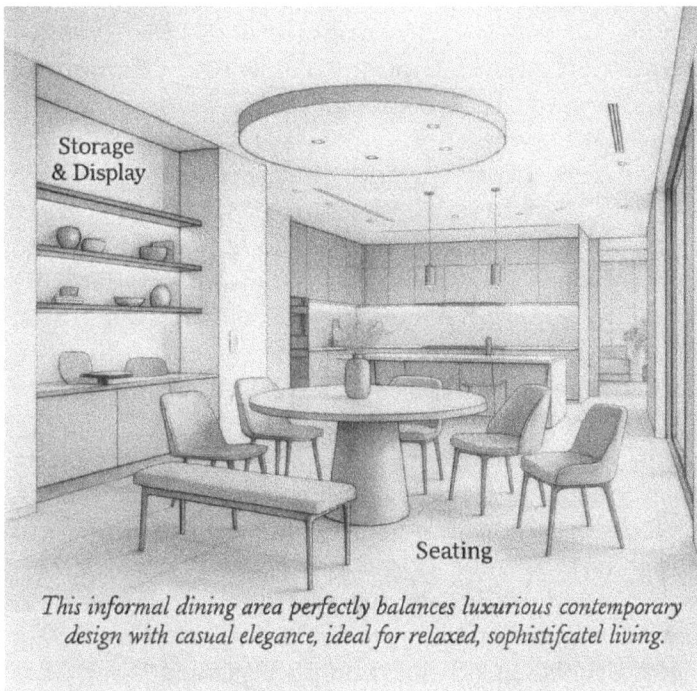

This informal dining area perfectly balances luxurious contemporary design with casual elegance, ideal for relaxed, sophistifcatel living.

CASUAL TABLE STYLING: PRACTICAL BEAUTY

Table Linens:
- Durable, washable fabrics in casual patterns or bright colors enhance daily usability.
- Placemats or runners provide informal texture and protect table surfaces.

Dinnerware & Glassware:
- Everyday ceramic or stoneware sets featuring playful patterns or rustic finishes.
- Versatile tumblers, sturdy glasses, or simple stemless wine glasses suited to daily use.

Flatware & Utensils:
- Durable, dishwasher-safe stainless steel or colorful handled flatware for daily practicality.

Centerpieces & Accessories:
- Simple, casual centerpieces like potted plants, seasonal fruits in decorative bowls, or small lanterns maintain visual charm without formality.

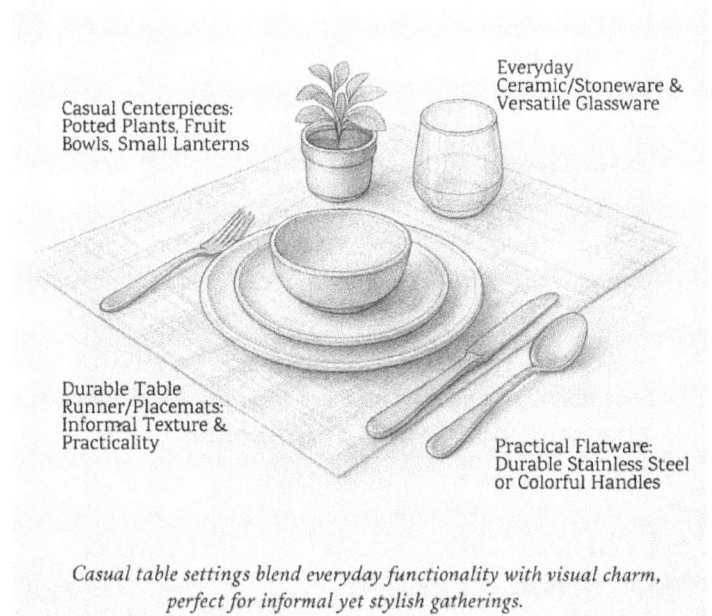

Casual table settings blend everyday functionality with visual charm, perfect for informal yet stylish gatherings.

LIGHTING & AMBIANCE FOR INFORMAL DINING:

- Mix overhead lighting (such as pendants or flush-mount fixtures) with natural light sources and adjustable accent lamps.
- Flexible lighting schemes that adjust easily from daytime meals to evening relaxation.

MAINTENANCE & SUSTAINABILITY

ELEMENT	FORMAL DINING	INFORMAL DINING
Table Shapes	Rectangular, Oval	Round, Square, Extendable
Furniture Style	Elegant, coordinated	Casual, eclectic, mixed
Seating	Upholstered, uniform sets	Mix-and-match, benches, casual seating
Lighting	Chandeliers, sconces	Pendants, flush mounts, accent lamps
Dinnerware	China, crystal stemware	Ceramic, stoneware, casual glassware
Textiles & Linens	Fine linens, matched napkins	Washable fabrics, placemats
Ambiance & Décor	Refined, structured, elegant	Relaxed, casual, comfortable

TIPS FOR FLEXIBLE DINING SPACES

Many modern homes require spaces that flex between formal and informal functions. Here are strategies for creating adaptable dining environments:

- **Versatile Furniture**: Extendable tables and stackable chairs accommodate both intimate dinners and larger gatherings effortlessly.
- **Convertible Lighting**: Adjustable dimming or smart controls facilitate transitions between casual brunches and formal dinners.
- **Modular Storage Solutions**: Mobile carts, convertible cabinets, or multipurpose sideboards that serve both formal and everyday needs.

STYLING CHECKLIST: FORMAL & INFORMAL DINING

Ensure your dining area meets its full potential using this practical checklist:

Formal Dining:
- Elegant dining furniture.
- High-quality table linens and napkins.
- Sophisticated dinnerware and flatware.
- Centerpiece and decorative accents.
- Adjustable layered lighting.

Informal Dining:
- Comfortable, flexible furniture arrangements.
- Durable, casual table linens and placemats.
- Practical, everyday dinnerware and glassware.
- Simple, casual centerpieces.
- Adaptable, relaxed lighting solutions.

CONCLUSION

Designing your dining space—whether for refined dinner parties, family breakfasts, or versatile use as a home office—unlocks opportunities for creative expression and thoughtful living. Thoughtful selection of table shapes and seating fosters convivial conversation, while layered lighting shifts the mood from daylight efficiency to candlelit warmth. Introduce texture via area rugs, upholstered chairs, or bespoke wallpaper to complement your home's architectural language. By weaving functional considerations such as traffic flow and storage into your aesthetic palette, you elevate everyday meals into lasting rituals.

Consider your lifestyle, entertaining frequency, and personal tastes when selecting chairs, table finishes, and decorative accents, transforming this room into the heart of your home. Whether you favor rich woods and sculptural centerpieces or linens and verdant greenery, curate elements that resonate with rituals and celebrations. Embrace adaptable layouts, artful textiles, and heirlooms to craft a dining haven where memorable experiences unfold at every gathering and occasion.

Bedrooms
AND CLOSETS

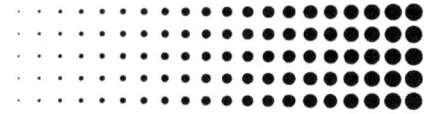

CHAPTER 8

DESIGNING THE PERFECT
Sleep Sanctuary

Your bedroom isn't merely a place to rest; it is your personal retreat—a haven where you begin and end each day. Inviting a sense of calm begins with a considered palette: muted greys, soft ivories, and whispering pastels create a tranquil backdrop, while accent hues in sumptuous textiles bring warmth. Layered linens and plush throws add tactile dimension, their gentle folds encouraging touch. Bespoke headboards, curved or geometric in form, anchor the space and reflect your individual style, while nightstands in contrasting materials—perhaps a lacquered finish against natural oak—elevate the tone. Lighting plays a pivotal role: a sculptural pendant overhead casts a soft glow, while bedside sconces offer adjustable illumination for reading or quiet reflection. Introduce a rug of artisanal weave beneath your bed to ground the design and soften footsteps.

Transforming your bedroom into a serene sanctuary involves careful orchestration of form and function. Position furniture to facilitate an easy flow around the bed, allowing movement to feel effortless. Conceal clutter with streamlined storage—consider built-in wardrobes with mirrored doors or under-bed drawers finished to match flooring. Carefully curated accessories—a single large botanical print, a handcrafted ceramic vase, or a cluster of decorative cushions—add character without overwhelm. Bring in living greenery such as a sculptural fern or a potted orchid to breathe life into the room. Finally, select window treatments that combine light-filtering sheers with blackout drapes to balance daylight and privacy. By weaving these elements together with intention, you'll craft the ultimate sleep sanctuary: a space that reflects comfort, tranquility, and your unique personality, inviting restorative rest night after night.

CREATING CALM THROUGH DESIGN PRINCIPLES

A truly restful bedroom should evoke peace from the moment you enter. Here's how to harness key interior design principles to foster calmness:

BALANCE AND HARMONY:

- Opt for symmetrical furniture arrangements or balanced asymmetry, which promote a serene visual flow.
- Consistent color tones and textures throughout the room enhance harmony.

SCALE AND PROPORTION:

- Choose furniture that matches the size of your room to prevent overcrowding or emptiness.
- A well-scaled bed acts as a comforting focal point without overpowering the space.

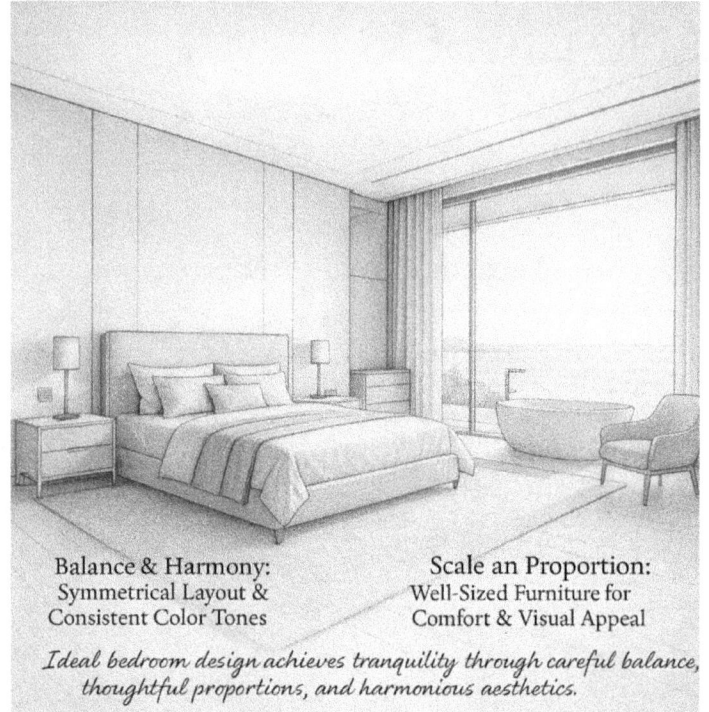

Balance & Harmony:
Symmetrical Layout &
Consistent Color Tones

Scale an Proportion:
Well-Sized Furniture for
Comfort & Visual Appeal

Ideal bedroom design achieves tranquility through careful balance, thoughtful proportions, and harmonious aesthetics.

COLOR CHOICES FOR A RESTFUL AMBIANCE

Colors profoundly impact our mood and sleep quality. Choosing the right palette is crucial:

COLOR CATEGORY	MOOD EFFECT	IDEAL USAGE IN BEDROOMS
Neutrals	Calm, grounding, timeless	Walls, bedding, upholstery
Cool Colors	Relaxing, tranquil, soothing	Accents, walls, textiles
Warm Colors	Cozy, inviting (in moderation)	Decorative accents, subtle touches

RECOMMENDED COLORS

Soft Neutrals		IVORY · BEIGE · TAUPE
Cool Shades		MUTED BLUES · LAVENDER · PALE GREENS
Warm Accents		SOFT BLUSH · TERRACOTTA · HONEY TONES

SELECTING THE PERFECT BED

The bed is the heart of your sleep sanctuary. Invest thoughtfully in your comfort:

BED FRAME & HEADBOARD:

- Upholstered headboards offer comfort and visual softness.

- Wooden or metal frames lend structure and timeless appeal.

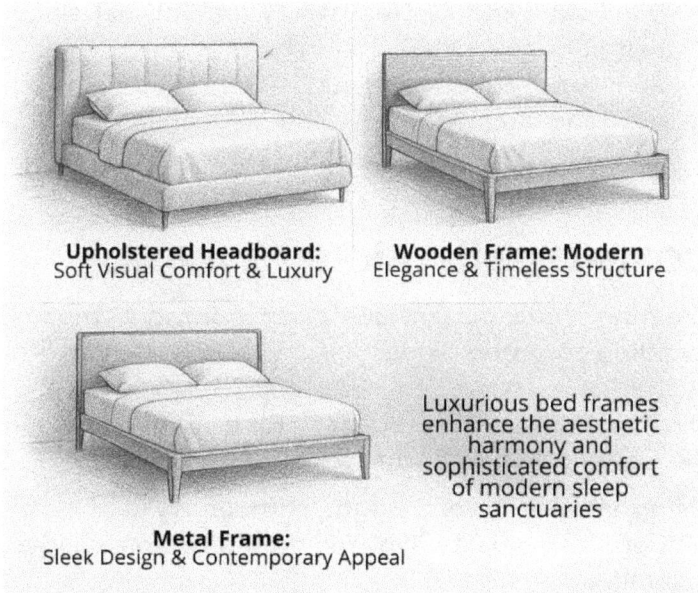

Upholstered Headboard:
Soft Visual Comfort & Luxury

Wooden Frame: Modern
Elegance & Timeless Structure

Luxurious bed frames enhance the aesthetic harmony and sophisticated comfort of modern sleep sanctuaries

Metal Frame:
Sleek Design & Contemporary Appeal

MATTRESS ESSENTIALS:

- Prioritize comfort, support, and durability. Explore memory foam, hybrid, or innerspring options to match your personal preference.

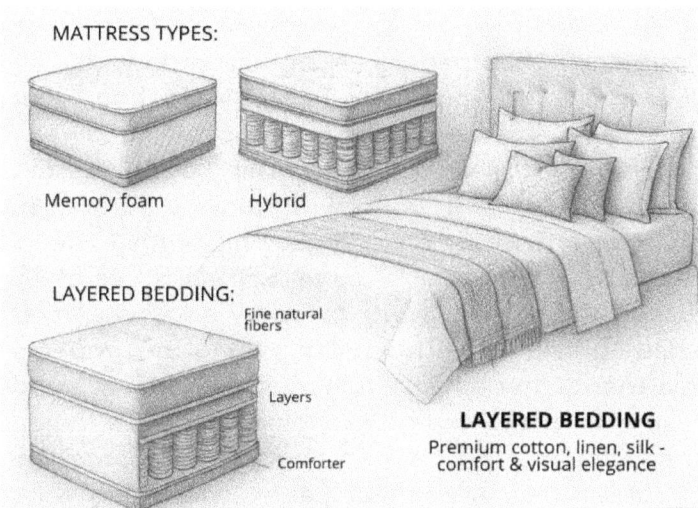

MATTRESS TYPES:

Memory foam   Hybrid

LAYERED BEDDING:

Fine natural fibers

Layers

Comforter

LAYERED BEDDING
Premium cotton, linen, silk - comfort & visual elegance

Luxury mattresses and thoughtfully layered bedding create the ultimate comfort and restful ambiance in ultra-modern bedrooms

BEDDING AND LINENS:

- Natural fibers like cotton, linen, or silk regulate temperature effectively.

- Layered bedding provides both visual appeal and flexibility in comfort.

OPTIMAL FURNITURE & LAYOUT

Furniture placement and choice contribute significantly to bedroom tranquility:

NIGHTSTANDS:

- Position bedside tables at arm's reach to comfortably accommodate necessities—lighting, books, and personal items.

DRESSERS & STORAGE:

- Utilize dressers, armoires, and under-bed storage solutions to maintain clutter-free serenity.

SEATING AREAS:

- Incorporate a cozy armchair, bench, or chaise lounge to create peaceful spaces for relaxation or reading.

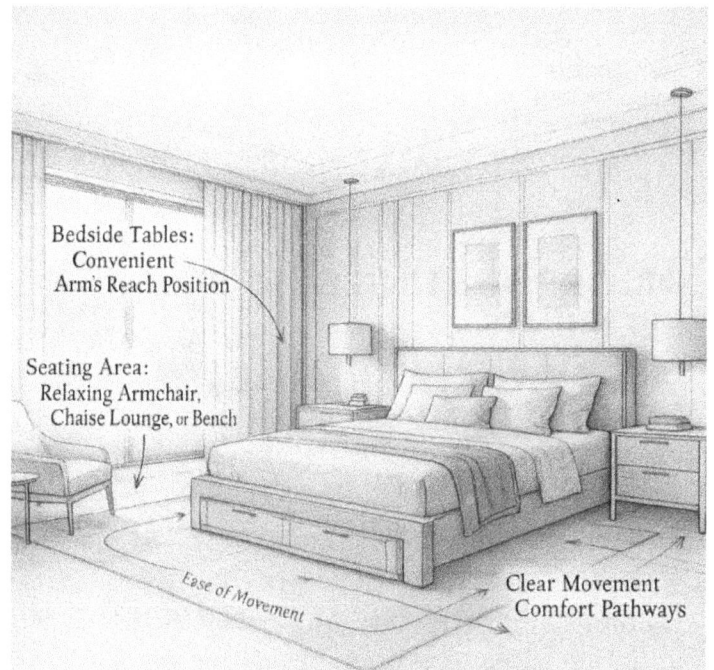

Bedside Tables:
Convenient
Arm's Reach Position

Seating Area:
Relaxing Armchair,
Chaise Lounge, or Bench

Ease of Movement

Clear Movement
Comfort Pathways

Thoughtful furniture arrangement creates a tranquil, luxurious sanctuary, ensuring both aesthetic harmony and daily comfort.

LIGHTING FOR RESTFULNESS

Lighting dramatically influences the bedroom's mood and sleep quality:

Ambient Lighting: Soft overhead fixtures or diffused lighting provide gentle illumination.

Task Lighting: Adjustable bedside lamps or sconces are essential for reading without disturbing your sleep partner.

Accent Lighting: Use subtle LED strips, candles, or decorative fixtures to create warmth and coziness.

Natural Light Control: Incorporate blackout curtains or shades to facilitate deep, uninterrupted sleep.

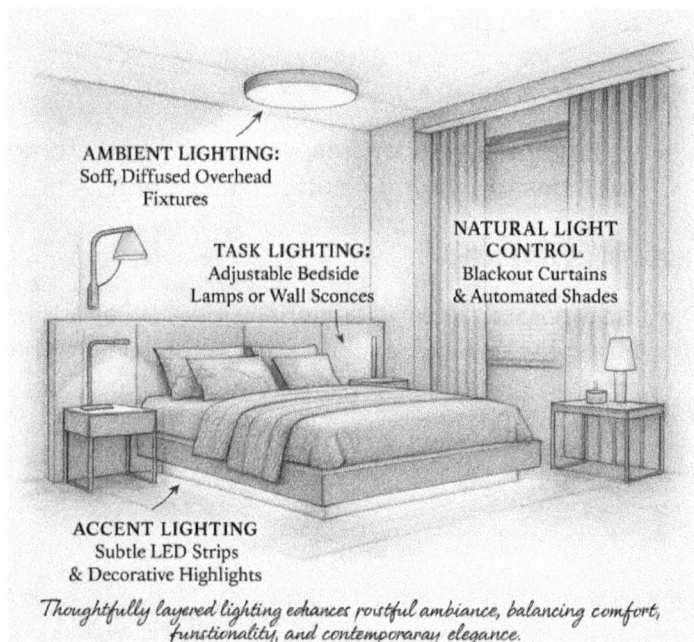

AMBIENT LIGHTING:
Soft, Diffused Overhead
Fixtures

TASK LIGHTING:
Adjustable Bedside
Lamps or Wall Sconces

NATURAL LIGHT
CONTROL
Blackout Curtains
& Automated Shades

ACCENT LIGHTING
Subtle LED Strips
& Decorative Highlights

Thoughtfully layered lighting echances restful ambiance, balancing comfort, functionality, and contemporaray elegance.

INCORPORATING SENSORY ELEMENTS

A true sleep sanctuary engages all senses:

Visual Calm: Minimalistic décor and simple wall art create visual serenity.

Auditory Relaxation: Soft ambient sound machines or gentle music enhance relaxation.

Tactile Comfort: Plush rugs, silky bedding, and upholstered surfaces offer inviting textures.

Aromatic Serenity: Essential oils, scented candles, or linen sprays with lavender, eucalyptus, or chamomile encourage relaxation.

BEDROOM SANCTUARY CHECKLIST

Ensure your bedroom meets sanctuary standards with this practical checklist:

- Comfortable, supportive mattress and bed frame.
- Calming, cohesive color palette.
- Well-organized, clutter-free storage solutions.
- Layered, adjustable lighting setup.
- Quality, comfortable bedding and textiles.
- Blackout window treatments for optimal sleep conditions.
- Sensory enhancements (aromas, textures, soothing sounds).

COMMON MISTAKES TO AVOID

Creating your perfect sleep environment means avoiding common pitfalls:

Overcrowding the Space: Excessive furniture disrupts visual flow and physical ease.

Using Intense Colors: Bright, stimulating colors can hinder sleep quality. Opt for muted or soft shades instead.

Neglecting Comfort: Prioritizing aesthetics over comfort can compromise restful sleep. Balance both for best results.

FINAL THOUGHTS

Designing the perfect sleep sanctuary is an investment in your well-being, impacting your physical health, mental clarity, and overall quality of life. Thoughtful selections of soothing color palettes, tactile linens, and layered lighting cultivate an environment that encourages restorative sleep. Integrating practical storage solutions, carefully chosen décor, and living greenery adds character while preserving tranquility. Prioritize window treatments that balance light control with style and ensure air quality through ventilation or the addition of a humidifier. By harmonizing form and function, you create a serene retreat. Let every element work in concert to envelop you in calm elegance, transforming your bedroom into a haven of comfort, rest, and rejuvenation. Always timeless.

Master Bedroom and
GUEST BEDROOM ESSENTIALS

The master bedroom and guest room are central to the home's comfort and hospitality. While the master suite serves as a personal oasis designed to cater to daily comfort, the guest room must effortlessly accommodate visitors with a warm, welcoming ambiance. Each space has distinct needs, yet both must prioritize restfulness and practicality.

ESSENTIALS FOR THE MASTER BEDROOM

01 COMFORT AND FUNCTIONALITY

Your master bedroom should feel luxurious yet practical, promoting rest and enhancing daily routines. Key features to incorporate include:

King or Queen-size Bed: Choose the largest bed your room comfortably allows, enhancing both visual appeal and sleeping comfort.

Comfortable Bedding: Invest in quality linens, pillows, and duvets tailored to your climate and personal preferences.

Adequate Nightstands: Matching bedside tables with ample surface area and storage enhance functionality.

Dresser & Wardrobe: Include a sizable dresser and wardrobe system for organized clothing storage, enhancing the serenity of your space.

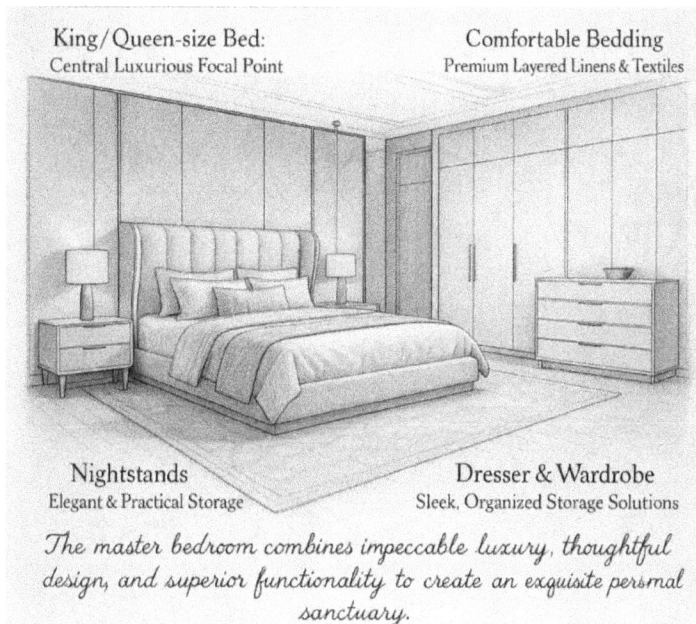

King/Queen-size Bed: Central Luxurious Focal Point

Comfortable Bedding: Premium Layered Linens & Textiles

Nightstands: Elegant & Practical Storage

Dresser & Wardrobe: Sleek, Organized Storage Solutions

The master bedroom combines impeccable luxury, thoughtful design, and superior functionality to create an exquisite personal sanctuary.

02 LUXURIOUS DETAILS

Attention to finer details elevates your master suite:

Ambient Lighting: Layered lighting options—ambient, task, and accent—transform your bedroom into a versatile retreat.

Sitting Area: Incorporate a cozy nook or seating area, perfect for relaxing, reading, or enjoying morning coffee.

Personalized Decor: Artwork, photographs, or decorative items that reflect personal tastes add warmth and character.

03 STORAGE SOLUTIONS

A well-organized master bedroom is fundamental to serenity and practicality:

Under-Bed Storage: Ideal for seasonal clothing, additional bedding, and infrequently used items, these drawers or rolling bins make efficient use of otherwise wasted space while keeping floors neat and dust-free.

Custom Closet Systems: Tailored designs with adjustable shelves, double-hanging rods, and integrated drawers ensure every garment and accessory has its place, promoting effortless outfit selection and reducing visual clutter.

Functional Furniture: Benches, ottomans, or beds with integrated storage help maintain visual tranquility.

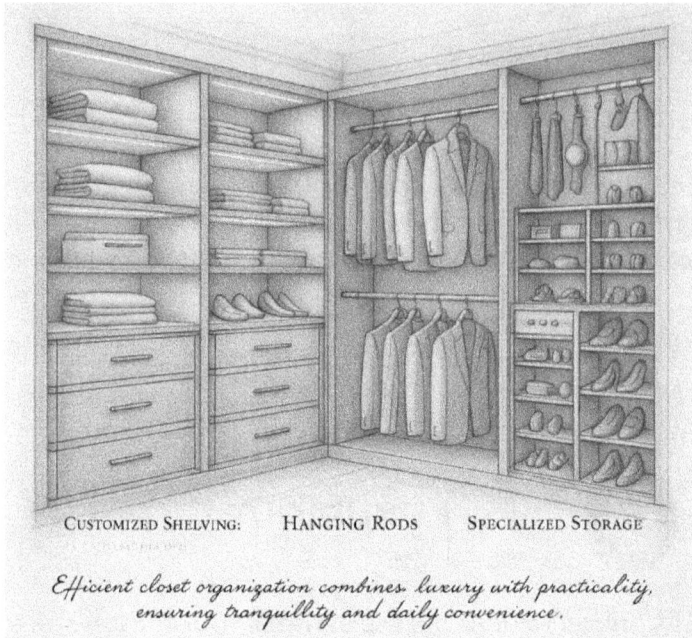

CUSTOMIZED SHELVING: HANGING RODS   SPECIALIZED STORAGE

Efficient closet organization combines luxury with practicality, ensuring tranquillity and daily convenience.

04 MASTER ENSUITE CONNECTION

When applicable, creating a seamless transition from bedroom to ensuite bathroom enhances functionality and luxury:

Consistent Design: Use complementary color schemes and materials in both areas to unify the aesthetic.

Accessibility: Ensure easy access and privacy between the two spaces with thoughtful door placement or partition designs.

ESSENTIALS FOR THE GUEST BEDROOM

A thoughtfully designed guest room instantly communicates hospitality and ensures visitors feel at ease. Here's how to expertly craft a welcoming retreat:

01 PRACTICAL FURNITURE & STORAGE

Ensure guests have ample space and feel at home during their stay:

Luggage Rack or Bench: A convenient spot to unpack or store suitcases off the floor, keeping pathways clear and providing a sturdy platform for luggage when organizing attire.

Nightstands with Essentials: Provide bedside tables equipped with adjustable lamps, alarm clocks, accessible outlets or USB ports, and surface space for personal items like phones, eyewear, and nighttime reading.

Closet and Drawer Space: Leave ample room in drawers and hanging rods, include a few wooden hangers and open shelves for folded garments, ensuring guests can unpack comfortably and access belongings with ease.

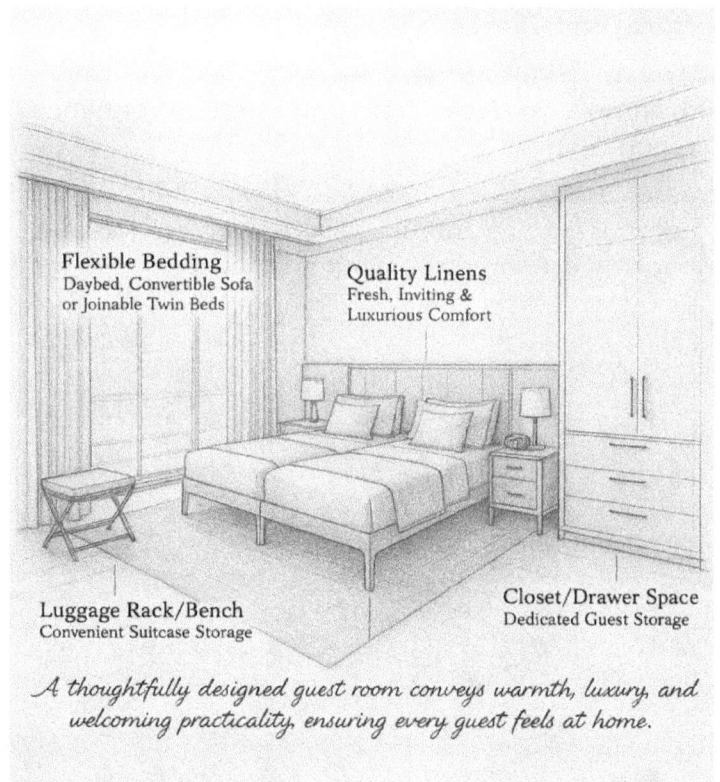

Flexible Bedding
Daybed, Convertible Sofa or Joinable Twin Beds

Quality Linens
Fresh, Inviting & Luxurious Comfort

Luggage Rack/Bench
Convenient Suitcase Storage

Closet/Drawer Space
Dedicated Guest Storage

A thoughtfully designed guest room conveys warmth, luxury, and welcoming practicality, ensuring every guest feels at home.

02 COMFORTABLE ACCOMMODATION

Flexible Bedding: Consider versatile options like daybeds, convertible sofas, or twin beds that can be easily joined.

Quality Linens: Always offer freshly laundered, inviting linens and additional blankets.

03 HOSPITALITY TOUCHES

Personal touches demonstrate thoughtfulness and warmth:

Welcome Tray: Arrange a small basket with essentials—water bottles, snacks, reading materials, Wi-Fi details, and toiletries.

Mirrors: A full-length or vanity mirror helps guests prepare for their day comfortably.

Privacy Solutions: Ensure adequate curtains or shades for guests' privacy and restful sleep.

04 LIGHTING AND AMBIANCE

Thoughtful lighting significantly impacts the room's overall feel:

Adjustable Lighting: Provide bedside lamps and adjustable overhead fixtures for convenience and comfort.

Ambiance Enhancers: Consider a lightly scented candle or diffuser for added warmth.

COMPARATIVE SUMMARY TABLE: MASTER BEDROOM VS. GUEST ROOM ESSENTIALS

FEATURE	MASTER BEDROOM	GUEST BEDROOM
Bed	King/Queen-size, luxurious bedding	Versatile sleeping arrangements
Storage	Extensive, personalized	Convenient, accessible storage
Furniture & Seating	Comfortable, personalized	Functional, welcoming
Lighting	Layered, customized ambiance	Adjustable, practical
Personal Touches	Personal art, memorabilia	Welcoming, universally appealing
Comfort Amenities	Everyday essentials	Hospitality items (snacks, Wi-Fi)

MASTER & GUEST BEDROOM CHECKLIST

Use this concise checklist to ensure nothing is overlooked:

MASTER BEDROOM ESSENTIALS

- Spacious, comfortable bed
- High-quality bedding and linens
- Nightstands and functional lighting
- Ample wardrobe and dresser space
- Seating or relaxation nook
- Personalized decor and accents
- Efficient storage solutions

GUEST BEDROOM ESSENTIALS

- Versatile sleeping arrangements
- Fresh, comfortable bedding
- Adequate storage for guests
- Welcoming hospitality basket/tray
- Privacy measures (curtains, blinds)
- Practical lighting options
- Clear information (Wi-Fi, emergency contacts)

AVOID THESE COMMON PITFALLS

Ensure your spaces meet their fullest potential by avoiding common missteps:

Neglecting Guest Privacy: Overlooked window treatments or missing locks can leave visitors feeling exposed; install elegant drapery and secure latches to foster a true sense of refuge.

Cluttered Master Suite: Excessive furnishings and decorative accents compete for attention and disrupt calm; select a curated few pieces and embrace negative space to uphold serenity.

Lack of Guest Amenities: A bare bedside or empty drawer can feel unwelcoming; offer thoughtful touches—plush towels, a small tray with water and glasses, and accessible charging ports—to ensure every stay feels effortlessly comfortable.

CONCLUDING THOUGHTS

Within the master quarters, sumptuous fabrics drape over an inviting bed framed by an upholstered headboard that reflects personal style and comfort. The gentle interplay of soft lighting across textured surfaces—velvet cushions, layered throws, and carefully selected area rugs—creates an intimate atmosphere that envelops the senses. Beside oversized windows, delicate draperies filter natural light into dappled patterns, while reflective finishes on nightstands and accent tables subtly amplify brightness without needless glare. Furniture silhouettes balance generous proportions with sculptural elegance, ensuring each piece contributes to a harmonious whole. A curated selection of artworks or decorative objets d'art brings a refined point of interest, punctuating neutral palettes with signature flourishes. Every detail, from hardware finishes to bespoke millwork, resonates with a quiet luxury that transforms the master suite into a retreat that honors both repose and restorative beauty.

In guest accommodations, a similarly thoughtful aesthetic unfolds, welcoming visitors with an effortless blend of refinement and ease. Crisp bedding in pure white or soft tonal shades complements a selection of plush pillows, while a modest bedside table, adorned with a simple vase or artful accent light, suggests thoughtful hospitality. Walls in soothing hues act as a backdrop for framed prints or understated sculptural details, infusing the space with character without overwhelming tranquility. The arrangement of furniture prioritizes openness, allowing guests to move freely and settle in at leisure. Storage elements, subtly integrated, keep personal items discreetly tucked away so that the room remains uncluttered and inviting. Textural contrasts—linen curtains, handwoven throws, and tactile cushions—imbue warmth and welcome without compromising elegance. In every gesture and hue, the guest quarters convey a spirit of generosity and grace, ensuring each visitor feels treasured and perfectly at ease within their temporary sanctuary, all infused with effortless elegance.

Kid's Rooms:
PLAYFUL & PRACTICAL IDEAS

Designing spaces for children is perhaps one of the most delightful yet challenging aspects of interior design. A child's bedroom must strike a careful balance between playful creativity and practical functionality. A well-thought-out kid's room not only sparks imagination but also promotes growth, development, and independence. Let's explore how to craft an inspiring and practical space where children will love spending time and parents will appreciate the thoughtful design.

01 ESSENTIAL ELEMENTS FOR CHILDREN'S ROOMS

SAFETY FIRST
When designing for children, safety is paramount. Ensure:

- **Rounded Edges**: Choose furniture without sharp corners to minimize injury risks.
- **Secure Furniture**: Anchor dressers, bookshelves, and other tall furniture securely to the wall.
- **Child-safe Window Treatments**: Opt for cordless blinds or safe curtain designs.

FLEXIBLE FURNITURE
Children grow quickly, and their needs evolve. Flexible furniture solutions help adapt to changing requirements:

- **Convertible Cribs and Beds**: Invest in beds that convert from toddler beds to full-size as your child grows.
- **Adjustable Desks and Chairs**: Select adjustable height options to accommodate children as they age.
- **Multifunctional Storage**: Use modular shelving or stackable storage bins that easily adapt as toys transition to books and hobbies.

Cordless Window Treatments
Safe & Stylish

Rounded Edges:
Prevent Injuries &
Ensure Safety

Secure Furniture
Wall-Anchored
Dressers &
Shelves

Secure Furniture
Wall-Anchored
Dressers & Shelves

Thoughtful safety design ensures children's rooms are playful, inspiring, and worry free.

02 PLAYFUL THEMES & IMAGINATIVE DESIGNS

CHOOSING A THEME
A theme can make a child's room magical and engaging. Popular and enduring themes include:

- **Adventure & Exploration**: Maps, globes, or safari-inspired decor.
- **Space & Science**: Starry ceilings, rocket ship furniture, glow-in-the-dark decals.
- **Nature & Woodland**: Forest creatures, tree murals, natural textures.

TIP: Select a flexible and adaptable theme to ensure longevity.

CREATIVE WALL TREATMENTS
Walls are ideal canvases to spark creativity:

- **Chalkboard or Whiteboard Walls**: Encourage artistic expression without worrying about permanent damage.

- **Interactive Murals**: Paint or apply wallpaper that incorporates educational elements like the alphabet, numbers, or maps.

- **Peel-and-Stick Decals**: Easy-to-change decals adapt to changing interests without permanent commitment.

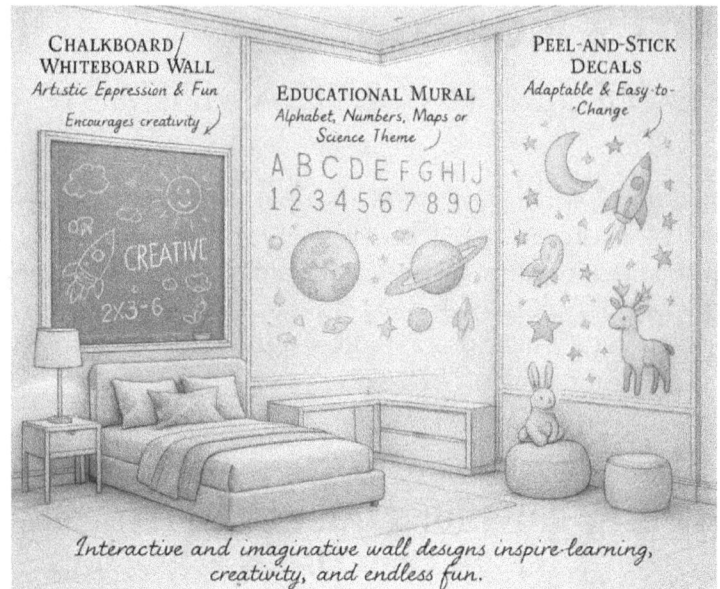

Interactive and imaginative wall designs inspire learning, creativity, and endless fun.

03   PRACTICAL STORAGE SOLUTIONS

Managing clutter in children's rooms can be a significant challenge, making efficient storage essential.

STORAGE TYPES & IDEAS

STORAGE TYPE	IDEAL USE & BENEFITS
Toy Chests/Bins	Easy clean-up, accessibility, and mobility.
Open Shelves	Showcase books/toys while promoting neatness.
Under-Bed Drawers	Utilize underused space for extra storage.
Hanging Storage	Perfect for soft toys, clothes, or shoes.

ORGANIZATIONAL TIPS

Clearly Label Storage: Use color-coded labels or illustrated tags to help children independently locate and store items correctly, fostering confidence and reducing morning scramble.

Accessible Height: Ensure shelving and bins sit at child-height, empowering kids to maintain order, choose toys or books unaided, and develop lifelong organizational habits.

Routine Clean-Up: Integrate daily tidying routines through playful incentives or rewards—such as sticker charts or brief cleanup songs—to make straightening up feel fun and reinforce consistency.

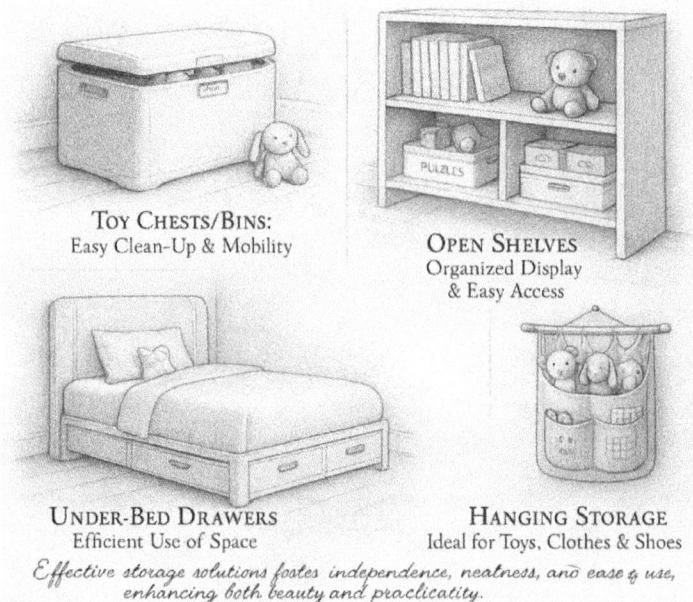

TOY CHESTS/BINS: Easy Clean-Up & Mobility

OPEN SHELVES Organized Display & Easy Access

UNDER-BED DRAWERS Efficient Use of Space

HANGING STORAGE Ideal for Toys, Clothes & Shoes

Effective storage solutions foster independence, neatness, and ease of use, enhancing both beauty and practicality.

04 LIGHTING AND AMBIANCE

Proper lighting transforms a child's room from a practical daytime area into a cozy nighttime retreat:

- **General Lighting**: Bright overhead lights facilitate play and learning activities.
- **Task Lighting**: Desk lamps or reading lights encourage study and quiet reading time.
- **Ambient Lighting**: Soft nightlights or fairy lights offer comfort during sleep or quiet moments.

TIP: Choose adjustable lighting with dimmers to easily transition between tasks.

05 ENCOURAGING LEARNING AND DEVELOPMENT

A child's bedroom can actively support their growth and education:

- **Study Corner**: A dedicated space with a desk, comfortable chair, and educational supplies promotes academic focus.
- **Reading Nook**: Create a cozy area with comfortable seating, good lighting, and accessible bookshelves.
- **Interactive Zones**: Areas designed for imaginative play, puzzles, arts and crafts, and other stimulating activities.

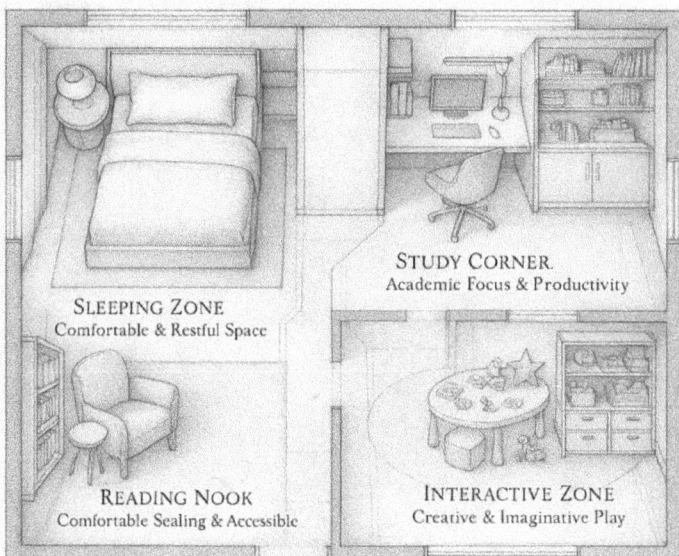

SLEEPING ZONE
Comfortable & Restful Space

STUDY CORNER.
Academic Focus & Productivity

READING NOOK
Comfortable Seating & Accessible

INTERACTIVE ZONE
Creative & Imaginative Play

06 LONGEVITY AND ADAPTABILITY

Children's interests and needs evolve, so designing rooms with flexibility ensures lasting value:

- **Neutral Foundations**: Keep wall colors and furniture basics neutral to easily update accents.
- **Adaptable Decor**: Use replaceable artwork, decals, textiles, and accessories to refresh the space without major redesigns.

KIDS' ROOM CHECKLIST: PRACTICAL & PLAYFUL

- **Safety**: Rounded furniture, anchored pieces, child-safe window treatments.
- **Adaptability**: Convertible furniture, adjustable seating, neutral base design.
- **Storage**: Clearly labeled bins, shelves, easy access solutions.
- **Themes & Decor**: Interactive murals, chalkboard walls, easily replaceable decor elements.
- **Lighting**: Overhead, task-specific, and ambient sources.
- **Learning Zones**: Study areas, reading corners, interactive play spaces.

COMMON PITFALLS TO AVOID

- **Overly Trendy Designs**: Avoid themes that children quickly outgrow, such as overly specific cartoon characters.
- **Underestimating Storage Needs**: Plan more storage space than you initially think necessary to handle increasing belongings.
- **Neglecting Child's Input**: Engage children in decision-making, ensuring they feel ownership and pride in their space.

Closet Organization
AND DESIGN TIPS (ILLUSTRATED)

Creating an organized, visually appealing closet transforms daily routines from chaos into calm. A thoughtfully designed closet maximizes space, improves functionality, and enhances your everyday life. Whether you have a spacious walk-in or a modest reach-in closet, effective planning, strategic storage solutions, and smart organization techniques can profoundly impact how you use and enjoy your wardrobe space. Let's delve into detailed strategies to create a closet that's as beautiful as it is functional.

01 ASSESSING YOUR NEEDS

Before starting any closet organization project, it's essential to assess your individual storage requirements clearly:

- **Inventory Your Items**: Categorize your belongings into clothing, accessories, shoes, seasonal items, and special garments.
- **Evaluate Closet Space**: Take precise measurements of your closet space—width, depth, and height.
- **Identify Your Habits**: Note how frequently you access various items. Place frequently used items within easy reach.

02 CLOSET LAYOUT FUNDAMENTALS

Efficient closet design considers your daily flow, maximizing the available space to its fullest potential. Here's a quick guide to different closet types:

WALK-IN CLOSETS
Ideal for larger spaces, walk-in closets provide luxurious storage opportunities.

- **Zones**: Clearly defined areas (e.g., dressing, shoe storage, accessories).
- **Central Features**: Island or seating area enhances usability.

CLOSET ORGANIZATION:
ASSESSMENT & CATEGORIZATION

STEP 1 INVENTORY YOUR ITEMS   STEP 2 EVALUATE CLOSET SPACE

Clothing   Accessories   Shoes

Seasonal   Special
Items   Garments

Closet Dimensions: Width, Depth, Height

STEP 3 IDENTIFY YOUR HABITS
Item Frequency: → Placed within easy reach
Frequently Used   → Placed at medium height
Occasionally Used   → Stored neatly in upper
                                 or lower closet areas

A thoughtful assessment transforms closet organization, making your wardrobe intuitive, functional, and beautiful.

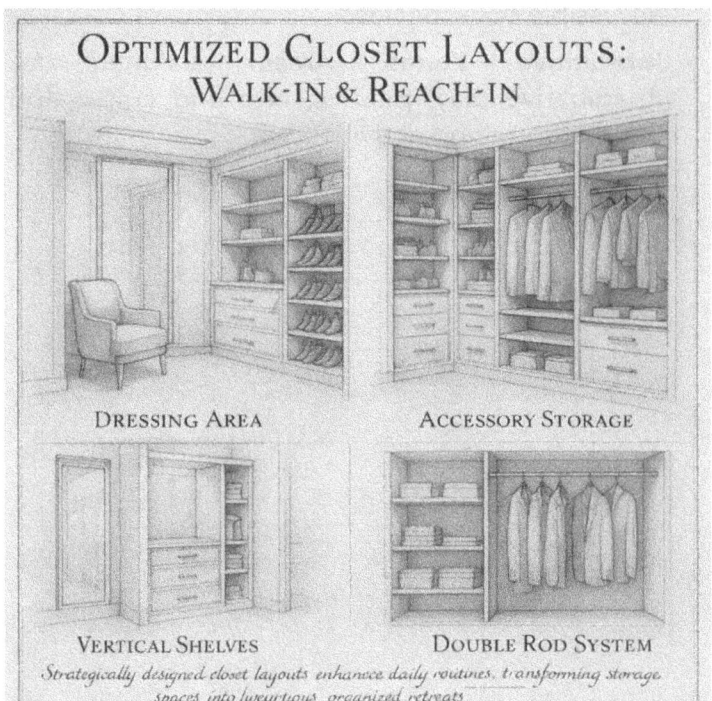

OPTIMIZED CLOSET LAYOUTS:
WALK-IN & REACH-IN

DRESSING AREA   ACCESSORY STORAGE

VERTICAL SHELVES   DOUBLE ROD SYSTEM

Strategically designed closet layouts enhance daily routines, transforming storage spaces into luxurious, organized retreats

REACH-IN CLOSETS
Common in apartments and smaller homes, requiring smart solutions.

- **Vertical Space Utilization**: Shelves and stackable units maximize storage.
- **Double Rods**: Install at varying heights for shirts and pants.

03 SMART STORAGE SOLUTIONS

Strategically chosen storage solutions dramatically enhance organization:

STORAGE TYPE	IDEAL USAGE & BENEFITS
Adjustable Shelving	Versatile heights for different items, ideal for folded clothes or accessories.
Double Rods	Efficiently doubles hanging space for shorter items.
Drawer Units	Perfect for storing smaller garments and accessories neatly.
Shoe Racks	Organizes footwear, maintains accessibility and visibility.
Door Storage	Great for smaller items like scarves, ties, belts, and jewelry.

04 ORGANIZATION TECHNIQUES AND TIPS

An organized closet simplifies your daily routine. Consider these proven strategies:

- **Categorize by Item Type**: Group clothes by type (shirts, pants, dresses), then further sort by color or season to streamline outfit selection, maintain visual harmony, and make daily decisions effortless.
- **Seasonal Rotation**: Store off-season items in clearly labeled bins or vacuum-sealed bags, placing them on higher shelves or under-bed drawers to free prime closet space for current essentials while keeping rarely used pieces accessible.
- **Visibility Matters**: Use transparent bins, open shelving, or wire baskets to facilitate quick access and easy identification of items, reducing time spent searching and encouraging you to keep the closet tidy.

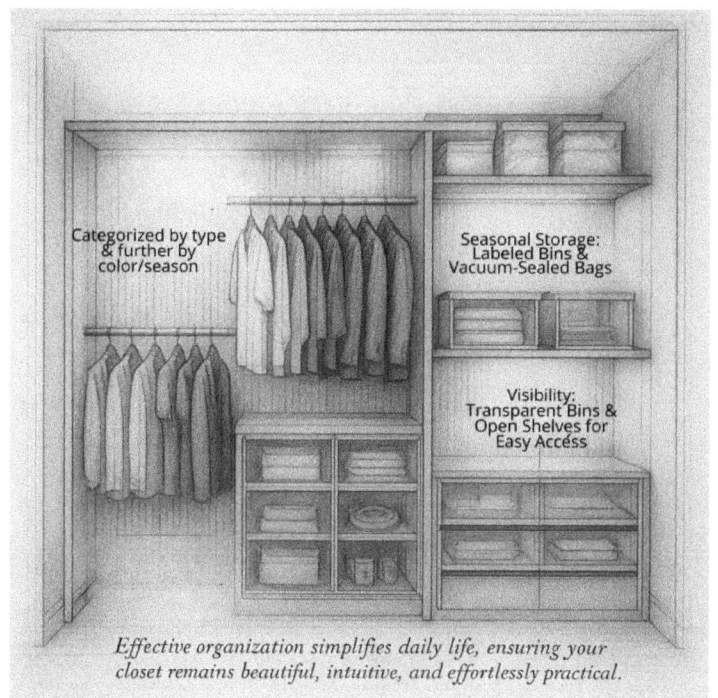

Categorized by type & further by color/season

Seasonal Storage: Labeled Bins & Vacuum-Sealed Bags

Visibility: Transparent Bins & Open Shelves for Easy Access

Effective organization simplifies daily life, ensuring your closet remains beautiful, intuitive, and effortlessly practical.

05 LIGHTING & VISIBILITY

Good lighting transforms a functional closet into a genuinely enjoyable space:

- **LED Lighting**: Install LED strip lighting along shelves or rods for even illumination.
- **Task Lighting**: Dedicated lights for jewelry trays or drawers enhance usability.
- **Motion-Sensor Lights**: Convenient in closets without accessible switches.

06 ACCESSORIES AND SPECIALTY STORAGE

Accessories require specific storage solutions to maintain order and prevent damage:

- **Jewelry Trays & Organizers**: Velvet-lined compartments keep delicate items safe and visible.
- **Tie & Belt Racks**: Mounted racks or pull-out trays provide neat and compact storage.
- **Purse & Hat Storage**: Shelf dividers or hooks ensure shape retention and organization.

SPECIALIZED CLOSET STORAGE FOR ACCESSORIES

JEWELRY STORAGE

VELVET-LINED COMPARTMENTS FOR PROTECTION & VISIBILITY

TIE & BELT STORAGE MOUNTED RACKS & PULL OUT TRAYS

PURSE STORAGE SHELF DIVIDERS & ELEGANT HOOKS

HAT STORAGE ELEGANT SHELVING & STANDS FOR SHAPE RETENTION

Tailored storage solutions preserve and display accessories tidily, making every item easy to find and end enjoy.

07 PERSONALIZING YOUR CLOSET SPACE

Your closet should reflect your style and preferences:

- **Choose Harmonious Colors**: Neutral or soft pastel colors provide a calming backdrop.
- **Custom Hardware**: Upgrading knobs, pulls, and rods enhances aesthetic appeal.
- **Decorative Touches**: Incorporate art, mirrors, or luxurious seating to create an inviting atmosphere.

Even small personal touches can dramatically improve how much you enjoy using your closet.

08 CLOSET ORGANIZATION CHECKLIST

Use this handy checklist to streamline your closet setup:

- **Measure and Assess**: Inventory items, measure space accurately.
- **Plan Layout**: Designate specific zones (daily items, seasonal items, specialty storage).
- **Choose Storage Solutions**: Select adjustable shelves, rods, drawers, shoe racks.
- **Implement Categorization**: Organize clothing by type, color, season.
- **Enhance Visibility**: Install appropriate lighting, use clear storage bins.
- **Specialty Storage**: Allocate dedicated spaces for jewelry, ties, belts, shoes, purses.
- **Personalize**: Select color schemes, hardware, and decorative touches.
- **Routine Maintenance**: Regularly declutter, maintain organization habits, periodic updates.

Bathrooms
AND POWDER ROOMS

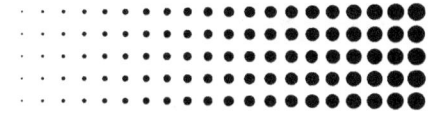

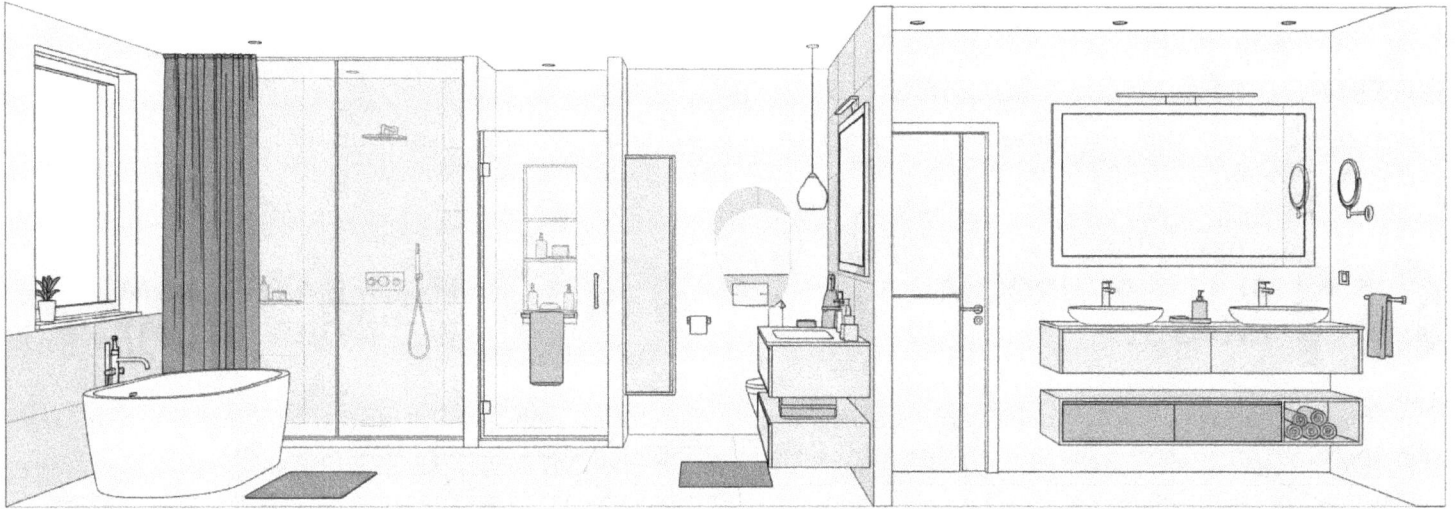

CHAPTER 9

Bathroom
LAYOUTS & ERGONOMICS

Elegantly orchestrating fixtures and finishes, a well-considered bathroom layout transcends mere visual appeal. When design dialogues with ergonomics, each element—from the gentle arc of a freestanding tub to the discreet curve of a vanity countertop—contributes to a fluid spatial choreography. Thoughtful placement of basins, showers, and storage zones cultivates ease of use, while generous clearances invite unhurried movement. Balanced proportions ensure that towel racks and shelving fall effortlessly to hand without intruding on circulation paths. Materials chosen for their tactile warmth and resilience—such as honed stone, finely grained woods, or hand-glazed ceramics—accentuate the harmony between human scale and enduring style. Every junction of tile, wood, and metal becomes not just a junction but a moment of sensory pleasure, reinforcing both comfort and refinement, and quiet moments of solitude.

Subtle shifts in elevation and careful sightlines transform routine rituals into moments of curated luxury. Warm underfoot lighting can cast gentle pools of glow beneath floating vanities, while wall-mounted mirrors framed in burnished metals reflect candlelight in shimmering patterns. Strategic recesses within niches keep daily essentials discreetly at hand, preserving the serenity of uncluttered countertops. Embrace ordinal symmetry or dynamic asymmetry to reinforce visual tension and comfort: twin basins balanced across a central axis, or a single sculptural basin that commands attention against a backdrop of rich marble veins. Safety and accessibility merge effortlessly in thoughtfully designed reach ranges and non-slip surfaces, ensuring every visit feels as intuitive as it is indulgent. The result is an environment that marries precision with poise, inviting repose with artful purpose.

UNDERSTANDING BATHROOM ERGONOMICS

Ergonomics in bathroom design addresses the efficient arrangement of fixtures and accessories to support comfort and ease of use. Here are key considerations:

- **Clearances**: Ensure enough space around fixtures to move comfortably.
- **Accessibility**: Fixtures and storage should be within easy reach.
- **Safety**: Non-slip surfaces, proper lighting, and grab bars for stability.

BATHROOM LAYOUT BASICS

Bathroom layouts depend largely on room size, shape, and personal requirements. Here are the most common layouts:

01 FULL BATHROOM LAYOUT

Typically includes a sink, toilet, and bathtub or shower. Ideal for master suites or family bathrooms.

- **Standard Minimum Size**: Around 40 sq. ft.
- **Optimal Size**: 50-60 sq. ft. for comfort and functionality.

Recommended Clearances:

- **Toilet**: at least 15" from centerline to adjacent wall or fixture, 30" total width.
- **Sink**: minimum of 20" clearance from any obstruction.
- **Bathtub or shower**: at least 24-30" of clearance in front.

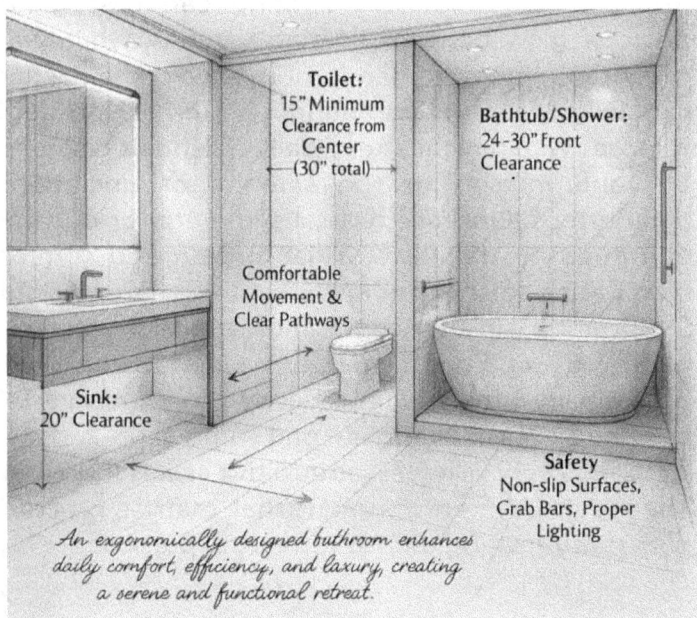

Toilet:
15" Minimum Clearance from Center (30" total)

Bathtub/Shower:
24-30" Front Clearance

Comfortable Movement & Clear Pathways

Sink:
20" Clearance

Safety
Non-slip Surfaces, Grab Bars, Proper Lighting

An ergonomically designed bathroom enhances daily comfort, efficiency, and luxury, creating a serene and functional retreat.

02 HALF BATHROOM (POWDER ROOM)

Includes only a toilet and a sink, ideal for guests or quick access in common areas.

- **Minimum Space**: 20 sq. ft.
- **Efficient Arrangement**: Toilet and sink typically positioned side by side or opposite each other for easy use.

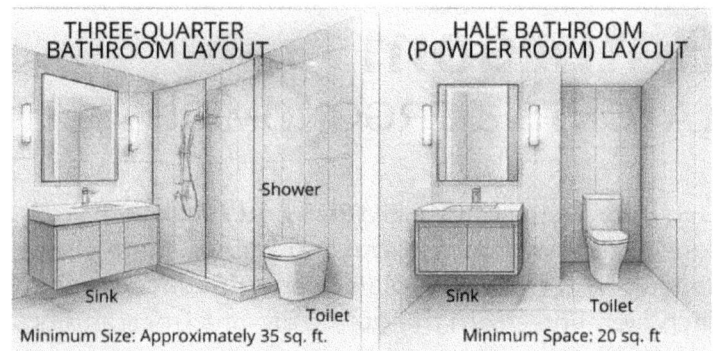

THREE-QUARTER BATHROOM LAYOUT

Shower

Sink

Toilet

Minimum Size: Approximately 35 sq. ft.

HALF BATHROOM (POWDER ROOM) LAYOUT

Sink

Toilet

Minimum Space: 20 sq. ft

03 THREE-QUARTER BATHROOM LAYOUT

Consists of a sink, toilet, and shower—perfect for guest or secondary bathrooms.

- **Minimum Size**: Approximately 35 sq. ft.
- **Optimal Arrangement**: Position fixtures to maximize usable floor space.

ESSENTIAL ERGONOMIC PRINCIPLES

Applying ergonomics effectively requires understanding user interaction with bathroom components:

FIXTURE	RECOMMENDED HEIGHT/DIMENSIONS	ERGONOMIC REASONING
Vanity & Sink	32-36 inches from floor to countertop surface	Ensures comfortable use without bending or stretching excessively
Toilet	15-17 inches from floor (comfort-height toilets)	Facilitates comfortable sitting and standing
Shower Controls	38-48 inches from floor (typically at waist-level)	Conveniently reachable from standing position
Towel Bars & Hooks	48 inches from floor	Easy access when drying hands or body
Mirror Placement	Bottom edge typically 40-45 inches from floor	Accommodates average eye levels

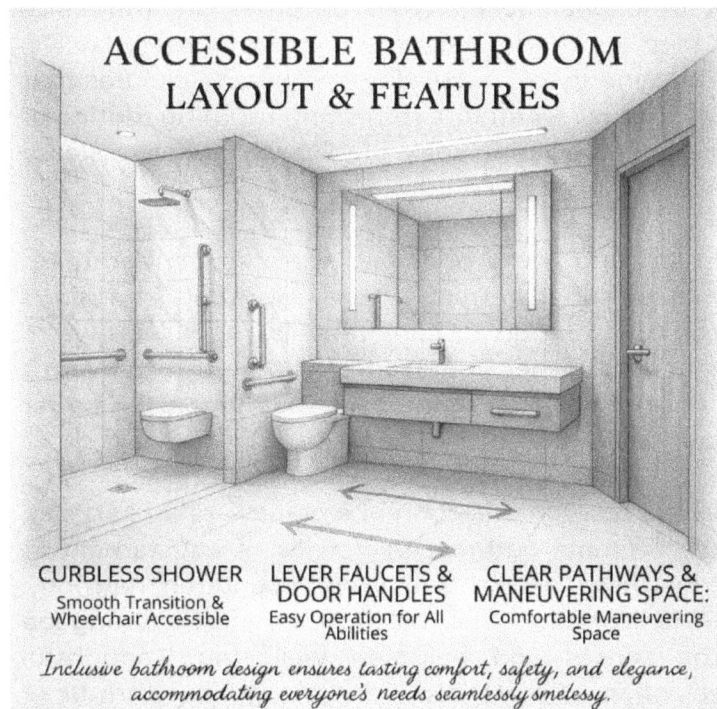

ACCESSIBLE BATHROOM LAYOUT & FEATURES

CURBLESS SHOWER
Smooth Transition & Wheelchair Accessible

LEVER FAUCETS & DOOR HANDLES
Easy Operation for All Abilities

CLEAR PATHWAYS & MANEUVERING SPACE:
Comfortable Maneuvering Space

Inclusive bathroom design ensures lasting comfort, safety, and elegance, accommodating everyone's needs seamlessly smelessy.

DESIGNING FOR ACCESSIBILITY

Inclusive bathrooms designed for all ages and abilities provide lasting comfort and functionality:

- **Curbless Showers**: Smooth transition prevents tripping, suitable for wheelchairs or limited mobility.
- **Grab Bars**: Essential near showers, tubs, and toilets to enhance safety and stability.
- **Lever Faucets & Door Handles**: Easier for all ages, including those with arthritis or limited hand strength.

SPACE-SAVING & FUNCTIONAL LAYOUT TIPS

Maximizing space while maintaining comfort can transform any bathroom, especially when working with compact dimensions and floor plans. Clever planning ensures every inch contributes to both form and function, delivering an environment that feels organized and stylish.

- **Wall-Mounted Fixtures**: Choosing floating vanities or wall-hung toilets not only visually expands the floor area but also simplifies maintenance by eliminating corners, making daily cleaning a breeze.

- **Corner Showers**: Perfectly suited to confined footprints, these enclosures tuck neatly into unused corners, creating a streamlined flow and maximizing open floor space for easier movement.

- **Pocket Doors**: Sliding doors that recess into walls preserve valuable square footage otherwise lost to swing arcs, offering seamless transitions between the bathroom and adjacent spaces.

- **Vertical Storage**: Tall cabinets or open shelving units mounted above vanities harness underutilized vertical surfaces, providing generous space for linens, toiletries, and decorative objects without encroaching on living areas.

COMMON MISTAKES & HOW TO AVOID THEM

Awareness of common pitfalls ensures a smoother design process:

MISTAKE	WHY IT'S A PROBLEM	HOW TO AVOID
Overcrowding Fixtures	Limits functionality, makes space feel cramped	Plan sufficient clearances and circulation paths
Poor Lighting Placement	Creates shadows, compromises safety	Layer lighting strategically (ambient, task, accent)
Ignoring Storage Needs	Leads to clutter and disorganization	Incorporate sufficient built-in storage early in planning
Inadequate Ventilation	Causes mold, mildew, and moisture issues	Plan for exhaust fans or windows to circulate air efficiently

ILLUSTRATED CHECKLIST FOR OPTIMAL BATHROOM LAYOUT

Here's a concise checklist to streamline the design process:

- **Define Usage Needs**: Daily routines, family use, guest access.
- **Select Appropriate Layout**: Full, three-quarter, or half bathroom.
- **Plan Fixture Placement**: Ensure ergonomic clearances and accessibility.
- **Integrate Effective Storage**: Cabinets, shelves, vertical space.
- **Prioritize Lighting & Ventilation**: Include multiple lighting layers and ventilation solutions.
- **Design for Accessibility**: Incorporate inclusive design features if required.

FINAL THOUGHTS ON BATHROOM LAYOUT & ERGONOMICS

Designing a bathroom that marries ergonomic precision with refined aesthetics transforms daily routines into moments of serene luxury. Each carefully considered dimension, from comfortable clearances that allow graceful movement to the interplay of light and material, contributes to an environment that nurtures both body and spirit. When fixtures align intuitively and surfaces resonate with tactile elegance, the space becomes more than a functional necessity—it becomes an immersive sanctuary that reflects the rhythms of everyday life. The synergy of practicality and beauty ensures that each ritual, whether a refreshing morning routine or a tranquil evening soak, unfolds with effortless ease and exquisite poise.

Embracing these principles elevates the bathroom into a refined retreat, where every detail whispers comfort. Subtle accent details, such as warm metallic finishes or artisanal tile patterns, cultivate a sense of bespoke refinement that lingers long after each visit.

In the quiet intersection of architecture and artistry, the ultimate bathroom emerges as a testament to thoughtful design and human-centered harmony. Fluid sightlines and balanced proportions engage the senses and heighten wellbeing. Thoughtful selection of materials—be it the gentle warmth of natural stone underfoot or the soft glow cast by artfully placed fixtures—imbues the room with enduring character. This orchestrated tapestry of form, texture, and light invites contemplation.

Ultimately, a bathroom conceived with both ergonomics and elegance in mind becomes a timeless expression of home, fostering restorative moments that endure long after each door closes. In thoughtful dimensions, the bathroom stands as a quiet celebration of personal well-being and artistic vision, inviting each day to begin and end with grace and serenity.

CHOOSING TILES,
Fixtures and Finishes

Selecting the right tiles, fixtures, and finishes can dramatically transform your bathroom, turning it into a space of tranquility, functionality, and visual charm. These elements, carefully chosen, define the aesthetic character, influence the perception of space, and determine the ease of maintenance. Let's explore in-depth the best strategies, considerations, and expert tips for choosing tiles, fixtures, and finishes that align seamlessly with your style, lifestyle, and budget.

TILES: BEAUTY AND FUNCTIONALITY

Tiles are foundational to bathroom design—equally aesthetic and practical. The right tile choice harmonizes durability, ease of cleaning, and visual appeal.

TYPES OF BATHROOM TILES

- **Ceramic Tiles**
  - Durable, affordable, and available in diverse colors and patterns.
  - Ideal for walls, floors, and showers.

HIGH-TRAFFIC FLOORS:
DURABLE & STYLISH

SUITABLE FOR HIGH-USE
ENVIRONMENTS

**WET AREAS &
SHOWERS:**
WATERPROOF &
SCRATCH-RESISTANT

Walls:
Durable &
Stylish

Floors:
Affordable &
Elegant

Showers:
Practical &
Beautiful

- **Porcelain Tiles**
  - Highly durable, waterproof, and resistant to scratches.
  - Suitable for high-traffic bathrooms, flooring, and wet areas.

- **Natural Stone Tiles** (Marble, Travertine, Slate)
  - Luxurious appearance and unique textures.
  - Require sealing to maintain their elegance and prevent staining.

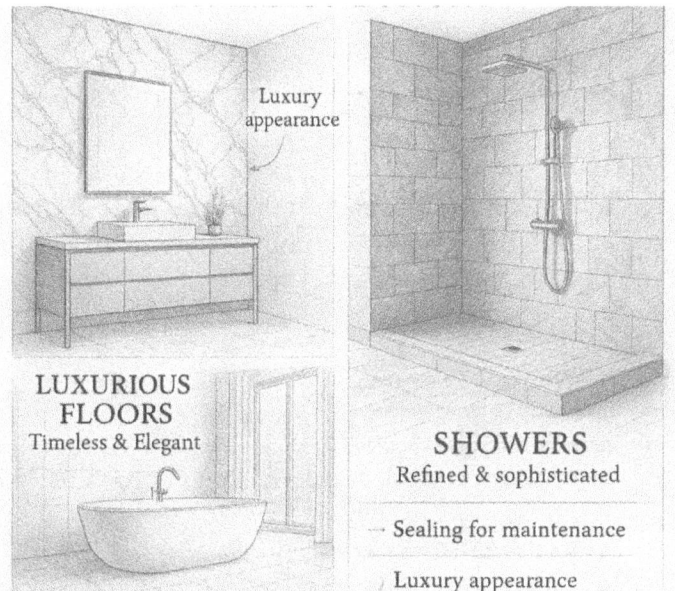

Luxury
appearance

**LUXURIOUS
FLOORS**
Timeless & Elegant

SHOWERS
Refined & sophisticated

Sealing for maintenance

Luxury appearance

- **Glass Tiles**
  - Ideal for backsplashes or accent walls.
  - Reflective properties add brightness and sophistication.

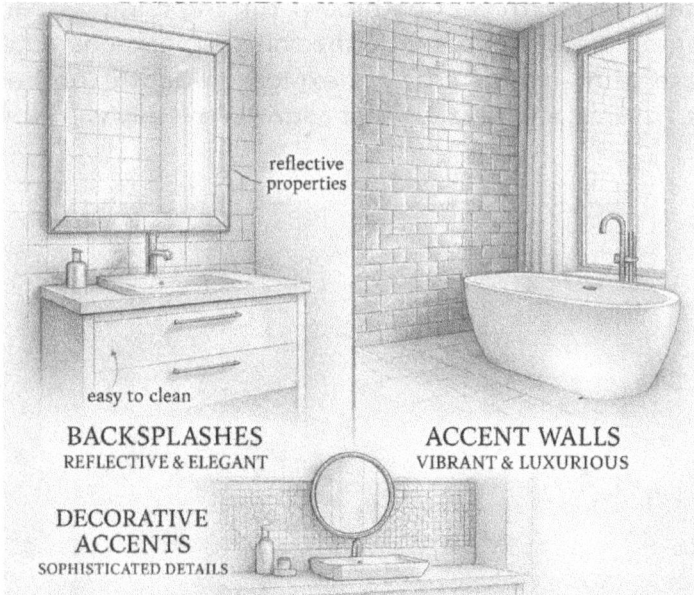

BACKSPLASHES
REFLECTIVE & ELEGANT

ACCENT WALLS
VIBRANT & LUXURIOUS

DECORATIVE ACCENTS
SOPHISTICATED DETAILS

TILE SELECTION TIPS

- **Size and Scale**: Larger tiles minimize grout lines, creating a spacious look. Smaller tiles are perfect for intricate patterns or detailed mosaic effects.
- **Texture and Safety**: Select non-slip textured tiles for shower floors to enhance safety.
- **Color and Aesthetic** Harmony: Complement your overall bathroom color scheme. Use neutral tiles for timeless appeal or vibrant options for a bold statement.

FIXTURES: FOCAL POINTS OF FUNCTIONALITY

Bathroom fixtures—sinks, faucets, toilets, showers, and bathtubs—combine functionality with design. Their styles, materials, and finishes greatly influence bathroom aesthetics.

KEY BATHROOM FIXTURES

- **Vanities & Sinks**
  - **Wall-mounted**: Modern look, enhances floor space.
  - **Pedestal**: Classic and minimalist.
  - **Integrated**: Seamless countertop-sink design for easy cleaning.

VANITIES & SINKS
MODERN ELEGANCE

WALL-MOUNTED SINK
Modern Look, Enhances Floor Space

PEDESTAL SINK
Classic, Minimalist Elegance

INTEGRATED SINK
Seamless Countertop-Sink Design, Easy Cleaning

Visual harmony   Practical elegance

- **Faucets**
  - **Single-handle**: Modern and sleek, easier temperature adjustment.
  - **Double-handle**: Traditional elegance, precise temperature control.
  - **Touchless/automatic**: Hygienic, convenient, ideal for modern bathrooms.

BATHROOM FAUCETS:
STYLE MEETS FUNCTION

Single-handle Faucet
Modern & Sleek, Easy Temperature Adjustment

Double-handle Faucet:
Traditional Elegance, Precise Control

Touchless/Automatic Faucet:
Hygienic & Convenient, Ideal for Modern Bathrooms

- **Toilets**
  - **Two-piece**: Traditional, affordable, easier repairs.
  - **One-piece**: Sleek, easier cleaning, higher-end appearance.
  - **Wall-mounted**: Maximizes floor space, easy cleaning, sophisticated appearance.

- **Showers & Bathtubs**
  - **Walk-in Shower**: Spacious, modern, easily accessible.
  - **Freestanding Tub**: Luxurious focal point.
  - **Tub-Shower Combo**: Space-saving and versatile, ideal for family use.

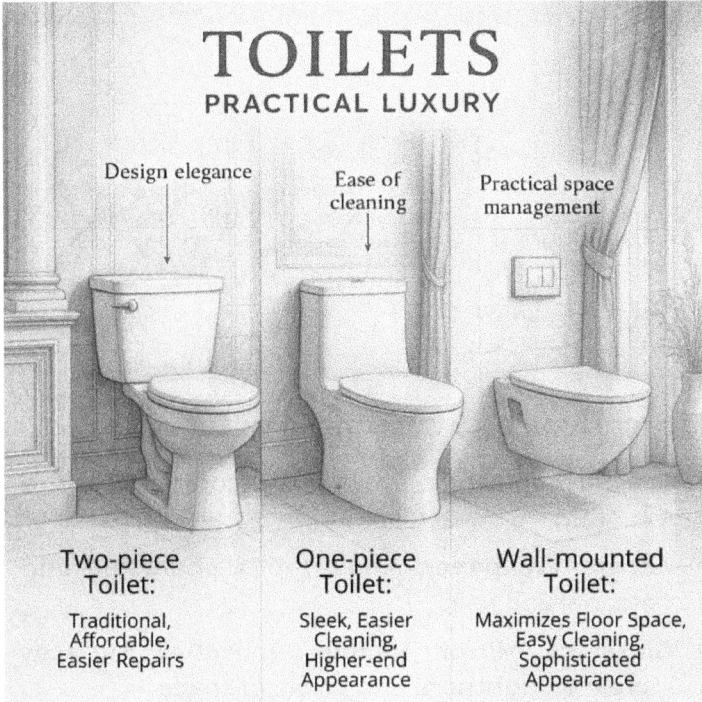

TOILETS
PRACTICAL LUXURY

Design elegance

Ease of cleaning

Practical space management

Two-piece Toilet:
Traditional, Affordable, Easier Repairs

One-piece Toilet:
Sleek, Easier Cleaning, Higher-end Appearance

Wall-mounted Toilet:
Maximizes Floor Space, Easy Cleaning, Sophisticated Appearance

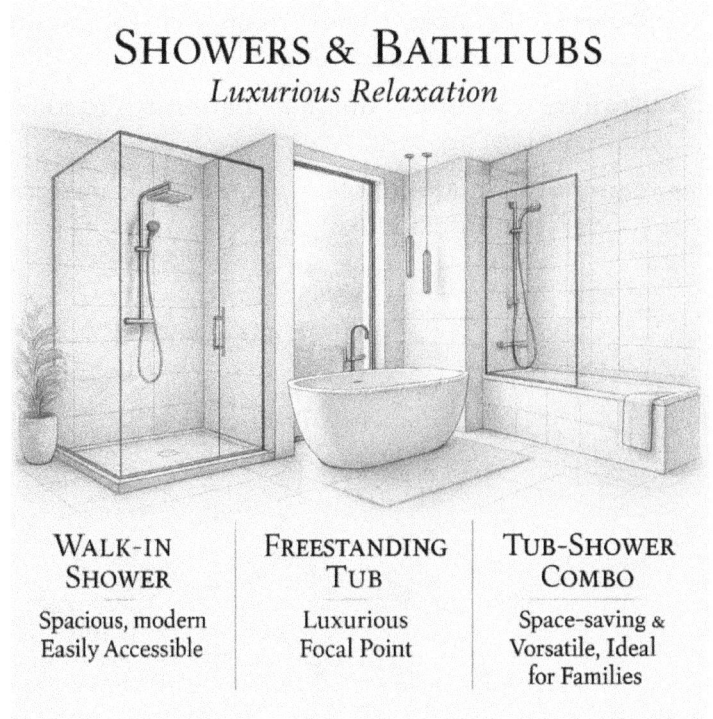

SHOWERS & BATHTUBS
Luxurious Relaxation

WALK-IN SHOWER
Spacious, modern Easily Accessible

FREESTANDING TUB
Luxurious Focal Point

TUB-SHOWER COMBO
Space-saving & Vorsatile, Ideal for Families

FIXTURE MATERIALS & FINISHES

Fixture finishes affect aesthetics, durability, and maintenance:

FINISH	STYLE	MAINTENANCE LEVEL
Chrome	Modern, bright	Low, easy cleaning
Brushed Nickel	Classic, subtle sheen	Moderate, resists fingerprints
Brass/Gold	Traditional, luxurious	Moderate-high, careful cleaning
Matte Black	Bold, contemporary	Moderate, requires regular care

SELECTING FINISHES: COHESION AND CONTRAST

Your finishes—encompassing cabinetry, countertops, and hardware—should enhance the overall aesthetic harmony. Here's how to select the perfect finishes for lasting appeal and practicality:

COUNTERTOPS

- **Quartz**: Durable, low maintenance, stain-resistant, versatile aesthetics.
- **Granite**: Natural, unique patterns, requires periodic sealing.
- **Laminate**: Affordable, versatile designs, moderate durability.

BATHROOM COUNTERTOPS
Luxury & Practicality

Quartz
Durable Low Maintenance
Versatile & Stain-resistant

Granite
Natural elegance. Unique patterns
Periodic sealing required

Laminate
Affordable. Versatile design
Moderate durability

Moderate durability

CABINETRY FINISHES

- **Wood**: Traditional charm, various finishes from rustic to polished.
- **Painted Cabinets**: Clean, contemporary look, easy to update.
- **Lacquer**: High-gloss finish, modern and luxurious.

CABINETRY FINISHES
STYLE & SOPHISTICATION

Wood Cabinets
Traditional Charm,
Rustic to Polished
Finishes

Painted Cabinets
Clean contemporary
Look, Easily updated

Lacquer Cabinets
High-gloss, luxurious
Modern Finish

Design Versatility   Ease of Care   Timeless Elegance

BACKSPLASHES & ACCENT FINISHES

- **Tile Backsplashes**: Practical, decorative, easy to maintain.
- **Accent Wallpaper**: Adds depth, character, and personalized flair.
- **Glass or Mirror Panels**: Reflective surfaces increase brightness and sense of space.

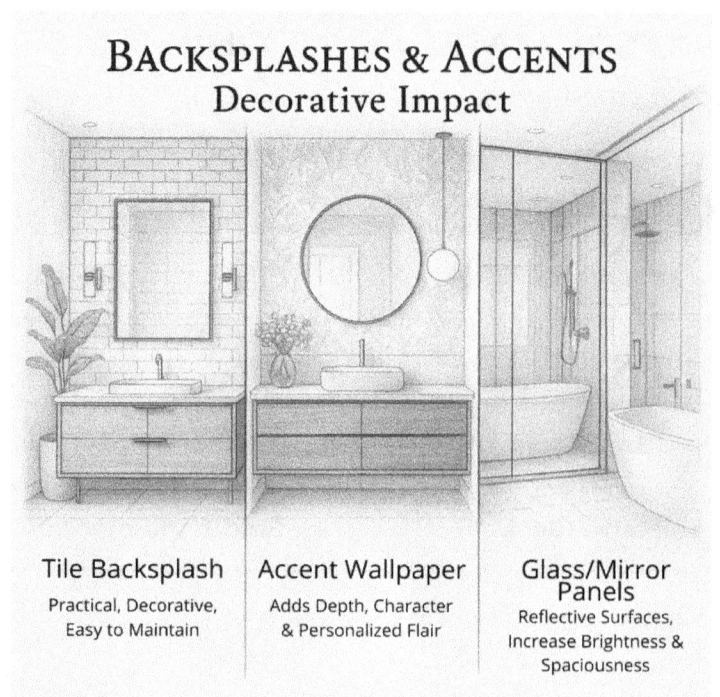

BACKSPLASHES & ACCENTS
Decorative Impact

Tile Backsplash
Practical, Decorative,
Easy to Maintain

Accent Wallpaper
Adds Depth, Character
& Personalized Flair

Glass/Mirror
Panels
Reflective Surfaces,
Increase Brightness &
Spaciousness

CREATING A UNIFIED BATHROOM AESTHETIC

Your bathroom tiles, fixtures, and finishes should coordinate beautifully. Follow these expert principles:

- **Unified Color Palette**: Establish a clear palette to ensure cohesiveness. Use complementary or analogous colors to achieve visual harmony.
- **Contrast and Balance**: Contrast textures—such as glossy tiles with matte fixtures—to enhance visual interest without overwhelming the eye.
- **Scale Consistency**: Balance large-scale elements (large tiles, freestanding tubs) with smaller-scale accessories and hardware to maintain visual proportion.

CHECKLIST: SELECTING YOUR BATHROOM ELEMENTS

Use this expert checklist as you finalize your selections:

Tiles
- Type chosen aligns with bathroom use (durability and waterproofing).
- Size and pattern harmonize with your aesthetic vision.
- Safety features (non-slip) are prioritized.

Fixtures
- Fixtures reflect the chosen style (modern, traditional, minimalist).
- Practical considerations (space, ease of cleaning) evaluated.
- Finishes selected for visual harmony and ease of maintenance.

Finishes
- Countertop material selected suits your daily needs and aesthetic.
- Cabinetry finish complements tile and fixture choices.
- Accent materials (backsplashes, wall treatments) enhance the overall design.

COMMON SELECTION MISTAKES & SOLUTIONS

MISTAKE	COMMON ISSUE	SOLUTION
Ignoring Maintenance	Choosing beautiful but impractical materials	Prioritize practical, easy-care finishes.
Excessive Contrasts	Elements clashing visually	Establish and follow a cohesive palette.
Overwhelming Patterns	Confusing, cluttered look	Limit patterns, use strategically as accents.
Poor Quality Fixtures	Reduced lifespan, frequent repairs	Invest in quality, durable fixtures.

FINAL THOUGHTS ON TILES, FIXTURES, AND FINISHES

The beauty and functionality of your bathroom are deeply influenced by careful selection and thoughtful coordination of tiles, fixtures, and finishes. Following these guidelines ensures your bathroom is not just beautiful, but practical, comfortable, and tailored to your personal style.

SPA-LIKE
Bathroom Features

A spa-inspired bathroom transcends ordinary functionality, becoming a sanctuary of relaxation and rejuvenation. Incorporating spa-like elements can significantly elevate your everyday experience, turning routine activities into moments of self-care and indulgence.

ESSENTIAL SPA FEATURES TO TRANSFORM YOUR BATHROOM

A spa-like bathroom embraces serenity, luxury, and comfort. Key features include elegant aesthetics, sensory details, and high-quality amenities that enhance relaxation.

01 LUXURIOUS SHOWERS & BATHS

Rainfall Showerheads: Provide gentle, soothing streams of water replicating natural rainfall, promoting relaxation and reducing stress.

Steam Showers: Incorporate a built-in steam generator for an authentic spa experience. Benefits include improved circulation, clearer skin, and muscle relaxation.

Soaking Tubs: Deep, freestanding tubs create a luxurious focal point, perfect for soaking away daily tensions.

02 NATURAL ELEMENTS & BIOPHILIC DESIGN

Bringing nature indoors enhances well-being by reducing stress and promoting mental clarity.

Plants & Greenery: Humidity-loving plants such as ferns, bamboo, or aloe vera thrive in bathrooms and purify air.

Natural Materials: Use materials like stone, wood, or bamboo for floors, counters, shelves, and accessories.

Rainfall Showerhead
relaxation, luxurious comfort

Freestanding Soaking Tub
stress reduction, indulgence

Steam Shower Setup
improved circulation, muscle relaxation

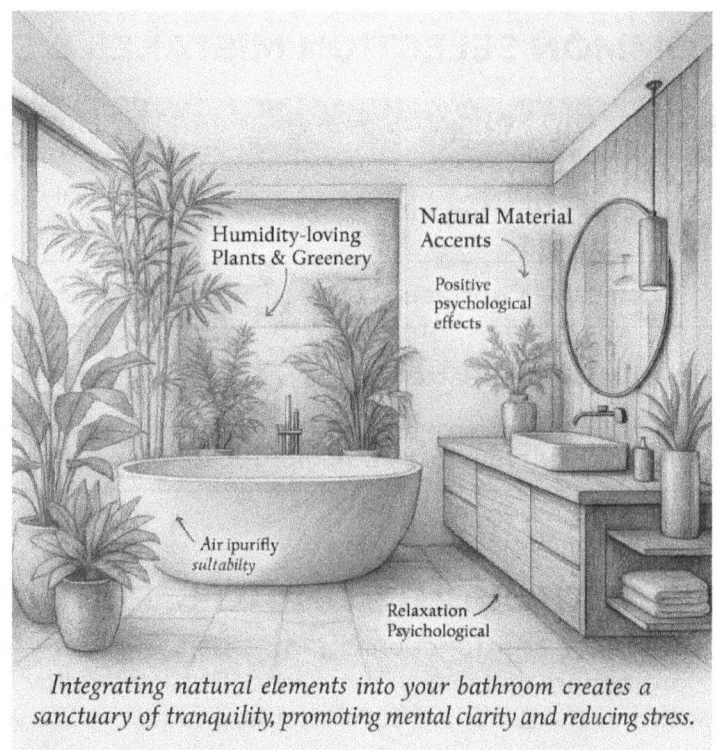

Humidity-loving Plants & Greenery

Natural Material Accents

Positive psychological effects

Air ipurifly sultabilty

Relaxation Psyichological

Integrating natural elements into your bathroom creates a sanctuary of tranquility, promoting mental clarity and reducing stress.

03 SOOTHING LIGHTING

Dimmable Ambient Lights: Adjustable lighting helps transition your space from practical daytime use to calming evening relaxation.

Accent & Candlelight: Incorporate subtle LED strips, wall sconces, and candles to create mood lighting and a warm, inviting atmosphere.

Lighting Checklist:
- Dimmable overhead lights
- Waterproof LED accent lights
- Elegant sconces near mirrors
- Candles (battery-operated or traditional)

04 HEATED FEATURES FOR COMFORT

Heated Floors: Radiant floor heating creates warmth and comfort, especially in colder climates, enhancing your relaxation experience.

Towel Warmers: Heated towel racks ensure warm, cozy towels, adding luxury and convenience.

Comfort Checklist:
- Radiant floor heating system
- Electric towel warmer
- Heated toilet seats (optional for ultimate luxury)

05 SENSORY DETAILS

Creating a spa ambiance involves carefully selecting sensory elements that elevate relaxation.

Aromatherapy: Use essential oil diffusers or scented candles featuring relaxing scents such as lavender, eucalyptus, or jasmine.

Music & Sound: Integrate waterproof Bluetooth speakers to play calming music or nature sounds.

Sensory Checklist:
- Essential oil diffuser
- Waterproof Bluetooth speakers
- Scented candles or wax warmers
- Soothing playlist ready-to-use

HOW TO ACHIEVE THE PERFECT SPA-LIKE BATHROOM: STEP-BY-STEP GUIDE

Follow these expert-recommended steps to transform your existing bathroom into a luxurious spa retreat:

STEP 1: DEFINE YOUR SPA VISION
- Consider your primary spa inspiration (luxury hotel, natural retreat, modern spa).
- Create a mood board of colors, textures, and features.

STEP 2: PRIORITIZE RELAXATION & COMFORT
- Identify key features (rain shower, soaking tub, heated floors) that maximize comfort.
- Budget your expenses for prioritized upgrades.

STEP 3: INCORPORATE NATURAL & SUSTAINABLE ELEMENTS
- Select eco-friendly, natural materials to boost your well-being and sustainability.

STEP 4: PLAN LIGHTING THOUGHTFULLY
- Layer your lighting (ambient, accent, and task lighting) to control the mood and enhance usability.

STEP 5: ADD LUXURIOUS TOUCHES
- Finalize your design with luxurious towels, bathrobes, spa products, and sensory enhancements like aromatherapy and soothing music.

COMPLETE SPA-BATHROOM CHECKLIST

Use this checklist to ensure every element contributes to your ideal spa experience:

FEATURE	IMPORTANCE	SELECTED
Shower/Tub	High	☐
- Rainfall Showerhead	Essential	☐
- Steam Shower	Luxury Option	☐
- Freestanding Tub	Luxury Option	☐
Lighting	High	☐
- Dimmable Lights	Essential	☐
- LED/Candles	Essential	☐
Natural Elements	Medium-High	☐
- Plants	Essential	☐
- Natural Materials	Essential	☐
Heated Features	Medium-High	☐
- Heated Floors	Recommended	☐
- Towel Warmers	Recommended	☐
Sensory Enhancements	Medium	☐
- Aromatherapy	Essential	☐
- Music/Sound	Recommended	☐

AVOIDING COMMON PITFALLS

Achieve your spa-like vision by avoiding common mistakes:

Clutter: Keep your spa bathroom minimal and serene by removing unnecessary objects and decorative excess; employ concealed storage or sleek baskets to maintain a calm, uncluttered environment. Ensure surfaces remain clear by routinely reassessing decorative items, stowing away anything that does not serve a functional or aesthetic purpose to preserve that sense of tranquility.

Poor Ventilation: A steam shower or frequent hot baths require effective ventilation to avoid mold and moisture build-up; integrate high-capacity exhaust fans or operable windows to ensure air remains fresh and invigorating. Consider installing a humidity sensor to automate extraction, protecting both décor and structural elements from long-term damage.

Overcrowding: Maintain a spacious, open feel—avoid cramming too many luxurious elements into limited space; select a few signature fixtures or materials and allow generous negative space to enhance the sense of calm. Resist the urge to display every towel, candle, or accessory at once; rotate accent pieces seasonally to keep the design feeling renewed and effortlessly elegant.

FINAL THOUGHTS: YOUR PERSONAL RETREAT

By incorporating thoughtfully chosen spa-like features, you will not only enhance your bathroom's aesthetics but also profoundly improve your daily wellness routine. Each morning or evening, your bathroom becomes a sanctuary for renewal, relaxation, and personal care.

CREATIVE SOLUTIONS FOR
Small Bathtooms

When space is at a premium, transforming your compact bathroom into a stylish yet functional oasis can seem daunting. However, with thoughtful design and clever strategies, even the smallest bathroom can feel spacious and luxurious. In this section, we'll explore a wealth of creative, practical, and visually appealing solutions to maximize every inch of your small bathroom.

MAXIMIZING SPACE: STRATEGIC LAYOUTS

Efficient layout planning is fundamental to enhancing small bathroom functionality. Careful placement of fixtures can make a compact space feel remarkably comfortable.

1. Corner Fixtures
Optimize awkward corners by installing corner sinks, toilets, or even showers. This clever approach frees up precious floor space, significantly improving flow.

2. Wall-Hung Fixtures
Wall-mounted toilets and vanities create the illusion of more space, revealing additional floor area and simplifying cleaning tasks.

3. Compact and Combined Fixtures
Consider fixtures designed explicitly for smaller spaces, such as narrow sinks or combination units that integrate the sink and storage.

SMART STORAGE SOLUTIONS

In compact spaces, creative storage is essential for maintaining order without sacrificing style.

Vertical Storage: Utilize tall, narrow shelving units, built-in wall cabinets, or over-the-door storage solutions. Vertical storage helps capitalize on underutilized wall space.

Built-in Niches and Recesses: Recessed shelving or niches within shower walls provide storage without protruding into the room. This approach is both practical and visually streamlined.

Floating Shelves and Cabinets: Wall-mounted shelves and cabinets enhance the openness of your space, creating a clean, modern look.

Storage Checklist:
- Vertical shelving units
- Recessed niches (particularly within showers)
- Wall-mounted cabinets and shelves
- Under-sink cabinetry tailored for compact spaces

Creative Solutions for Compact Bathrooms

CORNER SINK

WALL-MOUNTED TOILET
Increases visible floor space

COMPACT FIXTURES

Thoughtful, compact design transforms small bathrooms into spacious, luxurious retreats.

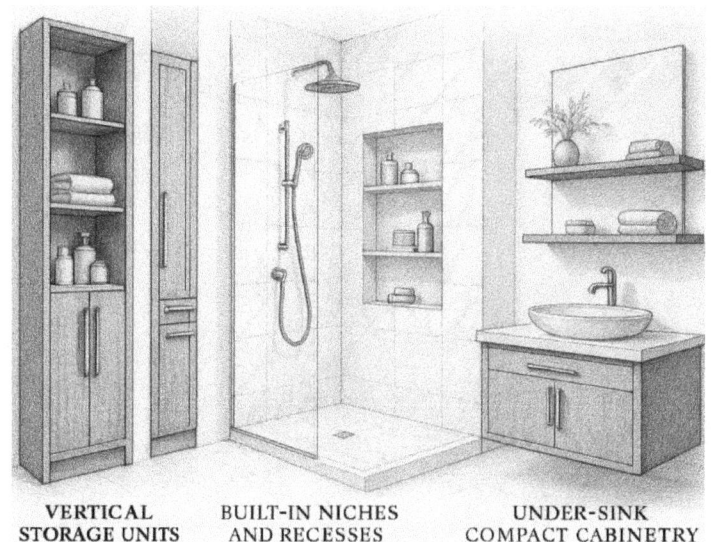

VERTICAL STORAGE UNITS

BUILT-IN NICHES AND RECESSES

UNDER-SINK COMPACT CABINETRY

ILLUSIONS OF SPACE: VISUAL EXPANSION TECHNIQUES

Optical illusions can dramatically enhance your bathroom's spaciousness.

MIRRORS & GLASS

Large Mirrors: Strategically placed mirrors reflect light and visually expand the space. A floor-to-ceiling mirror or a mirrored wall can double the apparent size of a small bathroom.

Glass Shower Doors: Clear, frameless glass shower doors or partitions maintain visual continuity, creating an unobstructed sightline that enlarges your perceived space.

COLORS AND FINISHES

Monochromatic Color Scheme: Use a unified color palette in soft, neutral tones to achieve visual harmony and openness.

Glossy and Reflective Surfaces: Reflective tiles and finishes increase perceived brightness and amplify the sense of space.

Visual Expansion Checklist:
- Oversized mirror
- Frameless glass shower doors
- Reflective or glossy tiles
- Neutral monochromatic palette

SPACE-SAVING FURNITURE & ACCESSORIES

Small bathrooms benefit significantly from fixtures and accessories designed specifically for tight quarters.

Folding and Retractable Elements: Consider fold-down seats, retractable towel bars, and extendable mirrors for functionality without compromising space.

Pocket and Sliding Doors: Sliding barn-style doors or pocket doors save valuable floor space that traditional hinged doors would occupy.

Multifunctional Accessories: Accessories that serve multiple purposes, such as mirrors with integrated shelving or towel holders, enhance both convenience and efficiency.

Furniture and Accessories Checklist:
- Foldable shower seats
- Sliding or pocket doors
- Multifunctional mirrors and accessories
- Retractable towel bars and hooks

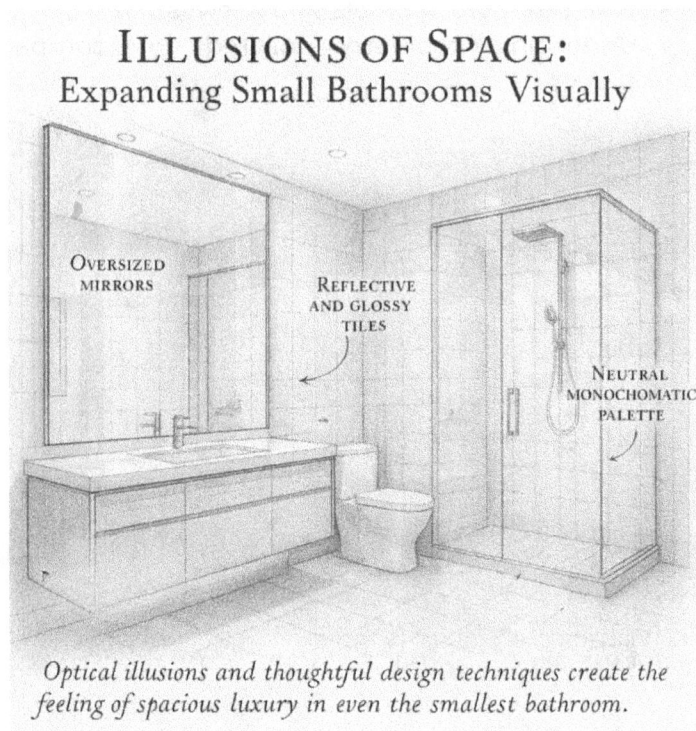

ILLUSIONS OF SPACE:
Expanding Small Bathrooms Visually

OVERSIZED MIRRORS

REFLECTIVE AND GLOSSY TILES

NEUTRAL MONOCHOMATIC PALETTE

Optical illusions and thoughtful design techniques create the feeling of spacious luxury in even the smallest bathroom.

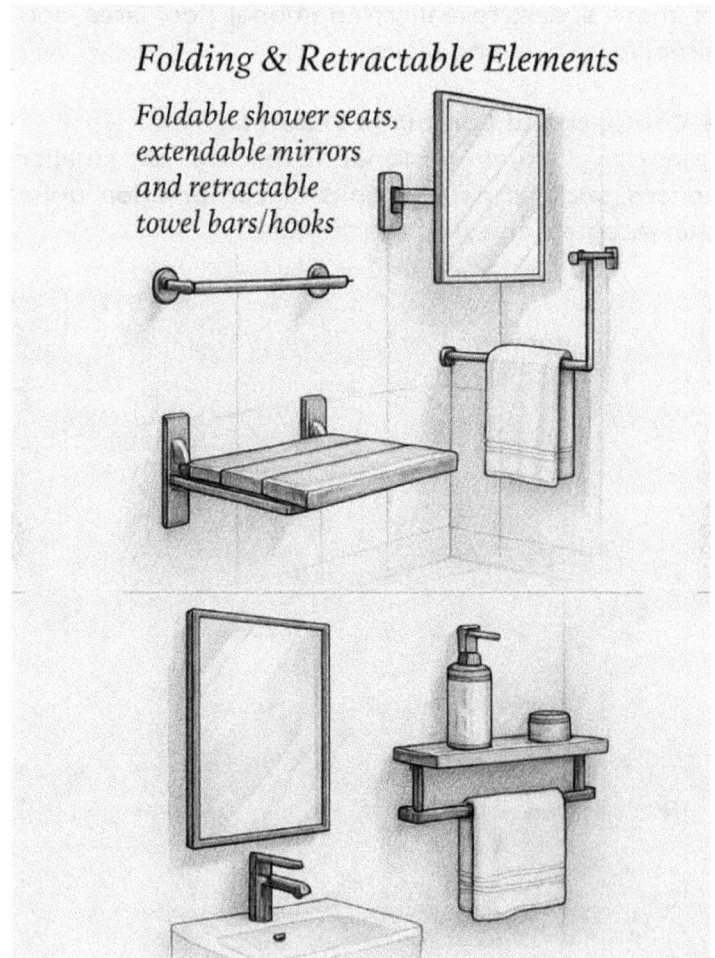

Folding & Retractable Elements

Foldable shower seats, extendable mirrors and retractable towel bars/hooks

Sliding and Pocket Doors

LIGHTING: ENHANCING DEPTH & AMBIANCE

Well-planned lighting profoundly influences the perceived spaciousness of your bathroom.

Layered Lighting: Combine ambient, task, and accent lighting to effectively eliminate shadows, brightening corners and visually opening up the space.

Natural Light: Maximize any available natural light sources. If windows are limited, consider skylights or solar tubes.

Recessed and Flush-Mount Fixtures: Utilize fixtures that don't intrude into the room, preserving ceiling height and openness.

Lighting Solutions Checklist:
- Recessed LED ceiling lights
- Wall-mounted sconces
- Skylights or solar tubes (if structurally feasible)
- Lighted mirrors or medicine cabinets

INNOVATIVE DESIGN TIPS FOR SMALL BATHROOMS

Follow this systematic approach to transform your compact bathroom into a space-saving sanctuary:

Step 1: Assess Your Space
- Carefully measure and map out your bathroom dimensions.
- Identify existing spatial limitations and prioritize your needs.

Step 2: Choose an Optimal Layout
- Evaluate corner and wall-hung fixtures to reclaim floor space.
- Sketch multiple layouts, considering flow and accessibility.

Step 3: Plan Storage Solutions
- Opt for vertical and recessed storage options.
- Plan custom cabinetry to maximize underutilized spaces.

Step 4: Enhance Visual Space
Select reflective finishes, large mirrors, and glass elements to amplify openness.

Step 5: Finalize with Smart Accessories
Incorporate foldable, retractable, and multifunctional elements to maintain flexibility and practicality.

AVOIDING COMMON SMALL BATHROOM MISTAKES

Oversized Fixtures: Avoid bulky vanities, large tubs, and heavy cabinets; they consume excessive space and shrink visual openness.

Poor Lighting: Don't rely solely on overhead lighting, as it creates shadows and makes the space feel smaller. A layered approach is essential.

Neglecting Vertical Space: Vertical areas are prime real estate in compact bathrooms. Ignoring this potential results in unnecessary clutter and decreased efficiency.

Home Offices
& CREATIVE SPACES

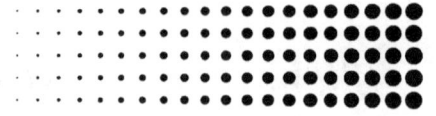

CHAPTER 10

Productivity
ENHANCING DESIGNS

Creating a workspace that elevates productivity requires more than functional furniture; it demands a synthesis of form, light, and materiality to inspire sustained focus. Arrange your desk and seating to capture natural light, allowing soft daylight to illuminate the work surface and uplift spirit. Integrate sculptural shelving and custom storage that conceals clutter while displaying curated objects, such as collection of artful books or personal mementos. A palette of muted neutrals punctuated by deliberate accents—perhaps a swath of deep indigo or a hint of metallic sheen—fosters a calm yet invigorating atmosphere. Underfoot, a woven rug defines the working zone and softens acoustics, while layered textures—from a tactile desk pad to plastered walls—add depth and warmth. When orchestrated thoughtfully, these elements transform the room into a blend of elegance and productivity.

By weaving ergonomic considerations into every design decision, you create an environment that supports effortless energy and clear graceful thinking. Carefully selected accent lighting casts a warm glow on key surfaces, elevating both mood and function, while integrated cable management preserves lines and harmony. Introducing artwork or sculptural elements at eye level fosters inspiration without distraction, and an assortment of planters or natural accents brings vitality to the space. Selecting a statement desk chair upholstered in fabric marries comfort with sophistication, inviting hours of work. Subtle contrasts between matte and glossy finishes animate surfaces and delineate zones without overwhelming senses. This harmonious fusion of tailored workstation, décor, and intuitive flow cultivates an atmosphere in which creativity thrives, tasks are completed with greater ease, and act of working becomes an inspired experience.

ESSENTIAL PRINCIPLES OF A
Productive Workspace

Designing your workspace around these core principles can significantly boost your productivity:

01 FUNCTIONAL ZONING

Divide your workspace into clear functional zones to support varied tasks, streamline workflows, and minimize distractions. Each zone should have a designated purpose, such as:

- **Task Zone**: Primary workspace for intensive work.
- **Reference Zone**: Area for materials, books, files, and resources.
- **Supply Zone**: Easy-access storage for frequently used tools and supplies.
- **Break Zone**: Comfortable, separate area to relax and recharge briefly.

02 MINIMIZING DISTRACTIONS

Creating an environment that limits interruptions is crucial for sustaining deep focus, reducing cognitive fatigue, and ensuring your attention remains fully on priority tasks throughout every work session.

Sound Management: Incorporate sound-absorbing materials like carpets, curtains, and acoustic panels. Consider white noise machines or noise-canceling headphones for focused sessions.

Visual Clutter: Opt for streamlined, hidden storage solutions to keep surfaces clear and maintain a sense of order.

LAYOUT AND SPACE PLANNING

Proper arrangement of your workspace directly affects your productivity:

Desk Placement: Position your desk in a spot that maximizes natural light without causing screen glare. Ideally, have a view of the room's entrance to feel secure and comfortable.

Clear Movement Paths: Ensure you have adequate space around furniture to move freely, which prevents feeling cramped or hindered.

Accessibility: Essential items and tools should always be within arm's reach. Secondary materials should be easily accessible without cluttering primary work surfaces.

LIGHTING STRATEGIES FOR PRODUCTIVITY

Appropriate lighting dramatically affects your efficiency, comfort, and health:

Natural Light: Capitalize on natural light sources, positioning desks close to windows when possible. Supplement with adjustable blinds or sheer curtains to control intensity.

Task Lighting: Incorporate adjustable desk lamps or floor lamps specifically for detailed work.

Ambient Lighting: Install overhead or wall-mounted lights to evenly illuminate the room, reducing eye strain and fatigue.

Lighting Checklist:
- Natural lighting optimization
- Adjustable task lighting
- Soft ambient lighting
- Dimmable fixtures to customize brightness levels

COLOR AND PRODUCTIVITY

Colors profoundly impact mood, focus, and creativity:

Blue and Green: Promote calmness, productivity, and concentration—ideal for extended periods of work.

Yellow and Orange: Stimulate creativity and innovation, beneficial in creative studios or brainstorming areas.

Neutral Tones (White, Beige, Gray): Foster simplicity, clarity, and flexibility, especially useful in multifunctional or shared spaces.

Choose your palette carefully based on your specific needs and the nature of your tasks.

TECHNOLOGY INTEGRATION

Streamlined technology significantly boosts productivity:

Cable Management: Conceal and organize cables neatly using cable trays, ties, and wireless technology to minimize clutter.

Connectivity: Ensure high-speed internet and reliable connectivity for seamless workflow.

Charging Stations: Dedicated charging hubs for devices reduce visual clutter and improve functionality.

Tech Checklist:
- Cable management solutions
- Reliable Wi-Fi or wired internet connections
- Device-specific charging stations

BIOPHILIC DESIGN: NATURE AND PRODUCTIVITY

Incorporating elements of nature boosts productivity, creativity, and mental health:

Indoor Plants: Integrate greenery to purify air, reduce stress, and enhance overall well-being.

Natural Textures: Use wood, stone, and natural fibers to create warmth, reduce stress, and stimulate creativity.

Views of Nature: If possible, position desks to overlook gardens, trees, or natural scenery to aid mental rejuvenation.

PERSONALIZATION AND MOTIVATION

Your workspace should reflect your personal style and inspire you daily:

Motivational Elements: Add meaningful quotes, vision boards, or personal goals to keep motivation high and reinforce purpose.

Personal Items: Include personal photos, artwork, or cherished objects to create emotional connection and a sense of belonging.

Organization Tools: Use aesthetically pleasing yet practical organizers to maintain efficiency and visual harmony.

ERGONOMICS AND COMFORT

Ensuring your workspace is ergonomically sound directly influences productivity and long-term health:

Ergonomic Chair: Choose a chair with adjustable height, lumbar support, and comfortable padding to prevent posture-related injuries.

Adjustable Desk: Consider standing desks or desks with adjustable heights to encourage varied working positions throughout the day.

Monitor Height and Distance: Your screen should be at eye level, roughly an arm's length away, to avoid neck and eye strain.

Keyboard and Mouse Positioning: Ensure your wrists remain straight and relaxed during extended use, reducing repetitive strain injuries.

ACHIEVING THE IDEAL PRODUCTIVITY WORKSPACE

Crafting an idyllic productivity workspace requires a harmonious interplay of form and function, where architectural precision meets personal expression. Thoughtful zoning defines areas for focused tasks, collaborative dialogue, restorative interludes, promoting seamless transitions throughout your day. Natural layered lighting illuminate surfaces without glare, accentuating refined materials reducing visual fatigue. Strategic positioning of storage and technology eliminates distractions while maintaining an uncluttered aesthetic. A subtle refined palette of soothing neutrals contrasted with deliberate accent hues fosters balance and inspiration. Through intentional design, each element coalesces to sustain creativity, efficiency, and well-being.

Ergonomic Home Office
ESSENTIALS

When it comes to crafting the ideal home office, aesthetics alone won't suffice. Ensuring that your space promotes healthy posture, minimizes physical strain, and enhances comfort is paramount. Ergonomics is the science of designing your workspace to match your physical needs, reducing discomfort and preventing long-term injuries caused by repetitive strain and poor posture. Here, I'll guide you through the critical ergonomic essentials that will transform your workspace into an optimal environment for sustained health, productivity, and comfort.

01 ERGONOMIC SEATING: CHOOSING THE RIGHT CHAIR

An ideal ergonomic chair should include:

Adjustable Height: Your feet should rest flat on the floor, thighs parallel to the ground.

Lumbar Support: Maintains natural curve in your lower back to avoid strain.

Seat Depth Adjustment: A proper seat depth ensures 2-3 inches of space between your knees and the edge of the seat.

Adjustable Armrests: Armrests should align with your desk height, supporting relaxed shoulders and arms.

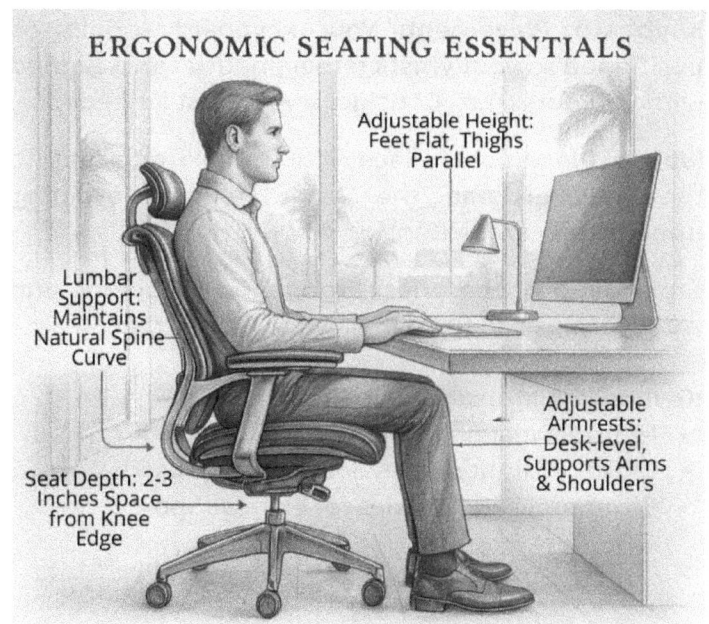

ERGONOMIC SEATING ESSENTIALS

Adjustable Height: Feet Flat, Thighs Parallel

Lumbar Support: Maintains Natural Spine Curve

Seat Depth: 2-3 Inches Space from Knee Edge

Adjustable Armrests: Desk-level, Supports Arms & Shoulders

02 DESK ERGONOMICS: POSITIONING MATTERS

The right desk significantly impacts posture and productivity:

Height Adjustable Desk: Enables alternating between sitting and standing to avoid prolonged sitting periods, boosting circulation and energy levels.

Proper Desk Height: When seated, your elbows should naturally rest at about 90 degrees when your arms are relaxed at your sides, and wrists should be straight while typing or using a mouse.

Desk Surface: Choose a non-glare, smooth surface to reduce eye strain and facilitate easy mouse movement.

Desk Ergonomics Quick Guide:
- **Desk Height**: Elbows at 90-degree angle
- **Standing Desk**: Height adjustable for flexibility
- **Non-glare surface**: Reduces visual fatigue

03 KEYBOARD AND MOUSE POSITIONING

Correct positioning prevents repetitive strain injuries (RSIs):

Keyboard Placement: Your keyboard should be positioned so your wrists remain neutral and aligned with your forearms. Consider a wrist rest if needed.

Mouse Placement: Place your mouse adjacent to the keyboard at the same height, avoiding unnecessary arm extension or wrist twisting.

Ergonomic Accessories: Ergonomic keyboards and vertical mice can further alleviate wrist strain.

Keyboard & Mouse Quick Tips:
- Neutral wrist alignment
- Close proximity to keyboard and mouse
- Ergonomic accessories for extra support

04 MONITOR AND SCREEN ERGONOMICS

Proper positioning of your screen is vital to reduce eye and neck strain:

Height: The top of your monitor screen should be at or slightly below eye level, approximately arm's length away.

Dual Monitors: If using two screens, position them side-by-side at the same height and distance, angled slightly inward.

Adjustable Monitor Arms: These tools provide flexibility, allowing easy adjustment of monitor height, distance, and angle.

SINGLE MONITOR
Top Edge at Eye Level

DUAL MONITORS:
Side-Side, Same Height & Distance, Angled Slightly Inward

05 FOOTRESTS AND ANTI-FATIGUE MATS

Supporting your lower body ergonomically enhances comfort significantly:

Footrests: Essential if your chair height causes your feet to dangle, footrests promote circulation and reduce lower back pressure.

Anti-Fatigue Mats: For standing desk users, these mats cushion feet, knees, and lower back, reducing fatigue from prolonged standing.

06 PROPER LIGHTING

Effective lighting reduces visual strain, a crucial ergonomic factor:

Adjustable Task Lighting: Adjustable lamps directed at specific tasks can reduce eye strain and headaches.

Ambient Lighting: Ensure consistent room illumination to avoid stark contrasts that strain your eyes.

Natural Light Management: Position monitors perpendicular to windows, minimizing glare while maximizing daylight benefits.

07 ERGONOMIC STORAGE SOLUTIONS

Efficient, ergonomic storage solutions minimize unnecessary movements:

Frequently Used Items: Store within easy reach to avoid excessive bending or stretching.

Storage Height: Arrange shelves and cabinets according to the frequency of item use—regularly accessed items at waist or eye level, less used items above or below this range.

Drawer Organizers: Help maintain order and quick access, reducing wasted time and physical strain.

Ergonomic Storage Quick Tips:
- Prioritize frequently accessed items
- Avoid overhead lifting
- Use organizers for quick access

09 REGULAR MOVEMENT AND STRETCHING

No matter how ergonomic your workspace, frequent breaks and movement are essential:

Micro-Breaks: Take short breaks every 20-30 minutes. Stand, stretch, and walk briefly to maintain circulation and muscle tone

Stretching Routine: Simple stretches targeting back, neck, shoulders, wrists, and legs significantly reduce discomfort and prevent long-term injuries.

Recommended Office Stretches:
- Neck rotations
- Shoulder shrugs and rolls
- Wrist rotations and extensions
- Standing hip flexor and hamstring stretches

09 ERGONOMIC ACCESSORIES AND TECH TOOLS

The right accessories can dramatically enhance your workspace ergonomics:

Document Holders: Position reading materials at eye-level to avoid neck strain.

Headsets: Reduce neck and shoulder tension caused by holding a phone.

Laptop Stands: Elevate laptops to the correct eye-level height, especially important if your laptop is your primary device.

BUILDING YOUR ERGONOMIC HOME OFFICE

An ergonomic workspace transcends mere comfort to become a deliberate investment in physical health, mental clarity, and enduring efficiency. Embracing ergonomic design principles in your home office fosters an environment where proper posture is supported by adjustable seating, desk heights align precisely with your frame, and screen positioning reduces strain on eyes and neck. Thoughtful inclusion of work surfaces, keyboard trays, and footrests encourages movement throughout the day, preventing fatigue and chronic tension. Tailor each element—from chair lumbar support to monitor arm flexibility—to your unique body metrics and work patterns. Regularly assess and refine your setup as tasks and preferences evolve, ensuring that the workspace continues to promote vitality, focus, and sustained well-being for hours spent at your desk daily.

Creative Corner
AND HOBBY ROOM DEISNGS

Whether you're an artist, musician, crafter, or avid reader, designing a dedicated space for creativity and leisure activities significantly enriches your quality of life. A creative corner or hobby room isn't just about aesthetics— it's about crafting a personal sanctuary that inspires innovation, boosts productivity, and supports your unique creative processes.

01 FINDING THE PERFECT SPACE

Your creative corner doesn't require an entire room —any underutilized area in your home can be transformed. Key places to consider:

- Under-utilized corners in living rooms
- Unused closets
- Attics or basements
- Spare bedrooms
- Garage conversions
- Sunrooms or enclosed porches

Space Selection Tips:
- Prioritize natural light.
- Ensure privacy and minimal noise disruptions.
- Evaluate proximity to necessary resources (water access for painting, electrical outlets, etc.).

TRANSFORMING SPACES FOR INSPIRATION

CLOSET ARTIST STUDIO
WITH INTEGRATED STORAGE

CORNER CRAFTING NOOK
WITH NATURAL LIGHT

ATTIC WORKSPACE
WITH SKYLIGHTS *and* EXPOSED BEAMS

SUNROOM CREATIVE RETREAT
WITH ABUNDANT GREENERY

Transforming overlooked spaces into lavurious creation, sanctuories inspires innovation and enhancces everyday living in upecals horres

02 ESSENTIAL ELEMENTS FOR CREATIVE SPACES

Regardless of your hobby, certain elements universally elevate the creative environment:

LIGHTING

- **Natural Light**: Enhances mood and reduces eye strain.
- **Task Lighting**: Adjustable lamps ensure adequate visibility for detailed work.
- **Ambient Lighting**: Creates a relaxing, inviting atmosphere.

STORAGE AND ORGANIZATION

- **Shelves**: Open shelves for easy access to materials.
- **Drawers**: For tidier storage of smaller items.
- **Bins & Boxes**: Clearly labeled containers for efficient retrieval of tools and supplies.
- **Pegboards**: For visible and adaptable organization.

COMFORT

- **Ergonomic Chair or Stool**: Essential for long creative sessions.
- **Anti-Fatigue Mats**: If you prefer standing.
- **Relaxation Zone**: Small seating area for breaks and reflection.

WORK SURFACE

- **Adjustable Tables**: Versatile options that accommodate various tasks and materials.
- **Durable Surfaces**: Easy-to-clean surfaces resistant to paints, glue, and general wear.

CREATIVE SPACE CHECKLIST

ESSENTIALS	RECOMMENDED OPTIONS
Lighting	Natural, task, ambient
Storage	Shelves, drawers, bins, pegboards
Seating	Ergonomic chair, stools, comfortable lounge
Work Surface	Adjustable height, easy-to-clean, durable

03 HOBBY-SPECIFIC ROOM DESIGNS

ARTIST & CRAFTER STUDIOS

An artist's space should encourage spontaneity and inspiration:

Ample storage: For canvases, brushes, paints, and other art supplies.

Large Worktable: Provides adequate space for laying out materials.

Washable Floors and Surfaces: For easy cleanup of paint spills and residues.

Art Display Area: Showcase completed works for motivation and inspiration.

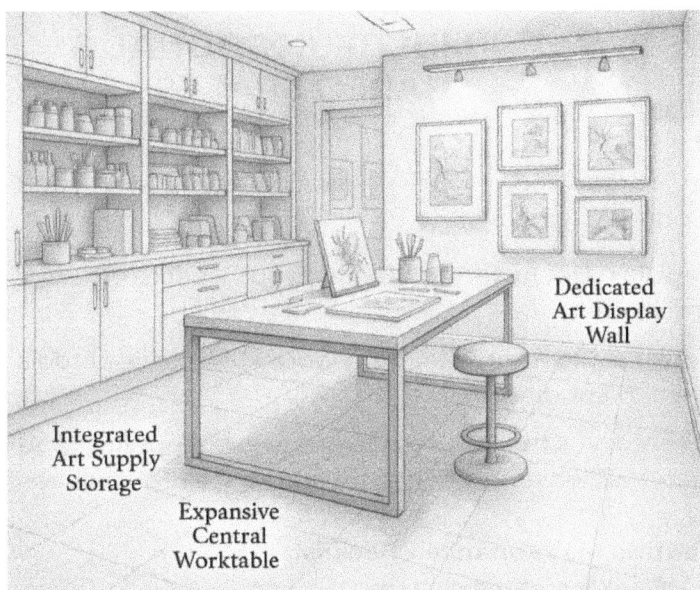

Integrated Art Supply Storage

Expansive Central Worktable

Dedicated Art Display Wall

MUSIC ROOMS

For musicians, room acoustics and instrument storage matter most:

Acoustic Treatments: Panels, rugs, or curtains to manage sound quality.

Instrument Storage: Stands, wall mounts, and protective cases.

Comfortable Seating: Essential for extended practice sessions.

Recording Setup: Integrated tech station for composing, recording, and editing.

MUSIC ROOM:
LUXURY MEETS SOUND

ACOUSTIC WALL PANELS & DRAPES

HIGH-END RECORDING WORTSTATION

LUXURIOUS SEATING AREA

CRAFT AND SEWING ROOMS

Tailored to sewing and crafting enthusiasts:

Dedicated Sewing Tables: Adjustable height, large enough for fabric cutting.

Fabric Storage: Open shelving, clear bins, or dedicated drawers.

Thread & Accessory Organizers: Pegboards or wall-mounted thread organizers.

Ironing & Cutting Stations: Integrated stations to streamline processes.

READING BOOKS

Comfort and tranquility reign supreme in reading corners:

Comfortable Seating: Plush chairs, chaise lounges, or cozy window seats.

Adequate Lighting: Adjustable lamps or strategically positioned overhead lights.

Book Storage: Built-in shelving or modular units to organize books attractively.

Side Tables: For drinks, reading glasses, and personal items.

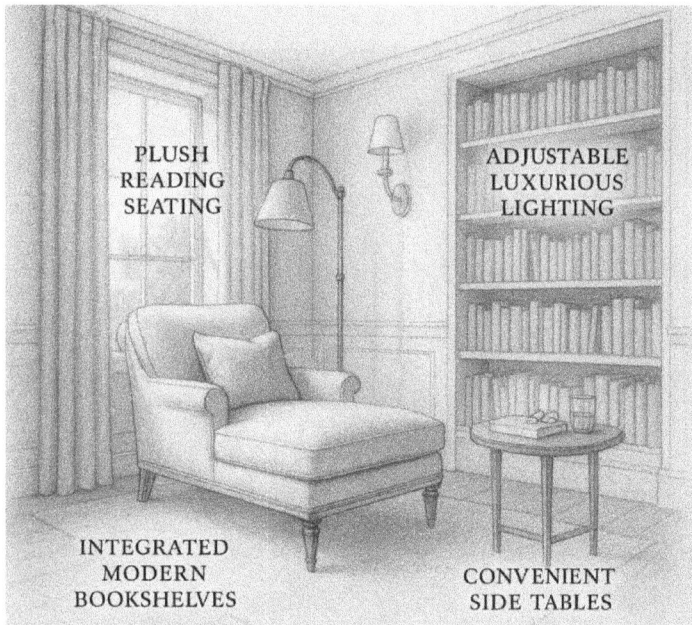

PLUSH READING SEATING

ADJUSTABLE LUXURIOUS LIGHTING

INTEGRATED MODERN BOOKSHELVES

CONVENIENT SIDE TABLES

04 ENHANCING CREATIVITY WITH COLOR AND DECOR

Colors significantly impact creativity and productivity:

Calming Colors: Blues, greens, and neutrals ideal for concentration-heavy activities (writing, reading).

Energizing Colors: Yellows, oranges, and reds suited for dynamic, expressive arts (painting, music).

Inspirational Decor: Quotes, mood boards, vision boards, personal art collections enhance the motivational atmosphere.

Color & Decor Guide:

ACTIVITY TYPE	RECOMMENDED COLORS	INSPIRATIONAL DECOR IDEAS
Writing, reading	Blues, greens, soft neutrals	Framed inspirational quotes, calming imagery
Painting, crafting, music	Yellows, oranges, reds	Vision boards, vibrant art prints

05 MULTIFUNCTIONAL & SHARED SPACES

If your home office doubles as your creative corner or family members share hobby spaces:

Modular Furniture: Easy to reconfigure for varying uses.

Clearly Defined Zones: Visual dividers or furniture arrangements that delineate different functions clearly.

Multipurpose Storage: Cabinets and shelves that accommodate diverse needs efficiently.

Tips for Multipurpose Creative Spaces:
- Use mobile carts or rolling storage solutions.
- Define separate areas using area rugs or room dividers. Opt for furniture pieces with built-in storage capabilities.

06 MULTIFUNCTIONAL & SHARED SPACES

An organized space sustains creativity and productivity:

Regular Decluttering: Keeps your space efficient and inviting.

Routine Cleaning: Maintain work surfaces and tools in good condition.

Inventory Checks: Regularly review supplies and materials, ensuring necessary items are replenished.

Routine Maintenance Checklist:
- Weekly surface cleaning
- Monthly inventory and declutter
- Quarterly deep cleaning

MULTIFUNCTIONAL
Workspace Solutions

In today's dynamic home environment, rooms often serve multiple purposes—balancing professional work, creative hobbies, relaxation, and sometimes even guest accommodation. Designing multifunctional spaces requires careful planning, thoughtful furniture selection, and innovative organizational strategies. A successfully designed multipurpose workspace not only enhances productivity but also seamlessly accommodates your evolving lifestyle needs.

01 ASSESSING YOUR SPACE & NEEDS

The first step is clearly identifying how your room needs to function. Consider these essential questions:

- What primary activities will happen here? (Work, crafting, studying, relaxation, guest hosting)
- How frequently will each activity take place?
- How many people will regularly use the space?
- Are any activities incompatible (noise, clutter, etc.)?

Example Needs Assessment:

ACTIVITY	FREQUENCY	PRIORITY	SPECIAL REQUIREMENTS
Professional Work	Daily	High	Quiet, organized, tech-ready
Crafting & Hobbies	Weekly	Medium	Ample storage, flexible workspace
Guest Accommodation	Monthly	Low	Comfortable sleeping arrangement
Relaxation	Daily	High	Comfortable seating, soft lighting

02 ZONING YOUR MULTIFUNCTIONAL SPACE

Clear zoning is vital for multifunctionality. Effective strategies include:

FURNITURE ZONING
Use furniture to naturally divide your space into distinct areas:

- **Bookshelves or Storage Units**: Dual-sided shelves define boundaries without closing spaces off.
- **Sofas and Armchairs**: Position to delineate conversation and relaxation zones.
- **Mobile partitions**: Portable screens or curtains offer flexibility.

VISUAL ZONING
Color and decor visually separate zones:

- **Area Rugs**: Define spaces by creating distinct areas with rugs.
- **Color Schemes**: Utilize complementary colors or patterns to differentiate between activity zones.

FUNCTIONAL ZONING
Grouping activities based on similar needs enhances efficiency:

- **Active Zone**: Work and crafting stations requiring task-oriented furniture.
- **Passive Zone**: Relaxation or sleeping areas demanding comfort and minimal distraction.

03 SELECTING MULTIFUNCTIONAL FURNITURE

Choosing versatile furniture maximizes space and functionality:

Convertible Furniture:
- Sofa Beds: Ideal for quick guest room transformation.
- Wall Beds: Excellent for compact rooms, providing comfortable sleeping arrangements without permanently occupying space.

Expandable Tables:
- Adjustable desks that transition from a workstation to a craft table.
- Drop-leaf dining tables for dining and craft sessions.

Storage Ottomans & Benches: Provide seating and concealed storage.

Mobile Storage Units: Rolling carts easily move from one zone to another, ideal for crafting supplies or office equipment.

Multifunctional Furniture Checklist:

FURNITURE TYPE	FUNCTIONALITY & BENEFITS
Sofa beds / Murphy beds	Guest accommodation and daily seating
Adjustable desks	Workspace for various activities
Drop-leaf tables	Space-saving dining/crafting area
Storage ottomans	Extra seating and concealed storage
Rolling carts	Portable organization of tools and supplies

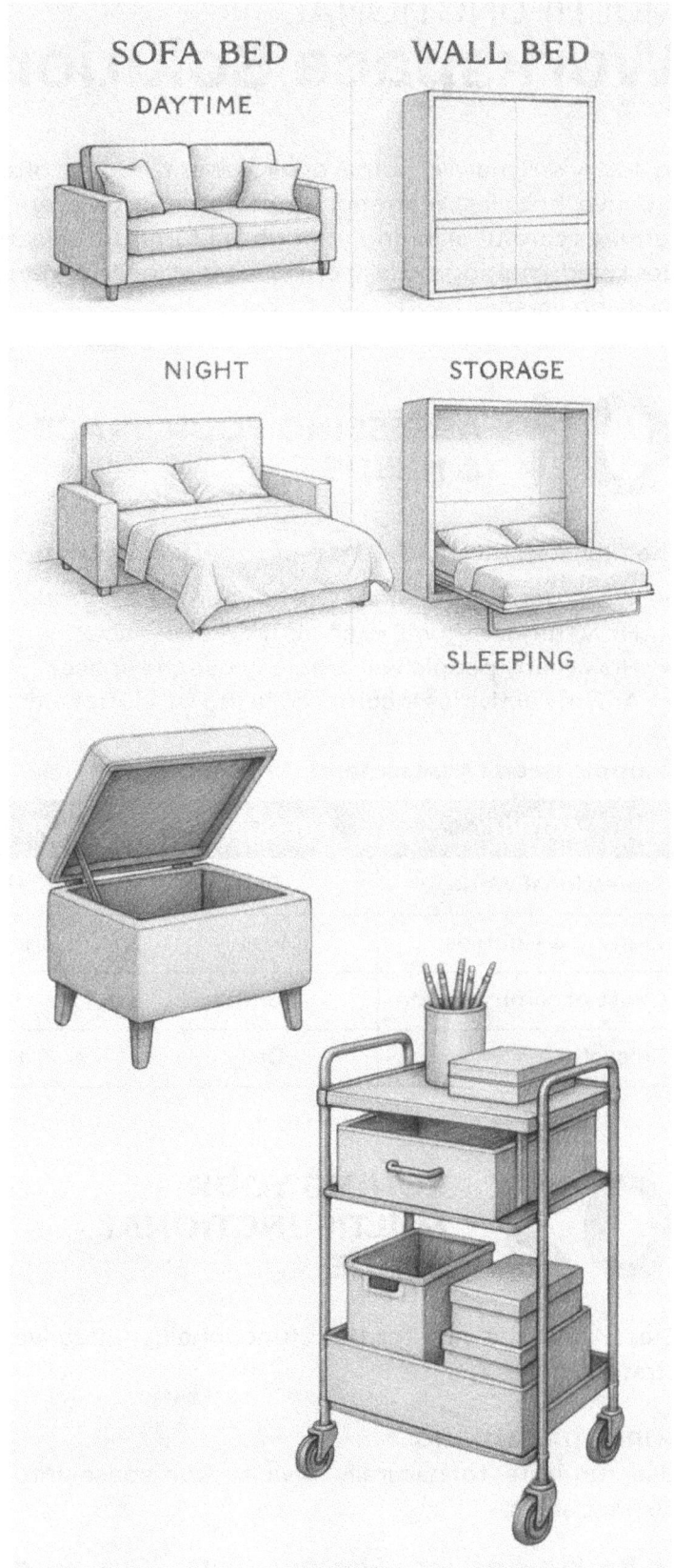

SOFA BED   WALL BED

DAYTIME

NIGHT   STORAGE

SLEEPING

04 EFFICIENT STORAGE SOLUTIONS

Smart storage solutions keep multifunctional spaces organized:

Vertical Storage: Wall-mounted shelves and pegboards for visible, accessible storage.

Modular Storage Units: Customizable storage for diverse organizational needs.

Hidden Storage: Under-bed boxes, lift-top coffee tables, and cabinets integrated into seating areas.

Digital Solutions: Digitize paperwork and resources, reducing physical storage demands.

Storage Strategies by Activity:

ACTIVITY	STORAGE SOLUTIONS
Office Work	Vertical file organizers, desk drawers, digital storage
Craft & Hobby	Pegboards, clear storage bins, modular shelving
Guest Area	Foldable storage boxes, dedicated closet space
Relaxation	Decorative baskets, concealed compartments in furniture

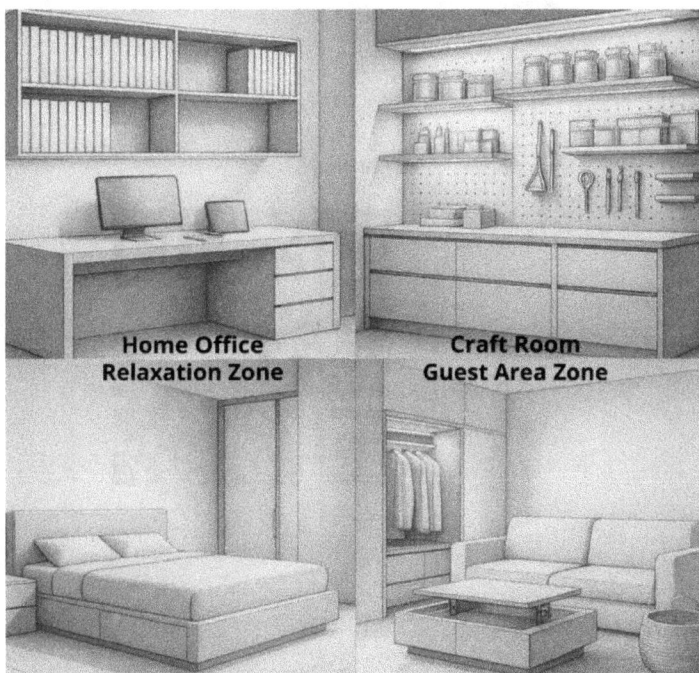

Home Office Relaxation Zone

Craft Room Guest Area Zone

05 LIGHTING & TECHNOLOGY INTEGRATION

Optimal lighting and integrated technology enhance comfort and productivity:

LAYERED LIGHTING:
- **Task Lighting**: Adjustable desk lamps/craft lights.
- **Ambient Lighting**: Dimmable overhead lights or lamps for relaxation.
- **Natural Light**: Strategically positioned workstations near windows.

TECH INTEGRATION:
- Multiple power outlets with USB charging ports.
- Smart-home tech for adjustable lighting and temperature control.
- Wireless charging stations for a clutter-free workspace.

Lighting and Technology Essentials:

FLEXIBILITY AND FUNCTIONALITY AT ITS FINEST

Multifunctional spaces represent the evolution of modern living—smart, adaptable, and reflective of diverse lifestyles. By assessing needs, implementing zoning, selecting versatile furniture, maximizing storage, and integrating lighting and technology, you transform any room into a harmonious, multifunctional haven. From a reading nook that converts to a meeting area to a workspace doubling as an entertaining zone, components must synergize seamlessly. Consider how finishes and fixtures perform dual roles without compromising style or comfort.

Your multifunctional workspace grows and adapts as life changes, remaining practical, comfortable, and inspiring. Embrace the creativity and innovation that multifunctionality offers, enjoying a space that accommodates every facet of daily routine and interests. Let each element combine to support productivity, relaxation, and social connection within a unified design narrative elegantly.

BECOME ICONIC — MAKE YOUR STYLE VIRAL WITH US!

You've selected **"The Interior Design Bible"**, a statement addition to your beautiful home.

Now it's your moment in the spotlight! Create a captivating video or sophisticated photograph featuring "Minimalist — The Interior Design Bible" and share your creation on Instagram, TikTok, or Facebook using the hashtag **#StudioLux**. Your elegant post might just spark the next big social media trend!

WHY PARTICIPATE?

- Showcase your exquisite taste and inspire a wide audience.
- Gain the opportunity to be featured by StudioLux for greater visibility and recognition.

And there's more to come...

CLAIM YOUR EXCLUSIVE GIFTS!

To celebrate your creativity, we've designed an exclusive bonus filled with practical and inspiring ideas you can immediately use to enhance your home's style. Don't miss this special opportunity—it's your next step toward achieving interior excellence.

FOLLOW THESE SIMPLE STEPS TO CLAIM YOUR REWARD:

- Capture your unique photo or create a compelling video featuring the book.
- Share your creation on Instagram, TikTok, or Facebook using the hashtag #StudioLux.
- Scan the QR code below to instantly unlock your exclusive bonus content.

Your moment of viral fame awaits!

With style and appreciation,

StudioLux

SCAN ME